SPORTS TOURISM

SPORTS TOURISM

Ravindra Verma

CENTRUM PRESS
NEW DELHI-110002 (INDIA)

CENTRUM PRESS

H.O.: 4360/4, Ansari Road, Daryaganj,
New Delhi-110002 (India)
Tel: 23278000, 23261597, 23255577, 23286875

B.O.: No. 1015, Ist Main Road, BSK IIIrd Stage,
IIIrd Phase, IIIrd Block, Bangalore-560085 (INDIA)
Tel: 080-41723429

Email: centrumpress@gmail.com
Visit us at: www.centrumpress.com

Sports Tourism

First Edition, 2010

ISBN 978-93-80540-03-0

PRINTED IN INDIA

Printed at Mehra Offset Press, Delhi

Contents

Preface

There are many different definitions of sports tourism, from those involving travel for the purpose of participating in competitive sports, to those involving more leisure or adventure sporting activities. Thus, the extent of sports tourism vary quite a bit. Sports tourism involves people travelling to participate or to observe sports. These activities may include people competing in an international event, such as the Olympics, or simply sitting amongst the audience watching the World Cup match.

Inevitably, following sports tourism, there will be consequential impacts. These may be classified under economic impacts, socio-cultural impacts, health impacts and environmental impacts.

The increasing and important impact sport has in economic terms requires a more multi-disciplinary approach. The economic sector of sport has transformed itself in the last decade from a traditional Spectators-Subsidies-Sponsors-Local (SSSL)-model to a more global Media-Corporations-Merchandising-Markets or MCCM-model. The new sport model has executed forms of vertical integration in the industry and has created synergisms as an outcome of the relations between business and sport. Some of the economic developments are - Broadcasting rights, merchandising, sponsoring, organizing of mega sporting events, multiplication effect of organizing a sport event, the mobile leisure society, sport tourism, sport and the impact on health, the public-private cooperation in building of sporting infrastructures, the betting industry, raising market share of sporting goods, shoes and clothing.

The British Tourism Authority claims that 20% of the tourist trips are for the prime purpose of sport participation, and 50% of the tourist trips include among other purposes sport participation. The data was also validated by 1998 Canadian Travel Survey which set an evaluation of 37% of the domestic trips for sport oriented activities.

The national pride and prestige one feels when a mega event is held in his country is perpetual. It is a proud feeling to know that your country is able to hold an international event, because it will be broadcast worldwide, and therefore known to the rest of the world.

"In Germany "national pride" ("Nationalstolz") is often associated with the former Nazi regime. Strong displays of national pride are therefore considered poor taste by many Germans. There is an ongoing public debate about the issue of German patriotism. The World Cup in 2006, held in Germany, saw a wave of patriotism sweep the country in a manner not seen for many years. Although many were hesitant to show such blatant support as the hanging of the national flag from windows, as the team progressed through the tournament, so too did the level of support across the nation. By the time the semi-final against Italy came around, the level of national pride and unity was at its highest throughout the tournament, and the hosting of the World Cup is seen to have been a great success for Germany as a nation.

This usually occurs among the spectators who are unsatisfied with the announced results. The spectators/ audiences usually from the losing side will create fights with the other side. Violence is one of the negative impacts that can arise from sports tourism. It is an unhealthy scene as this can sour the relationship between two counterparts. Violence in sports tourism does not only happen among countries, but also within one country itself.

There are so many books in sports Tourism but written almost by the foreign authors. This book is an unique painstaking effort by the author in the field of sports Tourism.

—*Ravindra Verma*

1

Sport Tourism—an International Overview

Sport Tourism is a prevalent and growing phenomenon. However it did not magically appear directly in the twentieth century. Connections between sports and tourism can be traced back to the ancient times. In this chapter, we will provide a brief overview of sport and tourism and will define three key terms: sport, tourism and of course sport tourism. Finally, we will look at the development of connections between the Olympic Games of ancient Greece to the increased access to, or democratization of, sport tourism in the twentieth century.

Overview of Sport and Tourism

Today vast numbers of people participate in or watch sports and almost everyone aspires to a holiday. Though the connections between sports and tourism have long been established, the relationship is now gaining global significance. Media attention has increased and people are becoming more aware of the health and recreational benefits that sport and tourism provide.

The growing number of travel companies that now produces brochures to advertise their sports and adventure holidays-for example, white-water rafting through the Arctic, scuba diving in Kenya, or trekking in Nepal-testify to the increasing interest in sport tourism. In travel and tourist magazines, resort advertising continues to emphasize the availability of sport facilities and opportunities. Spectator vacations are also increasingly popular with huge number of visitors attracted to sports events. Le Tour, France's prestigious three week cycle race, claims to be the world's largest annual sports spectating event, attracting several million spectators along its 2,500 mile route, while in Britain it is claimed that around 2.5 million people watch outdoor sport and another 1 million watch indoor sport while on holiday there. Congress, seminars and workshops on sport and tourism have been documented as taking place since 1971 when the International Council for Sport Science and Physical Education (ICSSPE) held a congress in Helsinki, Finland, on the topic "Activity Holiday Making". ICSSPE and the International Council for Health, Physical Education and Recreation (ICHPER) jointly sponsored the first congress that specifically addressed sport tourism which was held in Israel in 1986. The first journal dedicated to sport tourism, The Journal of Sports Tourism, began publication in October 1993. This journal is now produced quarterly in the E-zine format with access through the internet.

The relationship between sport and tourism in the modern world is symbiotic. It is not simply that sport furthers tourism by offering an ever-increasing range of valued visitor experiences; tourism also aids sport. This is an interdependent relationship. Sport is a special segment of the tourism industry. Sport and tourism are inextricably linked, and as globalization advances, new and exciting possibilities are opening up to enrich touristic experiences through sport development through tourism.

Adventure and activity holidays are a recognized and growing segment of the tourist industry and sports training is acknowledged and potentially health-enhancing activity for which tourism can be the catalyst. Health care and training of the body have become an important part of the tourist industry. From the start tourism was promoted for its health-improving functions.

People used to go to Seaside Resorts Because

of the "presumed health giving properties of sea bathing". Sea bathing lead to sun bathing, but the risk of the cancer has shifted emphasis toward a fit body, a body that is trained through exercise and sport. Sport as therapy is another growing segment of the tourism industry, with an estimated 15 million annual visits to the spas in Europe alone.

Sport as a part of business hospitality is big, profitable and growing with most of the Clients spectating at events miles away from their place of work. Active sport associated with the business tours is also increasingly widespread. However, due to space limitations and a strong commitment to sporting holidays, we must treat this type of sport tourism cursorily in this book.

Travel agents are always on the lookout for new markets as a way of broadening their business. It has become almost impossible for sportsmen and sportswomen to pursue their carriers without engaging in travel. Team tours are also popular with amateur clubs who engage agents to find matches and make accommodation and transport arrangements.

Definition of Key Concepts

It is important to clarify the humanistic perspective from which this book is written before we establish detailed definitions. Neither sport nor tourism are adequately described as industries; they are activities in which people engage. Sport is about an experience of physical activity, tourism about an experience of travel and place. Sports activity does not mean the same thing to all people; nor does its experience mean the same thing even for the same person at different stages of life. Likewise travellers do not all experience places in the same way. Yet the special significance of both sport and tourism is the meaning that each can have for different people, or for the same person at different times in life.

Such variations make definitions difficult. However, working definitions of the key concepts of sport, tourism are needed in Order to identify more adequately the phenomenon we are discussing.

Definition of Sport

There is no universally accepted definition of sport. Widely differing views are held as to which activities come under the heading of sport, although sport is often thought of as being highly competitive and organized. For example, North American definitions often characterize sport as a pursuit that:

a. requires complexity of physical skill and vigorous physical exertion.

b. involves some form of rule governed competition.

c. has organized and structured relations but keeps a sense of freedom and spontaneity.

The council of Europe defines sport as:

all forms of physical activity, which through casual or organized participation, aim at improving physical fitness and mental well being, forming social relationships, or obtaining results in competitions at all levels.

This definition does not separate competitive from noncompetitive activity or distinguish between professional and nonprofessional participation-all of these categories are referred to as sport.

In this text, however, we use the term sport in its widest possible sense to include the whole range of competitive and noncompetitive active pursuits that involve skill, strategy and/or chance in which human beings engage, at their own level, simply for enjoyment and training or to raise their performance to levels of publicly acclaimed excellence.

The advantage of this definition is that it embraces sports equity, the first principle Of the European Sports Charter. This was also considered to be important by the United Nations Educational, Scientific, and Cultural organization (Unesco).

Forms of Sport Involvement

Going beyond the definition of sport itself, involvement in sport can take different forms. A distinction is often made between active and passive sport involvement. Active sport involvement requires the participant to be physically active. This is the most common form of sports. Passive sport involvement comprises watching others engage in sport. In this book we focus on watching live performances, since only that type of passive sport involvement includes travel and thus tourism.

Definition of Tourism

Tourism is derived from the English word tour. The first characteristic of tourism is that travel is involved. However, travel is not a sufficient condition of tourism. Tourism and travel are not synonymous.

Tourism is a Modern Concept, Whereas Travel

Has taken place for as long as the earth has been inhabited. Tourism may be defined in terms of particular activities, selected by choice and undertaken outside the home environment. Tourism may or may not involve overnight stays away from home. The second characteristic of tourism is that stay away from home must be temporary. Essentially, tourism is a circular journey. The third element most scientists have adopted to describe tourism is the purpose of the trip. For the purpose of this text, definition of tourism is as follows: The temporary movement of people beyond their own home and work locality involving experiences unlike those of everyday life. The experiences might take place as part of a holiday or as an ancillary to business travel.

Forms of Tourism

Most countries accept that an international tourist is a temporary visitor who spends at least one night but not more than one year in a country other than his own for the purpose of leisure or business.

An international day excursionist is a visitor who does not stay overnight but who visits a foreign country for the purpose of leisure or business.

A domestic tourist is defined by World Tourism Organization as any person residing with in a country, irrespective of nationality, travelling to a place within this country other than his usual residence for a period of not less than 24 hours or one night.

A domestic excursionist is someone who meets the above definition but does not stay overnight.

Tourists are divided into three categories, according to the main purpose of their visit:

1. Holiday tourists.
2. Business tourist.
3. Other tourists.

Holiday tourists are those who travel to engage in a touristic experience in their leisure time including visits to friends and relatives.

Business tourists include those who travel as a part of their work obligation. The holiday visitor is free to choose time of departure and destination but the business traveller is usually highly constrained in terms of where and when to travel.

The category other tourists comprise those who travel for miscellaneous reasons, such as study or religious pilgrimages.

Definition of Sport Tourism

Love to participate in various sports? If you think you have that sportsman spirit in you, there are many destinations in the world where you will get to enjoy some of the most exciting and adventurous sports to your heart's content. Some of the most popular adventure and thrilling sports that you can avail includes rock climbing, sailing, cruise destinations, water rafting and kayaking to name a few. Here we will be discussing about the various top sports tourism destinations that can create memories which you will cherish throughout life. The popular sports of the world that are organized in various countries to attract tourists includes Snowboarding, Kitesurfing, Whitewater Rafting, Rock Climbing,

Skydiving, Trekking, Windsurfing, Scuba Diving, Surfing, Activity Weekends, Paragliding, Wakeboarding, Sailing and more.

Snowboarding: This is an extremely exciting game that is somewhat similar to skiing. In this game the players strap a composite board to their feet and ski down the mountain slops covered with snow.

It can be very adventurous if you are brave and love to indulge in sports that are bold and daring. To enjoy the thrill of snowboarding, you have to travel to the nations of Canada and United States. The various resorts of these countries organize snowboarding events in winter seasons.

Kitesurfing: This is another interesting and daring sport that involves a kite board along with a power kite that pulls the small surfboard. Apart from these, there are wheeled boats on land. With the powerful kite, the surfer is pulled in motion which seems similar to that of water skiing. Now a day, many countries are coming up with the sports of kitesurfing.

River Rafting: River rafting is a great recreational activity that more and more people are indulging in the rafting is basically navigating through rivers. Proper precautions need to be taken in river rafting as this daring sport can cause harm if proper safeguard is not taken in advance. Places like India, Nepal and Costa Rica can be your ultimate destinations for sports tourism.

Rock Climbing: Rock climbing is the most popular sports in this modern age. Lots of people throughout the world are opting for this sport that is not only daring but also hugely enjoying. For beginners, it is advised to get proper training from a professional trainer as this sport needs proper precaution and training. UK, Malaysia, India, Nepal, Bolivia, China are some of the top places to enjoy this sport. Set out and enjoy the thrills of this unconventional sport.

Sky Diving: Dream of flying in the open sky? Then sky diving can fulfil this wish of yours. Sky diving is basically jumping out of an aircraft or copter from an approximate height of 12000 feet. Proper precaution and training is a must in this daring sport as you will get to enjoy the thrill of free falling for a certain period of time. But one must always remember to activate the parachute in proper time to have a safe landing. Places which are famous for skydiving includes United States, United Kingdom, Australia, New Zealand and more. As a concept, sport tourism is often seen as of more recent origin than either sport or tourism. The 311 athletes who attended the first modern games came from 13 countries, although 230 were from Greece itself. Most of the visiting athletes travelled to Athens at their own expense, many on their own initiative, and between them won 17 out of the 22 first prizes.

The expenses of the first modern games were estimated to be about 200 drachmas; however, the games ended up costing more than a million. In order to meet such costs, Early games were linked to other tourist attractions. For example, the 1900 Olympic Games were held in conjunction with the Universal exhibition in Paris; the 1904.

Celebration was timed to coincide with St. Louis World's Fair. The distance, cost and difficulty of travel to St. Louis more than halved the number of competitors in 1904. Four years earlier, Paris had registered 1,330 contestants. St. Louis managed a mere 617 who represented 12 nations, but 525 of them were Americans and another 41 were Canadians, leaving just 51 overseas competitors.

Number of participants and countries represented in the Olympics climbed steadily as long as the games were held in Europe, clearly indicative of the greater ease of travel. In London in 1908, where the events were linked with an Anglo-French Exhibition, there were 2,056 competitors Representing 22 countries, and by 1912 in Stockholm this number had grown by a further 25 percent representing 28 nations.

In summary, sport's geographical diffusion around the world from its various "homelands" was closely tied to travel. Since sport is a part of cultural experience, as people travelled they took their sport with them and established it in new milieus. Thus much of the early development of sport can be attributed to the spread of travel and tourism.

Democratization of Sport and Tourism in Twentieth Century

The twentieth century has seen an unprecedented growth of travel and tourism. The period has been characterized by. Social diffusion and the development of mass tourism and mass sport, rather then their geographical diffusion characteristic of the nineteenth century. Democratization-the process by which increasingly more members of a community gain access to opportunities previously restricted to upper classes-has taken place.

Conditions that have Favoured the Democratization of Sport and Tourism

A number of conditions have influenced the democratization of sport and tourism. We have singled out some factors as major twentieth century developments that have encouraged mass tourism and mass sport:

- Economic forces.
- technological innovations.
- Political movements and.
- value changes.
- Economic Forces.

In order to take part in either sport or tourism, people must have adequate time and money.

Technological Innovations

Equally important in enabling sport and tourism to spread to a wider cross section of population are the technological innovations of this century. New methods of transportation have encouraged the expansion of tourism and this has had an impact on sport. There are many different definitions of sports tourism, from those involving travel for the purpose of participating in competitive sports, to those involving more leisure or adventure sporting activities. Thus, the extent of sports tourism vary quite a bit.

Sports tourism involves people travelling to participate or to observe sports. These activities may include people competing in an international event, such as the Olympics, or simply sitting amongst the audience watching the World Cup match. Inevitably, following sports tourism, there will be consequential impacts. These may be classified under economic impacts, sociocultural impacts, health impacts and environmental impacts.

Impacts of Sport Tourism

Sociocultural Impacts

Land Use: The use of land is necessary to sports tourism. Sports take up space. Some of these sports may even require facilities to be specially built. For instance, golf will definitely require land to be allocated to build its course. Singaporeans, who want to experience golf in a bigger and more fulfilling golf course, may seek to travel to nearby Malaysia instead, and this is a form of land use for Malaysia resulting from sports tourism.

Cultural Exchanges: It is certain that cultural exchanges will take place whenever people of different cultural backgrounds meet. Sports tourists will nevertheless learn about the culture of the country they visit when they arrive at their destination, although their main purpose of travel is to participant in sports, or to observe sports (but not for cultural purposes).

Preservation of Traditions: Once-dying traditions can also be 'revived' through sports tourism. The need to display these traditions to tourists will bring these traditions 'back to life'. Showcasing traditional food, traditional costumes, culture and ethnics will not only enrich these sports tourists' experience to the country, but also help preserve the traditions, instead of letting them gradually disappear from this world.

National Identity: The national pride and prestige one feels when a mega event is held in his country is perpetual. It is a proud feeling to know that your country is able to hold an international event, because it will be broadcast worldwide, and therefore known to the rest of the world.

"In Germany "national pride" ("Nationalstolz") is often associated with the former Nazi regime. Strong displays of national pride are therefore considered poor taste by many Germans. There is an ongoing public debate about the issue of German patriotism.

The World Cup in 2006, held in Germany, saw a wave of patriotism sweep the country in a manner not seen for many years. Although many were hesitant to show such blatant support as the hanging of the national flag from windows, as the team progressed through the tournament, so too did the level of support across the nation. By the time the semifinal against Italy came around, the level of national pride and unity was at its highest throughout the tournament, and the hosting of the World Cup is seen to have been a great success for Germany as a nation."

Violence: This usually occurs among the spectators who are unsatisfied with the announced results. The spectators/ audiences usually from the losing side will create fights with the other side. Violence is one of the negative impacts that can arise from sports tourism. It is an unhealthy scene as this can sour the relationship between two counterparts. Violence in sports tourism does not only happen among countries, but also within one country itself.

Health Impacts

There are various health impacts involved when looking at Sports Tourism, they are:

- Physiological impacts.
- Psychological impacts.
- Social health impacts.

Physiological Impacts

People are generally interested and motivated to play sports when participating in Sports Tourism. Many people all over the world travel to Hawaii to surf as it is a popular destination for big waves.

The physiological impact of Sports Tourism can be seen in athletes who are actively involved, going overseas to compete with other people. These athletes typically have a good physique as it is naturally normal for them to want to improve and train to be better. They lead a lifestyle which centres on their health and physical wellbeing.

Psychological Impacts

Sports allows for the mind to relax when done for recreation. People who engage in Sports Tourism in a noncompetitive environment typically use it as an opportunity to get away and recharge.

Sports also cause the brain to secrete endorphins, which prevents stress and strengthens the body against pain. At the same time, it makes people increase their self-confidence and boosts their self-esteem.

Social Health Impacts

The health risks involved in Sports Tourism applies to both the athletes and fans. They might train too hard to compete, risking injuries. Also, one needs time to adapt to another country and this may sometimes be difficult, sometimes even causing sickness.

For example, jet lag. Similarly, because of the internal time difference, fans all over the world purposely stay up to watch games, and this leads to an irregular sleeping pattern. Cases of fans falling ill during these periods are common, with increased consumption of junk food combined with late nights.

Environmental Impacts

The environmental impacts of sports tourism is classified as negative impacts. It consists of pollution and depletion.

Pollution: Pollution can occur in terms of air, land, water and sound. Air pollution happens basically due to the emission of harmful gases from vehicles. For example during major world games such as the Olympics and World Cup, there will be more vehicles than usual thus increasing the amount of air pollution. Sound pollution occurs due to the noise made by the spectators. As for land pollution, it usually occurs in natural habitats. For instance, sports like mountain climbing pollute the land as the equipments use can destroy the natural surroundings. Apârt from that, littering caused by the masses also contribute to land pollution.

Depletion: In this case, it refers to depletion of resources. For a sports events to be held (which is the main reason for sports tourism), many resources are required.

2

Sports Tourism in India

Sport tourism denotes tourism which is based on the theme of sports; this particular term and the movement associated with largely has been catered to by the western world comprising of North America, Australia and Europe. But nonetheless, it is revolutionizing the tourism sector in other corners of the world; India is a popular holiday destinations in the world where sports tourism is gaining immense prominence and popularity.

Sports tourism in India is being encouraged by the tourism providers in India. It means that vacations to India are sports-oriented. Sports tourism in India is indeed lucrative from the point of revenue-earning. Sports are an integral part of the Indian subcontinent.

India is top destination offering tourists with great and excellent scope for skiing in the Himalayan ranges, going on bicycle tour on the Indian roads or canoeing or whitewater rafting in the hilly streams and rivers. You can go in for mountaineering, rock climbing and aero-sports like hand gliding, ballooning and paragliding in places like Himachal Pradesh, Uttaranchal and Darjeeling. There are numerous water sports and activities in India, especially in Goa and other popular beach destinations.

Surfing the waves or water-scooting is great fun in the Indian seas. Scuba diving, angling and fishing are integral part of sports tourism in India. Golf courses in India largely encourage sports tourism in the Indian peninsula. Golf is an internationally acclaimed sports and favourite to people. The magnificent golf courses attract professional golfers and amateur golfers. Even the luxury resorts in India have private golf courses where tourist can tee off to a fun time during their leisure vacation to India. There are many traditional games in India which tourists take great interest; one such sport is the famous boat race of Kerala.

Business tours combined with active sports activities are becoming highly popular; here business meets leisure and such kind of sports tourism on business tours is a global corporate strategy for employee entertainment and wellbeing. Moreover sports tourism is nurtured by the professional sportsperson; they have to travel extensively for their career. Sportsmen and sportswomen come from all parts of the world to participate in international championships and tournaments like Cricket World Cup, Soccer World Cup or tennis events like Wimbledon. For instance ASEAN games and Commonwealth games have drawn sports professionals to India and will do so in all the future sports events in India.

It is an interesting fact of history... in the ancient past Romans and Greeks used to travel to several places to participate in sports. Hence sports tourism in the modern context is an offshoot of this very old practice; it can be said that is an adapted version of the theme. The only difference is that it leisure travel comes along with it

Sports tourism in India is an absolute must for all the thrill seekers. The geographical diversities of India open up great avenues for adventure sports and activities.

Sports Events in India

India has hosted many important sports events over the years. Many national and international sports events are held in India every year. One of the most important upcoming sports events coming up in India is the Commonwealth Games scheduled to held in New Delhi in 2010. Other sports events in India that are held every year include the Santosh trophy which is an annual football event where all the local teams and clubs take part from each states. The Durand Cup is another football tournament that is held every year in India. It is the oldest football tournament in India. Federation Cup is another popular football tournament held in India every year. IFA shield is also one of the major football tournaments in India.

Other sports events in India include various cricket tournaments. Cricket being the one of the most popular sports in India, the sports is played in both national level and international level. Ranji trophy is an annually held cricket tournament in India that is played between different states and provinces. The Ranji trophy is the first class domestic cricket which also act as doorway for players to get entry in the national team. Other notable cricket championships held in India include Challenger Trophy, Duleep Trophy, Irani trophy and Deodhar Trophy. India also hosted the 1987 cricket world cup along with Pakistan. India again hosted the cricket world cup along with Sri Lanka and Pakistan in 1996.

India also hosts many hockey tournaments throughout the year. Some of these include All India Aagha Khan Hockey Tournament, All India MCC Murugappa Gold Cup Hockey Tournament, Obaidullah Khan Gold Cup, All India Lal Bahadur Shastri Hockey Tournament and All India Beighton Cup Hockey Tournament.

Among other sports events in India, tennis tournaments that are held in India include Sunfeast Open, Chennai Open and Kingfisher Airlines Tennis Open.

Tournaments held in India in shooting include Asian Clay Shooting Championship... 2003, 2nd South Asian Shooting Championship... 1997, VI World Cup... 1997, ISSF World Cup... 2000, 7th South Asian Federation Games... 1995, ISSF World Cup... 2003, 1st Commonwealth Championship... 1995.

India has also hosted many world cup events from time to time in different fields of sports like football, cricket, hockey for both men and women. Other sports events in India include the 8th Asian Pacific Age Group Swimming & Diving Championships held in 1994. India also hosted the 7th SAF Games in 1995. In 1999, the 13th Asian Pacific Age Group Swimming & Diving Championships was also hosted by India. Some more sports events in India held in the past include 4th Women's Asia Cup in Hockey, 1999, Women's Hockey Tournament, 1996, 6th Indira Gandhi International Gold Cup, 1997 for Women hockey and so on.

Some more sports events held in India also include various table tennis tournaments like Commonwealth Table Tennis Championship, 15th Commonwealth Table Tennis Championship, 13th Asia Cup Table Tennis Tournament, VII Asian Junior Table Tennis Championship, VIth Asian Junior Table Tennis Championship, 15th Asia Cup Table Tennis Tournament, 14th Asian Cup Table Tennis Tournament.

Popular Sports in India

Hockey is the official sport in India. However soccer and cricket are the two most popular sports in India. There are also other traditional sports like kho kho and kabbadi that are quite popular and are even played in the national and international levels. India has excelled in sports since the time of the Vedas. Even in the great Indian epics we get to know about the sport activities of India. All the sports in India are played by both men and women and have earned fame for their country. Cricket is considered to be the most popular sports in India although hockey is the official sport of the country. Cricket became the popular sports from 17th century and still persists to be the most popular sports of the country. India won the cricket world cup in 1983 under the captaincy of Kapil Dev. India also won the ICC Twenty 20 world championship, a new form of cricket, in 2007 under captaincy of MS Dhoni. India also boasts in winning the World Championship of Cricket under the captaincy of Sunil Gavaskar in 1985.

Hockey is recognized as the official sport of India. India had been one of the top most names in hockey till the middle of 20th century. India also holds the record for winning gold medals in the Olympic games for 8 times. India also won the 1975 World Cup. India also became the runner up in the World Cup championship in 1973. One of the most notable names in Indian Hockey is Major Dhyanchand. India has also won the Asia in 2007.

Kabaddi is also noted among popular sports in India. This is also one of the traditional games in India. India really excels in Kabaddi and has bagged many awards. India won the gold medal in World cup and Asian Games for men held in 2006.

Badminton is one of the most popular sports in India. Badminton is played by both children and adult specially during the winter months. Some of the notable names associated with badminton in India are or

Prakash Padukone as well as Pullela Gopichand. Both of them bagged the All England Badminton championship and have earned fame and name for themselves as well as for their country. Saina Nehwal is one of the emerging badminton players in India.

Chess is one of the oldest sports in India. India has produced several grandmasters over the years. Famous chess personalities in India include Vishwanathan Anand, Parimarjan Negi, Koneru Humpy are only a few names to add on the list.

Football is another popular sports in India. Although introduced by the British, there are many clubs and teams apart from the national team that play football. One of the major championship won by India in football in the Nehru cup championship.

Boxing is not so much popular sports in India although India have own medals in the Commonwealth Games as well as the Asian Games. Notable Indian boxers are Kalpana Chaudhary, Sarita Devi, Aruna Mishra. Formula One is another sports though dominated once by the western countries, India is gaining popularity day by day. The one name that is associated with Formula One is Narain Karthikeyan. Other popular sports in India include long tennis, table tennis, golf, billiards, archery and so on.

Kerala Boat Race, India

Kerala boat race, India is defined by the several boat races in Kerala, the emerald state lying at the southwestern tip of India. Boat racing is one of the old traditional games of India; in Kerala you will get the full flavour of this sport. There is active participation of the Kerala folks in the boat races and tournaments; boat racing is no less than a community festival out here. Keralites look forward to the annual boat races and so does the tourist who flocks to this place to feel the pulse of this thrilling sport in southern India. Kerala boat race encourages the growth of sports tourism in India. Boat races in Kerala lure sports enthusiasts and leisure seekers to 'God's Own Country'. This sport, taking place in the backwaters of Kerala, represents team spirit and integration. The snake boat races in Kerala are marked by colourful fiestas and festivals and they take place during the harvest festival in the months of August and September. These snake boats or 'chundans' are rowed by 100-125 oarsmen and managed by four helmsmen. There are 25 singers who sing 'vanchipattu' or the boatman's song and rows simultaneously. There are thousands others who line the shores of the backwaters and cheer for their team.

The popular snake boat races of Kerala are:

- Aranmula Uthrattadi Vallamkali... This boat racing competition taking place at Onam is marked by colourful festivities. This colourful water carnival is a dramatic re-enactment of a legend where a religious Brahmin offered food to a pilgrim. It is connected to Aranmula Parthasarathy Temple and on the first day of the event the effigy of Shri Krishna is carried out in procession and on the second day colourfully decorated snake boats assembles; theses boats move in pairs and this magnificent assemblage is enjoyed by young and the old.
- Champakulam Moolam Boat Race... it is one of the ancient boat races in Kerala that is associated with the Shri Krishna temple at Ambalappuzha; in the Malayalam calendar on the 'moolam' day in the month of 'midhunam' this boat race takes place in Champakulam lake. This date is significant since the deity was installed on this day. The boats are exquisitely decorated with parasols.
- Payippad Jalotsavam... this is an annual fiesta of Kerala taking place for a stretch of three days on the Payippad Lake. It takes place in dedication to the deity at Subramanya Swamy Temple at Haripad.
- Nehru Trophy Boat Race... this is one of the popular boat events in Kerala. Punnamada Lake is the venue of Nehru Trophy Boat Race. This trophy is unique because there are separate competitions for women.

Other popular boat races of Kerala are:

- ATDC Boat Race.
- Rajiv Gandhi Boat Race.
- Neerettupuram Boat Race.
- Karuvatta Boat Race.

- Kumarakom Boat Race.
- Kavanattinkara Boat Race.
- Kottayam Mahatma Boat Race.
- Thazhathangadi Boat Race.
- Kottapuram Boat Race.
- The Indira Gandhi Boat Race.

Destinations in India offering Sports Tourism

Sports tourism in India is carving a niche for itself in Indian tourism industry. Sports tourism is broadly defined by the adventure sports and games in India. There are indeed several destinations in India offering sports tourism. There are varied sports activities that you can indulge during your leisure vacation to India. Mountaineering, rock climbing, scuba diving, white water rafting, kayaking, canoeing, sailing, surfing, water scooting, snorkelling and aero sports activities like ballooning, paragliding and hand gliding offer attractive scope for sports lovers and enthusiasts from all parts of the world.

Among the innumerable destinations in India offering sports tourism Himachal Pradesh, Uttaranchal, Goa and Andaman & Nicobar Islands are extremely popular and loved by tourists. The Himalayan state of Himachal Pradesh has become a prime centre of adventure sport activities. Sports tourism in Himachal Pradesh comprises of adventure sports like trekking, skiing, golfing, river rafting, para gliding and mountain cycling. The favourite places to ski are Manali, Shimla and Kufri. The snow covered golf course at Naldehra provides amazing golfing experience. Enjoy rafting in the mountain rapids and rivers of the state; Chandrabhaga, Ravi and Beas are the rivers where you can raft and kayak. In the Solang valley, lying close to Manali, you can enjoy aero sports like paragliding; Kullu and Kangra are good places to enjoy these sorts of aero sport activities. Mountain biking areas in Himachal Pradesh are Una, Kangra, Bilaspur and Hamirpur; you can enjoy mountain biking at Lahaul-Spiti and Kinnaur.

Sports tourism in Goa is marked by the numerous options of water sports; windsurfing, water-skiing, parasailing and dinghy sailing are popular water sports of Goa. The coastal stretches of Goa make this state in the western part of India simply a paradise for the aquatic sports lovers. Sports tourism in Andaman & Nicobar Islands, just like Goa, offers enjoyable and thrilling water games and activities to both national and international sports enthusiasts.

Jammu and Kashmir, Sikkim and Darjeeling in West Bengal also feature as destinations in India offering sports tourism. Skiing in Gulmarg is a thrilling and breathtaking experience. In the beautiful state situated in the foothills of Mount Kanchenjunga, Sikkim you can take great pleasure in adventure sports. You can trek to Bakhim and to Yuksam and Dzongri. Mountain biking can be done in North and West Sikkim. Tista and Rangit are two mountain rivers of Sikkim; you can look for a thrilling rafting and kayaking experience in these rivers. Jorethang in West Sikkim is a glider's favourite. Darjeeling blessed with panoramic views of Everest and Kanchenjunga has attracted thousands of trekkers.

One common point to be noted among the hilly states and regions of India is that the respective state governments are taking optimum measures to capitalize on the natural setting in order to promote sports tourism in India. States marked by presence of seas, oceans and water bodies are encouraging sports tourism through varied water sports. Goa, Kerala and Andaman & Nicobar Islands deserve mention in this regard. Hence destinations in India offering sports tourism promote and popularize adventurous sports activities in accordance to their geographical uniqueness.

Adventure Tourism in India

The endless scope of adventure tourism in India is largely because of its diverse topography and climate. On land and water, under water and in the air, you can enjoy whatsoever form of adventure in India you want. It is one opportunity for you to leave all inhibitions behind and just let yourself go. The mountainous regions offer umpteen scope for mountaineering, rock climbing, trekking, skiing, skating, mount biking and safaris while the rushing river from these mountains are just perfect for river rafting, canoeing and kayaking. The oceans are not behind in any manner as well. The vast and deep expanse of water provide tremendous opportunity for adventure sports in form of diving and snorkelling.

The forest and the desert region have their own distinct place in providing scope for adventure tourism in India. You can enjoy animal safari, jeep safari, bird watching, wild camp, wildlife safari and jungle trail in the forest region while jeep safari and camel safari are the most favoured adventure sports in the desert region. After all this, if you think the list of adventure sports in India has ended, think again. There is still much left in form of paragliding, hand gliding, hot air ballooning, etc.

Adventure tourism in India is meant to provide you an exhilarating experience for life. Many a times in process of having fun, an entirely new aspect of life manifests itself before you and an awareness and appreciation about the surroundings emanates somewhere from deep within your heart.

Trekking

If you love challenges and desire to tread the fascinating unexplored trails made by nature or wish to explore an entirely different culture and living style, then trekking in India is for you. Undoubetedly, the trails in the great Himalayan ranges are the ones that will attract you the most, but other parts of India also have vast opportunities for enjoying a trekking expedition. So much so that you will invariably feel drawn towards it again and again once you have experienced its magic.

So what do you exactly come across while trekking in India? Well, the snow capped mountains definitely have a prime place. Accompanying them are the rushing rivers, cascading waterfalls and lush tropical forests, brilliant with scented flowers, chirping birds and dreamily colourful butterflies. Offering a bit of contrasting beauty are the rugged terrains that have their own charm despite being devoid of any beauty. Adding more variety and fun to your trekking expedition in India are the villages where life is simple but carries a warmth that is unfortunately missing on the plains. The people residing here are not advanced and therefore offer you an opportunity to know, understand and enjoy a lifestyle that is at its most basic and unhurried self.

Moreover, there are a lot more other attractions in form of Hindu temples, Buddhists monasteries etc. in store for you while trekking in India. You just need to keep yourself ready for any kind of surprises that might spring up during your expedition. What is perhaps more interesting is that trekking in India offers every kind of trekker to enjoy himself. Whether you prefer an easy low altitude trek for simple fun or difficult high altitude trek for real challenge, India has it all. You just need to pick your choice and start off a journey off the beaten track.

Some Famous Trek Routes:

- Base Camp — Naitala.
- Bukki to Dokriani Glacier-23 km.
- Bukki to Bukki Village-2 km.
- Bukki to Kheratal-17 km.
- Kheratal to Dokriani Glacier-5 km.
- Bukki to Uttarkashi-34 km.
- Uttarkashi to Rishikesh-149 km.

Skiing

Skiing, as an adventure sport, has come a long way in India. Introduced by the Europeans, it started out as a purely elitist sport, which provided the foreigners an adventurous respite from the heat of the plains. However, it has today become a sport of the common man. People from within India as well as all around the world flock to the country in large number to enjoy the pleasure of skiing.

The fun, excitement and the thrill while sliding down the snow clad slopes of the Himalayans ranges in India is, in one word, fantastic. If you are a novice, you will scream, cry and laugh simultaneously as you speed down the slopes, whereas if experienced, you will enjoy your run down the challenging snowy slopes.

Moreover, the slopes in the skiing destinations in India give you an opportunity to enjoy both snow skiing as well as heli-skiing. In snow skiing itself, you can enjoy both Alpine and Nordic. This means that you can slide downhill in a straight route as well as in a zigzag course, jump from an elevated position, or for extreme adventure, hire a helicopter and have yourself dropped on the snow clad peak itself. From there, the fun and adventure of skiing downwards it enhanced multifold.

Assistance for skiers, in form of equipment, trained guides, pilots and even short courses are available, in an attempt to give them an unmitigated sense of joy when they come to India. So, next time when you feel like running down a snowcapped hill slope with cool icy breezes hitting your face, just think of India. It is here that you will have some of the best moments skiing down the snowy slopes.

Kerala Backwaters

The charm of Kerala lies in its unique attraction, something which is not seen or experienced anywhere else in the world. And there is not just one or two of these. You go on counting as Kerala springs surprises one after another from its treasure chest. You will get tired of witnessing Kerala's marvels, still Kerala will have more to show you.

Backwaters....One such unique attraction, or rather an exhilarating experience comes in the form of a trip to the Kerala Backwaters. For those who have come across the term backwaters for the first time, here's a bit of explanation as to what it actually is. Backwaters are formed when the sea water collects at the beach by the to and fro motion of waves. In Kerala, they constitute the canals, lakes, lagoons and estuaries. The entire network include five large lakes connected by 1500 km of canals. Most of them are natural, however, there are man made canals as well. These are supplied by 38 rivers that flow through the entire state.

A touch of legendary folklore is also interesting here according to which the land of Kerala sprung up as a result of the throwing of axe in the sea by the sage warrior, Parshurama. The distance covered by the axe dried up to give way to land which today is known as Kerala. So the link between Kerala's land and water is invariably strong and the water still takes care of and nourishes it unfailingly.

Significance of Backwaters-Past, Present and Future: In earlier times, when the technology was not much advanced and when roadways were not properly developed, Kerala's backwaters served as its main highway. Passengers and goods were transported from one place to another in equal measures by means of these backwaters. However, as of today, these backwaters are mainly used by the tourism industry to introduce tourists to the hidden troves of the state. The Backwaters is inextricably linked to its past history and culture, is an important part of the present and promises to remain so in future as well.

Backwater Tourism: A number of times, while you are on a trip discovering a new place, a sense of dissatisfaction dawns upon and makes you feel as if the happiness felt at knowing the place was not worth the effort put in to reach there. Not so with Kerala Backwaters. Kerala's Backwater experience will give you much more than just simple happiness. It will give you a feeling of elation-a feeling that has eluded you for a long time now. It is pristine, probably even child like where you feel like clapping with delight.

Plenty of clean water, refreshing greenery, amazing scenery around and a silence broken only by chirping of birds and waters moving below the boat-this is what you will definitely get on your Backwater trip to Kerala. Remote places that are otherwise disconnected from main areas seem to sail past like a dream. Fishing villages, tribal hamlets, people carrying on with their day to day work-scenes like this will be abundant.

The Backwaters of Kerala are also a venue for the annual boat races that take place in the different parts of the state. If you happen to visit during this season (which is around July to September), you can also witness the enthusiasm of the Backwaters as huge boats rush past each other to win the competition amidst loud cheers from the spectators.

The perfect way to explore the beauty and serenity of Kerala Backwater is to hire a boat or a canoe. For a little longer trip, houseboats, which are converted kettuvallom earlier used to carry cargo and passengers, can be hired.

Kerala Backwater Destinations:

Alappuzha: Start off from Alappuzha, a major Backwater Destination and the Venice of East. An intricate network of canals in Alappuzha, especially the ones that are a part of the Vembanad Lake are just the place if you wish to see some really awe inspiring beauty.

Scenes enroute are a varied lot-paddy fields, coconut lagoons, secluded islands, men on country boats busy fishing and shepherding their ducks to new pastures and school children being taken across the canal. Kuttunad, the rice bowl of Kerala, is at the centre of attraction here. This is perhaps the only place where farming is done on land below sea level. You can also step out of the boat and visit the village craftsmen while they are working to make coir. Taste the traditional Keralese food in one of these places, particularly the sea food. Boats are available from the jetty itself which is close to the KSRTC Bus Stand.

Kumarakom: Yet another Backwater destination on the banks of Vembanad Lake, the beauty of Kumarakom has inspired the likes of former Prime Minister, Atal Behari Vajpayee to state, 'Natures silent beauty provides a perfect setting here for contemplation'. Kumarakom Backwater, supposedly discovered just a decade ago, provides some splendid views of coconut groves, mangroves and paddy fields. The highpoint of your journey will be reaching the Pathiramanal Island which is around an hour's ride from the Kumarakom Bird Sanctuary.

Kollam: Fondly referred to as Swapnadesham by many of her faithful admirer, Kollam was once centre of cashew trade in Kerala. Today, the same industry has lost much of its zeal, nonetheless, the beauty and serenity of this little jewel of Kerala has not faded out even a wee bit. The Backwaters in the Ashtamudi Lake and its canals is still as mesmerizing as it was years back. Hire a boat and set out to explore the islands and villages that lie on way the route you have chosen to traverse.

Kozhikode: Located in the northern part of Kerala, Kozhikode has virtually unexplored backwater regions. As such, you can expect plenty of new discovery at each step. Elathur, the Canolly Canal and the Kallai river are favourite places for boating. Also popular are the Kadulundi Bird Sanctuary and Korapuza, the venue for Korapuzha Jalotsavam.

Kochi: The Queen of Arabian Sea, Kochi has one of the best natural harbours in the world. All the islands that constitute a part of Kochi are interconnected by a network of backwaters canals and lakes. Cruising through them and viewing the Chinese fishing net, particularly during sunset, will elate you beyond expression.

River Rafting

The challenge of holding your balance in the midst of speedy water is what river rafting is all about. And India, with a large network of rivers, is the place to be if you wish to enjoy the thrills of rafting. Originating from the great heights of the mountains, especially the great Himalayas, these rivers speed down in a way that makes you feel as if they are in a hurry to reach the plains and enjoy a long overdue freedom. Enroute they whirl, froth, foam and crash over rocky gorges and boulders. They make your raft wobble and wet you with an icy splash in an attempt to divert your attention.

In brief, the rivers in India exude every bit of their untamed qualities and challenge you to overpower them. Also, they put to test your strength, both physical and mental, and it is in this that the whole excitement of rafting lies. The river rafting destinations in India are comparable to the best in the world. Also, very much like trekking, rafting in India offers different levels so that both amateurs as well as trained and professional rafters can enjoy themselves. Moreover, for those, in need of a bit of training, there are quick courses on offer too.

Rafting

For adventure lovers, Himachal Pradesh in India is a destination par excellence. Amongst many adventure sports that can be enjoyed in Himachal, trekking, skiing, gliding and rafting are the most popular ones. The last one, rafting, is also known as the white water rafting and can be enjoyed to the maximum extent in the state of Himachal. The reason for this is the presence of a number of snow fed rivers in the state that rush down the Himalayan ranges and make their way through the various regions. These rivers bumping, swirling and rolling present wonderful stretch of water for rafting enthusiasts. As a matter of fact, the rivers of upper Himalayas are considered the best in the entire world for enjoying rafting. While rafting, the fun and thrill is at its peak. With water rushing at great speed and sometimes even splashing at your body and face, you feel completely delighted. Moreover, the sights enroute will give a new dimension and direction to your imagination.

Rafting Places In Himachal: There are four rivers in Himachal that offer opportunities to enjoy white water rafting. These rivers flow in the north westerly direction and are almost parallel to one another. The first of these, Beas has its genesis in the Rohtang Pass and flows through the Kullu valley. Rising from the Raigarh glacier, river, Ravi makes its way down Chamba valley. The third river, Chenab originates from the tributaries, Chandra and Bhagha and passes swiftly through the Chenab or Pangi valley. It finally enters the state of Jammu and Kashmir. Lastly, there is Satluj river that originates beyond Indian borders and enters the country near Shipkila and is later joined by the Spiti river at Khab. This river flows through Kinnaur and Shimla.

Amongst all these river, rafting in Beas has gained tremendous popularity. You can raft on the rapids of Beas, specially between Shamsi and Aut. This is around 20 km stretch and provides most thrilling rafting experience. This river is also the venue for many rafting competition in the state. And while talking about venues for rafting races, the Sutlej near Shimla, Ravi near Chamba and the Chandra in Lahaul are not behind. Only chances for rafting races are being found out on the Spiti river.

Tourists Info

The first important thing to know about rafting in Himachal is the season in which it can be enjoyed. Summers, spring and autumn are the time to go on a rafting since during winters and part of monsoons, this sport is stopped for a while. The equipments required for river rafting are provided by HTPDC, Himachal Tourism Development Corporation. These equipments include dinghy (inflatable rubber life raft), lifejackets and helmets. Apart from these, an expert guide is also provided for the benefit of rafters. There are certain things, that you will need to carry yourself as well. Amongst these items are sunscreen lotion, sunglasses, shorts, T-shirts, suitable shoes, a windproof jacket, a light sweater, towels, a flashlight and not to forget, a camera and first aid kit. Those who are under medication must carry their required medicine along. You can carry your personal items in a small dry box or a bag.

Uttaranchal River Rafting

River Rafting is an adventure sport which thrills and chills you at the same time. It is like a challenge to tame a wild river. When it comes to river rafting, Uttaranchal offers the broadest possible options for river rafting in the world, from milder river courses to wilder ones. Uttaranchal has in abundance rivers and terrains to suit all levels of river rafting. The challenge and thrill of flowing with the river and controlling yourself at the same time is the true thrilling experience.

Following the river course right from the time it emerges from the glacier upto the plains is a not just a fun water sports. Deep gorges, rocky course, boulders and moraines, all are in the your way.

Rafting in Garhwal

Garhwal is the origin land of many rivers in Uttaranchal, Ganga being the most significant one. The river courses in Uttaranchal are such that everyone from a novice to an amateur and expert can enjoy this watery thrill. At Devprayag when Alaknanda and Bhagirathi meet Ganga, the waters are frothy and racy. River rafting here in Grade IV to V is packed with a power punch of thrill, it is recommended for experts only. Down the course of the river, ahead of Devprayag, the river turns into a pool, just suitable for amateurs. The best thing about river rafting in Garhwal is the complimentary sight seeing. Rafting through the river, you closely follow the white sands where you camp in night. Also to be seen are the grassy terrains of oaks, pine spruce and fir, the terraced fields, and here and now glimpses of some wildlife. Not to forget the spiritualness of the river combined with the riverside ashrams. Since when did rafting got so much more then just wading in the frothy waters, well, the answer is for you to find in Garhwal.

The most popular stretch for rafting in Garhwal is between Kaudilya and Shivpuri. There are other stretches also including a variety of grades on rivers Alaknanda, Mandakini and Bhagirathi.

Rafting in Kumaon

Rafting in Kumaon is no less exciting. Infact, it has long stretches of dangerous waters where only the experienced can make a move. River Kali Ganga, also known as Sharda in the lower reaches, enters India from Nepal. At Jauljibi when it meets River Gori, it is then that the real adventure begins. The river gains volume and for the next 117 kilometres it is a taxing run. It passes through some dangerous rapids, hence this run is recommended only for experienced. It's a three day rafting to Tanakpur. Further down the course of river, rafting gets easier.

Find Out More: Garhwal Mandal Vikas Nigam, an undertaking of Uttaranchal government organises river rafting courses at Kaudilya which is 38 kilometres from Rishikesh. They offer courses, equipment etc. They have trained professionals to teach you river rafting in Ganges.

For more information about river rafting expeditions in Uttaranchal, you can contact GMVN.

Best Time To Go: The best time for river rafting if you have some hands on experience is during summer. It is at this time that water level rises due to melting of snow and the monsoons. For beginners, months of August and September are best as the water level is lower and manageable. Even springs and early summers can be considered for rafting. Rafting in winters is a complete no because many a rivers are frozen, the climate is chilled and getting soaked means inviting hypothermia.

Jammu And Kashmir Rafting

Rafting in J&K-Life in The Fast Flow: There are so many things to do in Jammu and Kashmir but nothing more challenging than rafting in the white waters of the many rivers that cut through the state of Jammu and Kashmir. The two most famous rivers where you can go for this extreme sport is River Indus and Zanskar river. River Lidder also has few stretches that are good enough to keep you enthralled. The rivers run trough few of the most mesmerizing landscapes, giving you the opportunity to explore those wonders of nature, which are otherwise unreachable through land routes. Few stretches are big enough that they take days to complete. And in between, you will stay in camps set up under the snowcapped mountains and hilltop monasteries, just by the sides of these roaring rivers.

Though there are rafting options in Jammu and Kashmir region but they don't compare up to rafting in Laddakh region, especially in Zanskar. There are many private agencies that offer these rafting trips. In other adventure sports, you get training sessions before you indulge in the real thing, but rafting is something where there can be no trial runs. All you get are few precaution tips and safety presentation. Here only the real thing prepares you for the real thing.

Famous River Rafting Destinations: The best place in Jammu and Kashmir where you can indulge in River Rafting is in River Lidder near Pahalgam. The river hosts the two different stretches, which are quite suitable for river rafting. They are great for rafting but they cannot be called treacherous as the slopes are not that steep, and this attribute of the river is idle location for the first timers and learners. One can go for a daylong excursion to the river. You can also take up white water canoeing in rivers like Sindh and Drass and Suru and in the many high altitude lakes like Gangabal, Kaunsarnag and Vishensar. The facilities for this sport are not very advanced since the sport is only just catching up in the state. But still, its worth the time and money that you will spend on it.

Rafting In Laddakh Region

This is the place where you will have an appointment with and the roaring and thrashing beast, the Zanskar river. The Zanskar is graded as a class IV, extremely rough river. But the first look of the river will be deceiving and the thought that the said difficulty of the river seems exaggerated will definitely cross your mind. The rafting trip will be few days long and the first two days might not feel that adventurous. But hold on, the real test begins after two days of rapids. The next few days you will be hitting fast rapids in the deep gorges and reveal it yourself why this rated so high. Apart from Zanskar River, Indus River also is a great option for thrilling white water rafting.

The best time for rafting in Jammu and Kashmir is during summer time when the rivers are full of water. In winters many rivers and lakes get frozen. Even in summers the water is freezing cold. So it is advised that you wear a wet jacket before you indulge in this sport. Rafting is an extremely challenging sport so do not ignore the precautionary measures and warning signs that your tour guide tells you to look out for. Make sure that there are adequate rescue measures before you embark on this adventurous thrilling sport.

Safari

The varied topography and climatic conditions of India ensure the lovers of safari, like you, a real treat. You can enjoy a safari on the back of a yak in the mountainous region and on the back of a camel in both the cold as well as the arid desert region of the country. Horse safari and elephant safaris are two other options for you to enjoy yourself on the back of an animal in India. A ride on a horse is as royal as it is on an elephant, the only difference being the speed of the two animals.

Leaving the animals behind, you can choose more speed and set out on a jeep or motorbike safari. These new modes of transportation allow you to see a great deal more in less time as compared to that of animals. This is not to say that the fun is more while you are enjoying a safari trip in a vehicle in India. Rather, it is more of a singular experience you get to enjoy in each of these that make your entire trip a memorable one. With animals it is their movement, which you are not accustomed to, that will make your safari trip interesting.

As for the locales that you traverse through while on a safari trip in India, there is a whole variety. If you are on a camel safari trip, then sand dunes are the major attraction in dry desert while the rugged mountain terrain, ancient passes and remote villages are the highlights in the cold desert region of India. In the mountainous regions of the country, riding on the back of yak can throw up sceneries like shimmering lakes, gurgling streams, glacial valleys, breathtaking cascades, towering snow peaks, meadows and forests. The beauties of the mountain regions can also be captured by undertaking a jeep or motorbike safari tour in India. Infact, given their convenience, these vehicles can be used to explore almost any part of the country. Jeep safari, additionally, is also quiet popular in the wildlife sanctuaries and parks.

That leaves us with the royal elephants and well bred horses. Elephant safari in the royal cities and the wildlife destinations is a classic means to enjoy the splendours of the places. And as for horses, they are perfectly suitable to discover the magic of plains as well as mountains.

If by now, you are thinking that it is just the landscape that can be enjoyed during a safari tour in India, you are in for a surprise. This is because what is more interesting and attractive about the safari tours in the country is the fact that they allow you to interact with local people regularly. They encourage you to understand their culture more closely and let you be a part of it, even if it is for a while. After, so much of information, there is hardly any need to stress the fact that safari, as an adventure activity in India, is not only famous but also growing more and more every day. Therefore, pick up any safari tour and get ready for an adventurous time ahead.

Polo Sports

The sport of polo had its beginnings in India, in the state of Manipur. Rajasthan's princely kingdoms adopted the sport and made it their own, with their natural proclivity for riding. Kingdoms kept special stables for polo ponies, and their teams included among the very best in the world. Very often, the players were the rulers and members of their families, though their armies also encouraged the sport. In the zenanas, even the women of the royal family were encouraged to play polo, and proved themselves adept at it. In fact, if the sport has a presence in the country today, it is because the former royal families have continued to provide encouragement for it, and the Indian Army has been able to contribute its mite to it. In recent years, corporate sponsorship too has been able to make a contribution to the sport.

Horse Polo

The Jaipurs were a formidable polo playing family, and the last maharaja of the state literally died with his spurs on, on a polo field. With the glamour of the game, they drew international publicity for India, and the sport has remained one of the most prominent in the elite social circuit. Along with Jaipur, there are also formidable polo teams in Jodhpur and Udaipur, while the 61st Cavalry, also based in Jaipur, has kept it alive in the army.

It is not possible to simply arrive and start playing polo, since the sport needs especially bred horses in large numbers. These are largely maintained by the players themselves, or with the help of their sponsors. You will therefore have to seek out an invitation to play, something you are best advised to do in advance. However, it is possible to send in a special request while planning your trip to Rajasthan, especially if you are a group with polo-playing members. This is important because, in season, when the game is played (September-March), the polo teams are often out (in Delhi, Calcutta or Mumbai) on the circuit, or may even be playing overseas. Of course, there is also the chance of having visiting teams in Rajasthan coinciding with the time of your visit. Even if you do not get the chance to play, there is every chance of being able to watch the sport as an observer which is almost as good as playing. There is something extremely satisfying about watching men on their horses as they pursue the ball with their sticks with skill and adroitness.

Camel Polo

At various tourist festivals in the state, camel polo has been introduced as a friendly, competitive sport. Perhaps the only place in the world where it is played, the game provides a great deal of amusement and mirth, but is not yet a serious pursuit. If you would like to have a game especially organised, request your tour operator to have it arranged.

Bicycle Polo

For those who like the fast pace of horse polo, bicycle polo provides an option that is at least as exciting. During the sixties and seventies, a lot of impetus was provided to the sport, particularly in Bikaner, though in recent years it has become somewhat dissipated. However, for those who may like to participate in a friendly match, or to observe one, special arrangements can be made on request. In more recent years, the sport has developed a following in the Shekhawati region.

Water Sports

Remember, when you were young, you loved to play in and with water. You loved to splash it at yourself or on your parents for the sake of fun. As you grew up, you began to learn newer ways of having fun with water. So much so that it has now become a huge attraction for you while you are planning a trip to any new destination during your vacation. If this is the case this time as well, just think of India.

With the Bay of Bengal in the east, the Arabian Sea in the west, and the Indian Ocean in the south, India has vast expanse of water bodies bordering its land. Additionally, there are towering mountains in the country that are origin point of the innumerable big and small rivers and streams. Some of the major rivers running through the length and breadth of the country include Ganga, Yamuna, Brahmaputra, Kaveri, Narmada, Godavari and Krishna. This piece of fact is enough to enthuse lovers of water-sports like you around the world. And, as for the various options available for water-sports in India is concerned, the list is long-sailing, boating, rowing, swimming, canoeing, kayaking, fishing, angling, yachting, surfing, wind surfing, kite-surfing, snorkelling and diving. Each sport offers you fun that is unique to it.

For example, if swimming offers you more of a refreshing round in water, snorkelling and diving offer you a glimpse of the colourful magical marine world in varying degree. There is surfing where you need to catch a good wave and then ride down the face of it while staying just ahead of its breaking part. In sharp contrast are rowing and kayaking wherein you just need to enjoy the beauty of the water and the feeling on being in midst of it while moving it with the help of oars or kayaks.

Equipment, trainers and guides and courses, anything that is required for enjoying water sports in India is readily available. You just need to choose the sport you will like to enjoy during your trip. The water sports destinations in India await to enthral you.

Aero Sports

There is a hidden desire in all of us to fly like a bird and aero sports give life to precisely this wish of ours. Aero sports have gained famed all over the world and India, too, attracts a whole bunch of aero sports lovers every year. Aero sports in India takes the form of paragliding, para sailing, hang gliding, hand gliding and hot air ballooning. Each is different from the other in one way or the other yet the basic intention is the same-to provide you that feeling of exhilaration while you soar above in the sky like a free soul.

The destination for aero sports in India range from the hilly to coastal regions and from plains to desert regions. This means that you have an opportunity to enjoy a bird's eye view of the vast expanse of blue sea, sandy desert and high mountain ranges, as per your wishes. You also get an opportunity to fly over and watch the cities as they move by in usual manner.

The risk involved while indulging in aero sports, except in perhaps hot air ballooning, is great and it is the same in India. You need to be physically fit and mentally prepared to enjoy any kind of activity in the air. As for the best time to enjoy aero sports in India, it is worth noting that the varied topography and climatic zone has made the country an year round aero sports destination. Moreover, there is no prior permission required to take up aero sports in India, except for in some restricted areas. So, if you nurture a desire to soar above in the sky, aero sports in India is definitely one of the best pick for you. Take it up and get ready to be enthralled.

3

The Business of Sport Tourism

Sport tourism is a multi-billion dollar business, one of the fastest growing areas of the $4.5 trillion global travel and tourism industry. By 2011, travel and tourism is expected to by more than 10 percent of the global gross domestic product. The economies of cities, regions and even countries around the world are increasingly reliant on the visiting golfer and skier or the travelling football, rugby or cricket supporter. In some countries, sport can account for as much as 25 percent of all tourism receipts.

Sport tourists are passionate, high-spending, enjoy new sporting experiences and often stimulate other tourism. Their direct benefit to a destination is cash-their indirect benefit can be years of follow-on tourists. Sport tourism is now a tool to make achieve many things-to make-money, create thousands of new jobs and even help change cultural perceptions such as in the Middle East and South Africa.

The Business of Sport Tourism is a Sport Business report which:

- Quantifies the size of the sport tourism industry.
- Assesses the benefits of event hosting.
- Identifies regions in the world that benefit from sport tourists.
- Highlights the key markets and players and their successful strategies.
- Analyses successful and unsuccessful sport tourism strategies.
- Forecasts the future industry.

The Caribbean economy is at a crossroads and Caribbean governments and the Caribbean private sector private must take deliberate and pragmatic actions to reengineer the productive and distributive processes, improve productivity and competitiveness in the face of increasing global competition.

It is unfortunate that the Caribbean economy has restructured but the development strategy of some policy makers are still locked in the colonial mode of production. Services have had the locomotive effect on the global economy since the 1980s. Global trade in agricultural products declined steadily, from 42% in 1950 to 8% in 1995, while trade in services expanded steadily, from 10% to 53% over the same period. Trade in traditional agricultural products is projected to decline to about 5% by 2010, while trade in services is estimated to increase to about 60% in the same period.

Tourism services export has had the locomotive effect on the rest of the economy but the persistence of protectionism had clouded the reality somewhat. Despite increasing pressure from emerging markets and the declining market share of international tourist arrivals, tourism offers the most viable economic option for the Caribbean region.

The stay-over sector has the multiplier effect since cruise tourism has not had the same economic impact even if the number of cruise ship calls has increased significantly. Information released by the St. Lucia Hotel & Tourism Association revealed that 'the cruise industry realized profits in 2005 in excess of US$6 billion of which the Caribbean generated 65% or US$4 billion. Yet only 2% of the taxes paid were to the Caribbean, 2% of materials sourced were from the Caribbean, and only 3% of the people they employ are from the Caribbean. ... In St. Lucia, "a boat trip by the cruise liners for US$80 results in benefits of only US$4 to the island; the rest remains "on board" as profits.

Studies by UWI, CTO and CTO member countries strongly suggest that the cultural products, particularly art, entertainment, music and sports drive activity in the stay over sector. Hotel occupancy and tourism receipts increase significantly in Antigua during the cricketing months. Tourism receipts for April 1995 and 1999 (when the West Indies cricket team played Australia at the Antigua Recreation Ground (ARG), totalled EC$75m and EC$76m respectively while receipts for the month that followed (May) totalled EC52m and EC$50m respectively. The annual St. Lucia Jazz Festival has generated significant economic activity during the tourism off-season. The 2004 Jazz Festival attracted 12,553 visitors, who spent an estimated US$17.7 million.

The Caribbean is known the world over for leisure, entertainment and sport. Sun, sea and sport fuse together with a contagious love, fun and joy to create the perfect environment for the business, entertainment or adventure tourist. The Caribbean sun is enjoyed on the greens, in the sea, in the football and cricket stands. The adventure seeker enjoys the non-stop nightlife in Jamaica, Antigua and Barbuda, St. Lucia, Barbados and Trinidad and Tobago, with entertainment including "back-in-time" parties, live groups in fun bars, mass camps and live performances featuring regional and international artistes.

Sport has become a socioeconomic phenomenon of considerable magnitude, influencing community life, business life, clothing styles, languages and ethical values, race relations and even automotive design.

Sport is part of the development of our human capital, as it promotes health, mental strength, develops character, neutralizes tension and social instability, builds international bonds, and earns revenue. Sporting successes cement a sense of community and allow the people a safety-valve for venting their economic frustrations.

My latest manuscript "Sport Tourism" sponsored by the UNDP amplifies the importance of sport in the social and economic development of the English-speaking Caribbean countries in the light of the painful macroeconomic adjustment that they are going through, and establishes the importance of sport tourism as an important emerging sector with the capacity for entrepreneurial development, foreign exchange earning, employment creation and youth empowerment.

The case studies confirm the viability of golf and cricket as internationally competitive products. Sporting teams must be coached, trained and disciplined for the purpose of professionalizing exceptional players for overseas contracts, and for providing sustained high-value performances that attract visitors and fill the hotel rooms. Where commercial sporting facilities are developed, they must be sold in the international marketplace as ideal venues for major events.

Sport is an ideal avenue for the empowerment of our restless youth population. It is a vehicle for arresting youth antisocial behaviour, creating employment, lifelong education, and for providing opportunities for career and enterprise development.

The study argues for a paradigm shift in the conception and approach to the development of sport in the Caribbean. It calls on policy makers to clearly define the role of recreational and commercial sports in the national development strategies.

This study develops three typologies of "sport tourism activities" in the English-speaking Caribbean – the "economic boosters," the "employment creators", and the "potential cash-cows." The economic impacts of the sporting activities are analysed using case studies.

The work perceive CWC2007 as galvanizing the modernization of the society and economy, facilitating the shift from the 'weighted economy' to 'weightless economy,' creating the milieu for the takeoff of the tourism industry (the economic conveyor belt), reengineering the production and distribution of commercial cricket, and laying the platform for the growth of sport business industry in Antigua and Barbuda, Barbados, Grenada, Guyana, Jamaica, St. Kitts and Nevis, St. Lucia and Trinidad and Tobago (LIAT, February 2006).

It argues that the policies geared at liquidating the legacy associated with the reorganization of production and distribution could create the platform for the competitiveness of the regional economy.

"Sport Tourism" calls for a paradigm shift in our conception and development of sports in the Caribbean. And this new vision must become part and parcel of our personal, national and regional development vision. Policy makers must clearly define the role of recreational and commercial sports in the development strategy. The first is an imperative, and forms an integral part of the program for building a harmonious and productive society, and lays the foundation for the successful growth of the political and economic systems, while the second is selective and targeted towards foreign exchange earning.

A holistic approach to sports development is critical. It is the continual socialization of the people in these formal and non-formal curricula which improves health and wellbeing, preserve mental balance, overcome traumatic experiences, perpetuates core social values, produces acceptable behaviour types, builds good ethnic and race relations, reinforces gender equality, and reduces generational gaps in our society. And increasingly, these curricula are opening avenues for life skills and entrepreneurial training for many in poor communities.

There are many different definitions of sports tourism, from those involving travel for the purpose of participating in competitive sports, to those involving more leisure or adventure sporting activities. Thus, the extent of sports tourism vary quite a bit. Sports tourism involves people travelling to participate or to observe sports. These activities may include people competing in an international event, such as the Olympics, or simply sitting amongst the audience watching the World Cup match.

Inevitably, following sports tourism, there will be consequential impacts. These may be classified under economic impacts, sociocultural impacts, health impacts and environmental impacts. The increasing and important impact sport has in economic terms requires a more multi-disciplinary approach.

The economic sector of sport has transformed itself in the last decade from a traditional Spectators-Subsidies-Sponsors-Local (SSSL)-model to a more global Media-Corporations-Merchandising-Markets or MCCM-model. The new sport model has executed forms of vertical integration in the industry and has created synergisms as an outcome of the relations between business and sport. Some of the economic developments are-Broadcasting rights, merchandising, sponsoring, organizing of mega sporting events, multiplication effect of organizing a sport event, the mobile leisure society, sport tourism, sport and the impact on health, the public-private cooperation in building of sporting infrastructures, the betting industry, raising market share of sporting goods, shoes and clothing.

The concept of sport related tourism has become more prominent in the last few years both as an academic field of study and an increasingly popular tourism product.

The purpose of this paper is to review and critique the sport tourism literature as it stands in 1998, and to suggest a future research agenda. Disparities in the definition of sport tourism are addressed and some of the difficulties which scholars have faced in establishing a standardized definition are outlined. In answering the question why has sport tourism suddenly become so prominent, a look back at history shows that people have engaged in sport related travel for centuries.

However, in the past ten years, the popularity of this form of travel has increased. Various explanations, such as the increased emphasis on health and fitness and increased use of sports events by cities to attract tourists, are examined. The question of what is known about sport tourism includes a review and critique of the literature in the three domains of sport tourism: active sport tourism, which refers to people who travel to take part in sport; event sport tourism, which refers to travel to watch a sports event; and nostalgia sport tourism, which includes visits to sports museums, famous sports venues, and sports themed cruises.

The overarching conclusion from this review is that the field suffers from a lack of integration in the realms of policy, research, and education. At a policy level, there needs to be better coordination among agencies responsible for sport and those responsible for tourism. At a research level, more multi-disciplinary research is needed, particularly research which builds upon existing knowledge bases in both sport and tourism. In the realm of education, territorial contests between departments claiming tourism expertise and those claiming sport expertise need to be overcome.

India Tourism Industry is Gearing up for Commonwealth Games 2010

The Commonwealth Games 2010 will be held at New Delhi, the Capital of India. Delhi is a modern metropolis that has hosted Asian Games twice before– in 1951 and in 1982. After nearly three decades, it will host the prestigious sports event in October next year.

The prospects of international travellers and tourists who will come to India during the period is already keeping India tourism and hospitality industry with its allied sectors on toes. Besides those who will come here to participate and watch the sports events held here, experts in tourism industry bet that other tourists will also prepone and postpone their visit to India to coincide with the Commonwealth Games so that they can optimize their tour experience. Hospitality, aviation and hotel industries in Delhi and National Capital

Region (NCR) are developing their infrastructure, improving their service quality and facilities, and promoting their brands at a record pitch.

Tour operators and hotel booking agents expect a sharp rise in the sale of Golden Triangle tours, Rajasthan Tours, and North India tours too. Other major tourist attractions of India that include Taj-fame Agra, Jaipur, Mumbai, Goa, Bengaluru, and Cochin are also preparing for the influx of tourists during Commonwealth Games. Commonwealth Games 2010 are also being seen as a grand opportunity for promoting India Tours among international tourists. Government is going through all possible antics to project an image of clean, green, safe and friendly India that is easily accessible by world-class transport systems.

Rich historical architecture and cultural diversity of Delhi sets an ideal base to arouse curiosity in tourists about the splendour and opulence that lies in the royal forts and palaces of Rajasthan. Rajputs of Rajasthan were either friends or foes of great Mughals who dominated Agra, Delhi and surrounding areas.

The most lavish palaces can be seen in the princely states that chose to have friendly ties with Mughals but most legendary forts can be found in the regions where bloody battles were fought and Rajputs refused to let Mughals enter their territory. India Travel agencies are preparing specialized tour packages for the Commonwealth Games of 2010 that feature quick-to-reach destinations such as Taj Mahal, Khajuraho Temples, Golden Temple of Amritsar, Ranthambore and Corbett National Parks and Tiger Reserves, and idyllic mountain resorts like Shimla, Mussoorie, Nainital, and Manali in Uttaranchal, Himachal Pradesh, and Jammu & Kashmir. With high hopes set on 2010 Commonwealth Games, India tourism industry is also preparing itself to cash the opportunity to promote lesser-known tourist destinations such as Northeast Vacations, Virgin Islands of Andaman and Nicobar, Monasteries of Leh and Laddakh, and Pilgrimage Tours that offer true taste of culture and traditions in India.

Travel experts say that since the sports event is to be held in October, it gives an excellent opportunity to tourism industry to prop up its Fairs and Festivals Tours. October and November is the time of festivities in India. Pushkar Fair Tours, Durgapuja and Diwali Tours, Mysore Dussehra Tours, and several other such packages will be able to attract foreign visitors to India by offering them an opportunity to share the colourful and musical celebrations of Indian festivals and observe the traditions and lifestyle of people from close.

When Narain Karthikeyan veered his yellow Jordan into an outlap during a practice session at the Sepang Grand Prix in Malaysia a month ago, he was surprised to see Indian flags fluttering around the track. "Narain was taken aback, as a few years ago Indian faces were not a familiar sight at Grand Prix events," says Yohann Sethna, the founder of India's only Formula One (F1) fan club. This year, however, Sepang Grand Prix had about 1,000 Indians flying to Kuala Lumpur to see the Coimbatore racer rev up the engines down the F1 track.

It's not just happening at Grand Prix events, the number of Indian spectators crowding world stadia is on the rise as India begins its innings in sports tourism. "Sports tourism is a growing niche market in India and in the next three years, over 100,000 Indians are expected to travel abroad exclusively to watch sports-related events," says Gaurav Sundaram, CEO of the Bangalore-based GET Lionel India, a K K Birla group company which recently got into sports tourism. Sundaram adds that the market for sports tourism is currently pegged at Rs 20-25 crore. And the future? "A jump of nearly 500% to approximately Rs 100-150 crore can be safely estimated," he says.

According to market observers, sports tourism got the much-needed impetus with the rise in popularity of sports like golf, F1 and tennis which typically attract the well-to-do crowd. Says I Nissim, a Chennai golfer who did two golf tours to China last year, "These days it's not uncommon to run into an Indian at a golf course or at F1 events held abroad. Thanks to sports channels and newspapers, cricket is no longer the only game which attracts the ready-to-travel sports enthusiast."

Sethna would agree. When this avid F1 fan backpacked his way with two friends to the 1990 Silverstone Grand Prix in London, they were the only Indians present in the stadium. "In the early '80s, not many knew about these races as even newspapers didn't carry F1 reports," he recalls. According to Zakir Ahmed, a former rally driver who is also the first travel agent in India to conduct F1 package tours: "Around 300 Indians went for the 2000 Malaysian Grand Prix, about

500 for the Australian 2002 Grand Prix and over 1000 went to Sepang last month."

The number of sports enthusiasts may have gone up, but what got them to travel abroad to watch sports events? The tourism analysts say that the growth in sports tourism has been influenced by the thriving economies of the Middle East and South East Asian countries.

"Till the late '90s, Grand Prixs were only held in not-in-use World War II airfields in UK, Europe, the streets of Monte Carlo and places in the West," says Ahmed. Tickets were expensive and difficult to book. Then in 1999 Kuala Lumpur came up with a state-of-the-art race track followed by Bahrain and China in the year 2004. Ahmed adds that F1 race tickets are cheaper in Asia. "A F1 tour package including airfare, race tickets and sightseeing came for as low as Rs 30,000 to 35,000 per head," he says.

In the late '90s, golf tours here, the tourists prefer to tee off, became the in thing, especially for corporate customers. "In the last decade, a number of golf courses have come up in Malaysia, Thailand and China which have recently started attracting small Indian groups of 30 to 40 people," Ahmed says.

Even though golf and F1 events have been drawing Indian crowds, it's the cricket World Cup which expectedly gets the maximum Indian sports tourists. Though the market figures for outbound travel for watching cricket matches were unavailable, one prominent travel agent says the number of bookings from India went up from 900 for the '99 World Cup to 1,500 for the '03 World cup. "Unlike other sports events, the cricket World Cup tour packages have to be booked a year in advance. The closer the host country, the more the demand," he says. With the number of cricket tours, F1 races and golf tournaments on the rise, it won't be long before the niche sport tourism market edges rapidly towards the mainstream.

The study was carried out in Mumbai, Maharashtra state, India during winter 2004-05 with a view to promote sports tourism in the country and discussed in detail its benefits in terms of sustainable economic development, the promotion of peace and understanding between people. The respondents opined both positive and negative impacts of sports tourism on heritage sites and nature based ecotourism spots.

It was observed that 78% of the respondents were very much interested in the sports cum heritage and nature based tourism. 22% of the tourists were somewhat interested only in sports tourism. Only 1% of the respondents stated that they did not possess an understanding of the concept of the sports tourism. Over 80% of those surveys in each category perceived sports tourism as beneficial with enhanced employment opportunities both directly and indirectly to the vast spectrum from highly trained managers to unskilled workers.

The respondents (11%) expressed awareness that the development of sports cum tourism may have impacts on the natural and cultural environment as well as social impacts on the community that may not be easily mitigated if at all. It can be concluded that sports and tourism are interdependent, educational and enjoyable and play a significant role in promoting the socioeconomic development of the society in particular and country in general.

Back in 1997 it was first suggested that sport tourism could be categorized and better defined by adopting a consumer motivation approach. It was posited, albeit briefly, that sport tourism could firstly be divided into two areas of focus; differentiating between those who travel primarily for sport (sport tourists) and those where sport is perceived as a secondary consideration (tourism sport).

Each section was segmented further through the use of hard and soft definitions, which differentiated between competitive and recreational considerations in sport tourism, and the secondary and incidental components of tourism sport (all of which will be explained in more detail later in this article).

Clearly what was missing from the original paper was, firstly any discussion relating to theoretical perspectives which would help underpin and explain the consumer motivational approach, and secondly an example(s) of its likely application to both destinations and particular sports. Therefore this paper aims to highlight the secondary reinforcement properties of sport-related tourism and its consequent implications to sport tourist categorization, destination profiling, tourism planning and education.

Sport, Tourism and Motivation.

When reviewing literature pertaining to sport and tourism motivation it becomes clear that the plethora of explanations offered are often dependent upon the interpretation of what constitutes motivation and in some cases whether it is important to distinguish motive from motivation. For example within the tourism literature alone it soon becomes clear that the motivation to take a vacation cannot be even partially explained as a straight forward need to take a break. Such simplistic explanations fail to take into account the cultural, sociological and psychological reasons as to why an individual feels it necessary to take a break, as well as failing to discover whether the motivation is based upon a need to escape from a present environment or the desire to escape to another (or indeed a combination of both). Furthermore, it is unclear whether the tourists themselves are aware as to why they are making a trip:

> *For some, tourist motivation results from deep, psychological needs often unrecognized by tourists themselves, whereas others equate motivation with the purpose of a trip or the choice of holiday. In addition, it is equally ambiguous whether motivational approaches to tourism should focus upon the expressed motives of travellers or the underlying motive which initially drives them. Therefore a tourist may express the reason for travelling as a desire to be pampered-but perhaps this need to be pampered stems from self-esteem issues caused by negative childhood experiences.*

To help illustrate this point, Iso-Ahola (1980), when describing expressed leisure needs, uses an iceberg analogy to help illustrate the layers of differing motives. The tip of the iceberg (i.e. what is visible) represents expressed motives whilst the overwhelming majority of the iceberg, which remains unseen below the waterline, accounts for the underlying motives such as those pertaining to socialization and personality factors.

Fascinating though these underlying motives may be, it is arguably unrealistic to identify all the often contradictory reasons for travel which are specific to individuals' own biographies and in any case are so deep rooted as to be practically imperceptible by those who experienced them. Unsurprisingly, therefore, tourism motives mooted in the literature tend to categorize reasons for travel as escaping from and/or escaping to particular destinations in order to experience preconceived outcomes. This has led to a variety of both similar and competing cultural, social and psychological suggestions of what drives individuals and groups to travel. For example Krippendorf (1987) lists 8 primary reasons for travel: recuperation and regeneration; compensation and social integration; escape; communication; freedom and self-determination; self-realization; happiness and to broaden the mind.

Alternatively McIntosh and Goeldner (1990) offer 4 broader categories, which would undoubtedly encompass the more specific reasons, mentioned above, these being: physical motivators; cultural motivators; interpersonal motivators; status and prestige motivators.

Whilst Ryan has argued the case of utilizing research in leisure motivation (based upon Beard and Ragheb 1983) in order to identify motives in tourism; these being intellectual, social, competence-mastery and stimulus-avoidance component.

It is important to point out that with all the approaches detailed above (and others elsewhere in the literature) a single motive is rarely identified as the sole reason for travel; rather there are a number of motives for travel – though there may be one which takes precedence over the others. This multiple motivational position is discussed by Swarbrooke and Horner (1999) who suggest that the many reasons for travel can combine collectively:

Most people's holidays represent a compromise between their multiple motivators. Either one motivation becomes dominant or a holiday is purchased which ensures all the motivators can at least be partly satisfied.

Therefore, tourism motivational research demonstrates the myriad of conscious and sub conscious reasons for travel, which in-turn effectively illustrates the complexity of this area of study. Not only does this research account for the many causes as to why an individual may wish to take a vacation but also the often contradictory reasons for specific destination choice. Furthermore, it has been suggested that motives do not act independently; but rather combine, into collective primary and secondary tourism drives.

Similarly sport suffers from a multitude of approaches to motivation; some of which (e.g. recuperation, escape and self-determination) are also used in tourism methodologies. However, there are also some very specific motives, which are peculiar to sport such as a need to compete, a desire to win and the opportunity to develop current skill levels. These motives tend to be linked to achievement behaviour and incorporate a number of theoretical positions including: need achievement theory, test anxiety, expectation of reinforcement, and cognitive and social cognitive approaches (for a comprehensive coverage, see Roberts, 1992). To add further complexity, motivational explanations in sport do not just focus upon the actions of the active participant but also aim to explain the motives of the sport fan. For example Wann et al (2001) has identified the 8 most common sport fans motives to be:

- group affiliation.
- family.
- aesthetic reasons.
- self-esteem.
- economic motives.
- escape and entertainment.

In contrast, visits to sport related attractions may be founded upon motives linked to nostalgia, pilgrimage and/or education.

As discussed above, concerning the tourism-motive literature, there will undoubtedly be differences in the expressed motives to participate (actively or passively) in sport and the underlying motives that originally led to them. It would appear safer at this point to focus upon the basic expressed motives outlined in the literature: namely that sport participation is competitively or recreationally driven – and that such participation may be achieved through passive or active involvement. Of course this is a somewhat undemanding and simplistic synthesis of the many reasons why people are involved in sport, but nevertheless may act as a starting point to explain the primary and secondary motives of sport related travel.

Such diversity in both the sport and tourism literature illustrates the multifaceted nature of motivation which is contextually and theoretical dependent. However, these differing theoretical approaches should be viewed as neither conflictive nor competing, but rather reliant upon the motivational focus taken. It may be useful to refer to Neulinger's (1981) comments when confronted by the definitional inconsistency and diverse research approaches found in the field of "leisure" (i.e. whether it should be defined as free time, an activity, or state of mind etc.): The primary task is not to discover what leisure is, but rather to make a decision as to which of the phenomena labelled by this term, one intends to address oneself to.

Perhaps the same approach should be taken with the sport and tourism motivation literature; namely that the motivational approach chosen is dependent upon the aims and objectives of the research – whether they be psychologically, sociologically or culturally driven.

4

Motivational Synergy in Sport Tourism

Attempting to accurately identify sport tourism motivators seems to be plagued with a number of difficulties. The complexity and copious number of motives for participating in sport and tourism are well documented. Additionally the fact that these motives change over time and cover broad and disparate areas of study further exacerbates the problem.

In sport tourism context the multiple nature of motivators can easily be described. For example the sport tourist travelling to the Euro 2004 soccer championship may want to see their team competing, enjoy the pleasant summer weather, participate in associated cultural festivities or take advantage of the local hospitality. These combined collective motives illustrates that at this point in time it is unrealistic to identify and link up the almost countless motivational variables found in both sport and tourism.

It may be wiser to take a broader view of the sport-tourism nexus by first suggesting that there exists a motivational duality which is both synergetic and reciprocal. Standeven and De Knop highlight this relationship by observing that, '...the nature of sport tourism is about an experience of physical activity tied to an experience of place.' However, Standeven and De Knop's (1999) explanation of the sport-tourism relationship errs on the side of geographical theory rather than a psychological one that addresses the method by which this synergy takes place.

The idea originally proposed was that the sport tourist could be categorized depending upon their primary and secondary reasons for travel. Furthermore, referring to the wider literature concerning intrinsic and extrinsic motivation, it was suggested that secondary motives had an enriching affect upon the primary ones:

Secondary reinforcement refers to a process by which an originally neutral stimulus acquires reinforcing properties through its association with a primary reinforcer. In these terms, an intrinsically motivated activity is simply one in which the reinforcement value of the goal has associatively rubbed off on the behaviour itself".

Therefore secondary motives should not be perceived as inferior or second rate, but rather as sources of enrichment to the primary ones. For example, whilst the primary motive maybe to play golf, the experience of playing will be reinforced by a number of contextual indicators that the environment engenders.

These could include climate, scenery, social elements, the quality of the course or indeed a host of other indicators which add to the overall experience of playing golf (an experience which collectively differs from the experience back home). This example illustrates that for some individuals (in this case active sport tourists) sport tourism offers them the opportunity to experience the best of both worlds. As Ryan (2003:31) succinctly observes, 'Finding something you love to do, of course, creates both meaning and pleasure.' What could be better than to participate in your favourite activity in your favourite place – or in a place that you had always wanted to go to? Whilst it is suggested that sport and tourism motives combine additively it is less clear to what extent they interact during the experience(s).

For example, it is not known in what ways (if any) negative touristic experiences affect sport related ones and vice versa. Such questions of course focus upon the experience rather than the motive but nevertheless generates some important considerations for both the sport tourism manager and researcher.

A Sport Tourism Framework

Drawing upon the observations of Swarbrooke and Horner (1999); that tourism motives are generally made up of primary and secondary reasons for travel. And that secondary motive positively affect (in terms of reinforcing properties) the primary reasons for travel a sport tourism consumer framework can be outlined.

The main aim of the framework is to, firstly, illustrate the bisectional nature of the subject area, i.e. either from a sport or tourism base (a supposition supported in the sport tourism literature whilst, secondly, highlighting the segment list structure of sport tourism in order to delineate further areas of focus.

Although categorizing sport tourism is not new the subdivision to soft and hard categories attempts to demonstrate four distinctive sport tourist types, each with quite different organizational, financial and methodological implications.

For example, the organizational and marketing processes within the Sport Tourism hard definition differs greatly from those utilized in the Tourism Sport hard definition. The following section introduces in a little more detail the four proposed categories.

Sport Tourism

The left-hand side of the framework focuses upon Sport Tourism. This section is devoted to the analysis of individuals and/or groups of people who actively or passively participate in competitive or recreational sport, whilst travelling to and/or staying in places outside their usual environment. The qualifying criteria are that sport is the prime motivation to travel, though the touristic element may act to reinforce the overall experience.

Hard Definition

A hard definition of the sport tourist includes those individuals who actively or passively participate at a competitive sporting event. We can therefore classify a hard sport tourist as someone who specifically travels to and/or stays in places outside their usual environment for either active or passive involvement in competitive sport.

In this case sport is their prime motivation for travel and would encompass participation at sporting events e.g. the Olympic Games, Football World Cup. The competitive nature of these events is the distinguishing factor.

Soft Definition

A soft definition of the sport tourist would be someone who specifically travels to and/or stays in places outside their usual environment for primarily active recreational participation in a chosen sport; for example skiing and cycling holidays. The active recreational elements are the distinguishing factors here.

Tourism Sport

Tourism sport comprises persons travelling to and/or staying in places outside their usual environment and participating in, actively or passively, a competitive or recreational sport as a secondary activity. The holiday or visit being their prime motivational reason for travel. Similarly this can be broken down into two distinct categories:

Hard Definition

Here one can identify holidaymakers who use sport as a secondary enrichment to their holiday (passive or active). Competitive or noncompetitive sport may be applied, examples of which are Centre Parcs, Eurocamp and beach holidays. So for these tourists whilst the holiday is their primary motivation to travel, they will also expect to participate in some sport. Therefore sport will act as a secondary reinforcement to their vacation.

Soft Definition

A soft definition of tourism sport involves visitors who as a minor part of their trip engage in some form of sport on a purely incidental basis. For example whilst visiting a seaside resort for the day they play or watch bowls (jeu de boule) or play tennis in a local park; or visitors to Cambridge (UK) may wish to punt on the river. This is deemed "soft" because their participation is purely incidental. The framework was designed in order to first identify four distinct categories of the sport tourist (based upon primary and secondary motives) and secondly, to propose that there are a number of varying facilities and resources that each category of sport tourist would be mostly likely be drawn to.

This is not to suggest that competitive sports events are only going to attract those individuals and groups whose primary motive for travel is sport, for certainly major events will attract a diverse cross section of visitor, but rather to argue that it is these sport tourists that such events are more likely to attract. Since publishing the first article, it became clear that the original framework did not account for either sport tourism attractions or the ever popular sports fantasy camps. Halls of fame, sport museums and stadia tours have been treated as "secondary visitor attractions" and have consequently been included in the hard "Tourism Sport" category.

Of course, similar to the other categories, this is a somewhat uncomfortable generalization, as undoubtedly some of these attractions (e.g. Noucamp in Barcelona, Baseball Hall of Fame in Cooperstown) have become primary draws for domestic and international tourism alike. In contrast, sports fantasy camps can be classed, as soft Sport Tourism activities as the primary aim of these products are active recreational participation.

Application of the Framework

Implicit in the design of the framework is its applicability to a number of motivational, planning and marketing related contexts. Sport today represents a serious consideration to national, regional and urban re-imaging and marketing strategies unsurprisingly, such strategies involve a number of diverse stakeholders from both public and private sector organizations each wishing to establish and enhance their sport and tourism profiles. Indeed, since 1997 and the publication of the original article, we have been approached by local governments, major international entertainment organizations and political policy makers all interested in the applicability of the framework.

It soon became apparent that further clarification and adaptation was necessary. The framework has been revisited since 1997 to provide a more international flavour of activities around the world and of course to illustrate ways of how the framework could be applied to specific sports and places.

The framework can indicate the sport tourism components of a country through including major sporting, leisure and tourism activities that take place there. This could be based on a number of criteria. For example attendance figures, frequency, bookings, number of sports clubs, participation rates, tourism statistics or a combination of these.

Similarly this principle can also be applied at a regional level (province, county or district).

In addition cities and towns can also show their sport tourism and tourism sport components by the inclusion of what it has to offer through the definitions described.

In this way specific sport, leisure and tourism components could be identified as potential areas to develop, or indicate areas as inadequate or weak. It may useful to refer back to Rooney's (1974) approach which helped identify a large number of hotbeds of sports activity in North America which compared regional variations with the national per capita level – as well as region to region comparisons.

Cities could potentially analyse their own sport tourist numbers, local sports events or sport attractions and compare them with either the national average (suggesting a need for a sport tourism index) or a host of other domestic and/or international urban competitors.

The inclusion of distinct categories and definitions forms a basis for exploring the motives of the sport tourist, providing a blueprint for further analysis and investigation. National sport and tourism agencies, local government and private leisure companies could use this approach as a starting point for developing their portfolio of sporting products.

Equally tour operators can monitor and evaluate their primary and secondary sporting products. Alternatively one sport could be analysed through the motivational framework. The sport could then be applied at any of the levels described above. This could benefit particular sport organizations, national governing bodies, tour operators and of course private companies.

The national framework example, incorporating the Netherlands was chosen because the majority of the sport tourism literature features sporting destinations that have developed a relatively sophisticated sport tourism portfolio e.g. Britain, France, Portugal, Australia, USA etc.

Little attention has been paid to those destinations that are not in the media limelight as either a consequence of hosting major international events or as being recognized as major tourism destinations. Similarly, sporting cities such as Barcelona, Sheffield and Sydney have been cited numerous times in the sport tourism literature at the expense of smaller, or lesser known towns.

Although, not immediately associated with sport, for a country its size the Netherlands has achieved considerable sporting success. The fervour with which the Dutch also support and follow their sports (in many ways in a carnival /party atmosphere) is second to none. However this example also serves as a reminder of the ease with which the framework can be applied to any country.

According to the Dutch Central Bureau for Statistics about 25% of the 16 million people are registered to one of the 35,000 sports clubs in the country. About two thirds of the population older than 15 years participates in sport weekly. Additionally, many Dutch enjoy watching sports events. The most popular sports, both for active participation and audience are football, cycling, speed skating and tennis.

In addition in 2003 recreational activity (being away from home for at least two hours) accounted for 1 billion day trips with walking (75% of the population) and cycling (66%) being the most popular and on the increase. The Dutch spend about 16% of their holiday budgets in their own country. Revenues from incoming tourists account for 1.7% of the Dutch gross domestic product (GDP). This is significantly less than the European average of 2.3%. The potential therefore to increase sport tourism revenue is high.

Cruises, walking holidays and cycling opportunities are popular and are well catered for. A range of water sports are also available. These range from swimming, windsurfing, sailing, water-skiing and fishing. There are many canal and river tours. With 300km of coastline, walking is very popular. Walking routes are available for long and short distances and a unique experience is mud walking over the Wadden Sea to the islands offshore.

There are 17000 km of special cycling lanes and paths with a number of long distance routes. Bikes can be hired everywhere and railways allow bikes on trains. In 2003 More than 40% of day trips undertaken by children were connected with sports activities.

Choosing a city to apply the framework did not pose too much of a problem as there are a number of well-known sporting cities whose particulars are well documented but the usefulness of the framework is not just in identifying the array of existing sport tourism offerings in major urban areas but also to indicate possible future developments in 2nd tier cities. Groningen is not a big sport tourism city, yet exemplifies effectively the dilemma many small cities face when examining their sport tourism and tourism sport profiles. They show possible gaps, over dependence and a different emphasis and perspective on the sport tourist. Groningen is the major city of the Northern Netherlands with a population of 179,000, and is the seventh largest city in the country. From an inspection of figure 3 it soon becomes apparent that there is further potential for Groningen to develop a sport tourism base. This is particularly emphasized by the fact that Groningen is the 'youngest' city in the Netherlands with over half the population being under thirty-five!

"Golf" was selected as the sport to apply to the framework because it not only illustrates well the different categories in the framework but also exhibits a range of different forms and activities. Profiling a particular sport provides an overview for possible market penetration for many organizations interested in developing a sport tourism product.

The application of the framework provides countless opportunities to examine aspects of sport tourism at many levels. These include local, regional, national and international dimensions. However in addition different sports organizations, private companies, tour operators and local government can all utilize the flexibility of the framework to increase their understanding of the sport tourism phenomenon.

Implications of the Framework

Many of the implications discussed in 1997 are unsurprisingly still relevant today. Undoubtedly the primary implication of the Sport Tourism Framework is that it attempts to delineate the sport tourist into four clearly identifiable categories based upon the combination of primary and secondary motives for travel. Consequently the framework may help to better understand the consumer through further research into the individual segments of the sport tourism categories. It also provides a starting point for profiling tourism destinations, places, cities, sports, and potentially private companies for sport tourism and tourism sport opportunities. For example, by undertaking a stock-take of what a destination currently offers in the way of sport tourism and comparing it to what is offered elsewhere, managers can either focus their efforts in maintaining and building upon what they already have or to develop particular products and services they may be weak in.

The framework continues to provide a discussion point for the future development of the subject both academically and industrially. From an academic perspective it us hoped that it will help stimulate the sport-tourism nexus debate by illustrating the breadth and diversity of the subject area. Similarly, the framework will aid sport tourism planners and managers in the innumerable opportunities open to them, as well as offering a window into both the motives and possibly the complex expectations of their customers.

Conclusions

The multitude of explanations detailing why people choose to actively or passively participate in sport, together with the many touristic motives for travel illustrates the multi-facetedness of the sport tourist. In sport tourism no single motive can account for the variety of multiple and shared motives prevalent at any one time. It may be over ambitious and indeed obfuscatory to detail the almost innumerable combinations that these primary and secondary motives generate. However, it may be safer to argue that there exists a motivational and indeed experiential synergy which denotes, at a basic level, the beginning of a sport tourist typology. The Sport Tourism Framework aims to illustrate this relationship by categorizing the sport tourist consumer based upon primary and secondary motives, linked to competitiveness, recreation, activity and passivity. Furthermore it also acts as an indicator to those organizations offering sport tourist experiences; outlining what they currently offer against what they might want to develop for the future.

Of course this is only a starting point to building a better understanding of the motives and experiences of the sport tourist. It is still relatively unknown in what ways sport and tourism motives combine and interact and how this might affect consumers' expectations and satisfactions. Nevertheless, the proposed framework aids in our understanding and knowledge of the sport-tourism relationship by outlining four clearly defined and applicable motivational categories. Research now needs to focus more on these categories to examine further the motives of the sport tourist and to assess in more general terms the utility of the framework Sports tourism refers to international trips specifically taken to watch sporting events.

Common examples include international events such as world cups, the Olympics and Formula 1 Grand Prix, regional events (such as the soccer European Champions League), and individual (non-team) participant sports such as tennis, golf and horse racing.

Estimate of Global Market Size

The most popular global sporting events are the soccer FIFA World Cup and the Olympics, followed by the European Football Championships. However other popular sporting events also attract a large number of international visitors. These include the Rugby Union World Cup and Formula 1 Grand Prix.

- The FIFA Football World Cup held in France in 1998 attracted 900,000 international football fans and generated $12.3 billion.
  - It is estimated that the 2000 Olympics in Sydney generated 111,000 additional international arrivals to Australia specifically travelling for sports tourism.
  - Euro 2004 (the European Football Championships) attracted 500,000 sports tourists to Portugal, generating $320 million for the Portuguese economy.
- The Monaco Grand Prix (which alongside the Indy 500 and Le Mans is one of the most famous motor racing fixtures of the year) attracts 200,000 visitors over its four-day duration.
- The 2007 Cricket World Cup staged in the Caribbean was thought to have generated an additional 100,000 visitors who travelled specifically for the tournament.

Whilst the number of sports tourists fluctuates on an annual basis depending on the events taking place (it is greatest during FIFA World Cup and Olympics years), on average an estimated 12 million international trips are made for the main purpose of watching a sporting event.

Potential for Growth

Increased media exposure of sporting events over the last decade has raised the profile of many sports, and although TV coverage is better than at any time in the past, an increasing number of sports fans want to experience live events.

The media also has the ability to make national and international icons of sporting stars, thereby generating greater demand, as fans want to see their sporting idols "in the flesh".

Sporting events themselves are being made increasingly appealing to attend, with greater levels of comfort, and other events – such as festivals-being created around them (such as horse racing weekends, boating regattas, etc.).

Low-cost regional airlines (and more affordable long haul flights), are also driving demand for sporting events as flights become more convenient, more regular, and of course more affordable. Overall, the sports tourism niche market is expected to grow annually at around 6% for the next five years.

Brief Profile of Consumers

Sports tourists are more easily profiled according to the sports they follow. However, in general terms the bulk of the market tends to be young-between 18 and 34 years, and in the C1 and C2 (middle) socioeconomic groups. This would also be the typical profile of a sports tourist following soccer matches.

Rugby and cricket followers tend to be slightly older and with greater disposable income. Horse racing has a broad range of followers with no clear demographic structure. Followers of athletics tend to be young, low spenders, whilst those following the Formula 1 Grand Prix circuit tend to be skewed towards males in their 90s with above average disposable income.

Main Source Markets

The main source markets for sports tourism are those that are most interested in the main international sports. These include:

- United Kingdom.

- United States.
- Germany.
- Italy.
- Spain.
- Scandinavia.
- Australia.
- South Africa.

Main Competing Destinations

The main competing destinations tend to vary depending on where the large events, such as the FIFA World Cup and Olympics are held. However, those holding key annual tournaments of global sporting interest include:

- United States.
- United Kingdom.
- France.
- Australia.
- Spain.

For specific sports, such as golf, motor racing, or yachting, this list of competing destinations would vary considerably.

Key Tour Operators

There are a large number of sports tour operators. However most of them operate at a very local level, principally serving a specific soccer club for example. However, there are a few that operate as international sports tour operators offering a wide range of sporting events in different countries. It is not uncommon, in particular for the much sought-after events, to find tour operators offering flights and accommodation but without tickets.

An overview of sport tourism: Building towards a dimensional framework. The notion of people travelling to participate and watch sport dates back to the ancient Olympic Games and the practice of stimulating tourism through sport has existed for over a century. Just recently, however, sport and tourism professionals alike are realizing the significant potential of sport tourism and are aggressively pursuing this market niche.

Although the definition of sport tourism may vary based on different people's interpretation of sport and travel, for the purpose of this article sport tourism refers to travel away from home to play sport, watch sport, or to visit a sport attraction including both competitive and noncompetitive activities.

Sport tourism can be broken down into five main categories: attractions, resorts, cruises, tours, and events. Each of these categories draws from other tourism sectors such as adventure tourism, health tourism, nature tourism, educational tourism, and leisure tourism. This article outlines the benefits and reasons for growth of sport tourism; provides examples of the scope and opportunities within the sport tourism field; and suggests ways to maximize potential by understanding all elements integral to sport tourism.

Sports Tourism Strategy in Australia

Tourism has in recent decades become firmly established as a major Australian industry, providing significant economic and employment benefits. It accounts for 8% of employment, 5.8% of Gross Domestic Product and nearly 15% of export earnings. Forecast growth, especially for inbound tourism, is very strong.

Similarly, the sports sector has a major economic impact, contributing billions of dollars to the economy and employing tens of thousands of Australians. Furthermore, sport occupies a central place within Australian culture and identity, based on a long history of achievement across a wide range of sports.

It is not surprising then that travel for the purpose of participating in some manner of sporting activity is both significant and growing– in Australia and worldwide.

The Key Elements of the Strategy

The aim of the Strategy is to facilitate a viable and internationally competitive sports tourism industry which can maximize its contribution to Australia's economic and social wellbeing, especially in regional Australia. The draft strategy identifies a number of issues that impact on the development of the sports tourism industry, and discusses developments in these areas and possible actions. The issues include:

- industry coordination.
- education and training.
- government regulation.
- sport and tourism.
- infrastructure.
- evaluation of the economic benefits of sports tourism.
- research and data and
- Strategy implementation.

What is Sports Tourism?

Estimates of the size of the sports tourism sector vary, mainly because there is no single, agreed definition of what constitutes "sports tourism". While definitions of tourism are well accepted and fairly consistent throughout the world, definitions of sports tourism range from narrow ones involving travel solely for participation in competitive sporting activity to broader definitions where the "sporting" activity might be more leisure or adventure activity incidental to the main purpose of travel.

For the purposes of developing a National Sports Tourism Strategy, a relatively narrow definition has been adopted. It is:

- Domestic sports tourism: any sports-related trip of over 40 kms and involving a stay of at least one night away from home; and
- International sports tourism: any trip to Australia a prime purpose of which is to participate in a sporting activity, either as a spectator, participant or official.

The sport or sporting activity under this definition are organised activities – unstructured activities undertaken by individuals have been excluded, as governments' ability to influence such activities is relatively limited. Under such a definition, it appears that sports tourism in Australia might represent about 5% of the overall tourism market, equating to tourism expenditure of about $3 billion per annum.

Tourism and Sport – The World and Australian Markets

Tourism and travel have grown to become not only one of Australia's, but also one of the world's most significant industries. The World Tourism Organization predicts that global international tourism, which in 1999 generated, directly and indirectly, 11% of global GDP, will expand by 4.1 per cent per year over the next two decades. Australian international visitor arrivals are predicted to grow more quickly at around 7 per cent per year through to 2008. Based on these predictions, tourism is destined to continue playing a vital role in Australia's economic and social development. Accompanying the growth in tourism has been a significant expansion in the worldwide sport and recreation industry. These industries come together in the sports tourism sector, and with the emergence of "niche" markets as a major factor in tourism development, the potential for growth in the sector is considerable.

Apart from economic factors, notably increases in disposable income, there is a range of other factors influencing the future growth. These include: continuing increases in the number of sporting events and accompanying media exposure; increased professionalism in sport and consequent demand for training camps; the growth of mass participation events such as Masters Games; and the growth in "manufactured" events – both made for television and made specifically to help promote tourism to a region.

Opportunities for Australia at the International, National and Regional Levels

The hosting of the Sydney 2000 Olympics also provides Australia with a unique opportunity. Apart from showcasing Australia to the world, both as a tourism destination and as a country with the ability to successfully stage major sporting events, the Olympics will leave a legacy of expertise in a range of sports-tourism related fields as well as a legacy of world-class sporting venues. The challenge for sports tourism development is to take advantage of all the opportunities this presents.

Industry Coordination

Sports tourism opportunities, and especially the tourism benefits, are sometimes lost or not maximized because the linkages between the sports and tourism sectors are not well established.Sporting activities, especially events, have historically been organised by sporting organizations for purely sporting purposes. Maximizing the tourism potential of the events has often not been a major consideration for the organizer, representing a potential failure of the market. Further, many sporting organizations rely on volunteers, and may not have well developed business or organizational skills or experience. Both of these factors can lead to lost tourism opportunities.

To overcome this, better linkages need to be established between the sporting and tourism groups at all levels – regional, state/territory and national. Regional "sports tourism clusters" provide a model for building these linkages at the local level. Similar groupings at state and national levels would also be beneficial. While the State and Territory events units are working to improve linkages, there may be a role for the Commonwealth to disseminate information and take on a coordination and facilitation role at the national level.

Education and Training

Education and training is critical to the success of both the sports and tourism sectors. For sports tourism, the issue of education and training is especially important in ensuring that sporting bodies in particular have the requisite business skills both to run successful events and to recognize and take advantage of the tourism opportunities which accompany the hosting of those events. While training in this area is certainly available, there may be an issue with ensuring such training is appropriate to the needs of the sector and is affordable and accessible.

Regulatory Issues

Government regulation can and does impact on the sports tourism sector– at the local, State/Territory and Commonwealth levels. This can range from the need to obtain permits for road closures etc. at the local level, to visa requirements for international athletes or international visitors generally, involved in a sporting activity. It is important to try to minimize any adverse impacts of such regulation. A basic problem for many organisers is simply trying to deal with what can seem like a maze of different agencies with differing requirements. While some States/Territories have developed information kits to help address this issue, the Commonwealth could also play a major role in assisting organisers to navigate through this maze.

Infrastructure

Most if not all sporting activities and events rely on there being appropriate infrastructure in place. The most obvious form of infrastructure is the sporting facilities themselves, however other infrastructure is often more important if sports tourism opportunities are to be maximized.

Adequate accommodation and transport are often critical to the success of events where large numbers of people may need to be moved and accommodated. This can provide difficulties in regional areas, where accommodation may be in short supply and where transport links, both to and within a region, may be expensive and/or suffer from inadequate capacity.

A starting point in addressing these issues, and one which the Commonwealth and a number of States and Territories have already embarked on, would be to conduct facilities audits to identify just what sporting facilities and at what standard, are available. A further logical step down this track would be to conduct a broader "asset audit" of all relevant infrastructure, to assist organisers in assessing the ability of a region to support a particular sporting activity or event.

Research and Data Collection

Like many niche tourism sectors, the sports tourism sector suffers from a lack of reliable data on which to base strategic decision-making. Even data which might help measure the size of the sector is not readily available. Indeed, there is no agreed definition of just what constitutes "sports tourism", hence any discussion of research and data needs must start with the need to come to some consensus as to just what "sports tourism" comprises. Limited data is available from the major tourism surveys-the International Visitor Survey and the National Visitor Survey. At best, however, the picture they draw is very partial but does indicate that sports tourism is significant in the overall tourism market.

A further issue is that most of the available research tends to focus on individual events and not on improving our overall understanding of the sports tourism market and how it operates at a national or regional level.

Evaluation of Events

There are numerous "models" employed to evaluate events which can lead to different outcomes and a consequent inability to compare results. A more consistent methodology, and in the case of smaller regional events, a simplified methodology, would be of considerable benefit.

The Cooperative Research Centre for Sustainable Tourism, through its events sub-program and its recently established sports tourism "node", may be able to better coordinate activity in this area, and help provide a more "macro level" focus.

Australia can learn from international experience in the sports tourism field. The United Kingdom, through the British Tourist Authority, has developed a sports tourism marketing strategy and has recently appointed a sports tourism coordinator in their Sydney office.

Canada has been pursuing a program of developing sports tourism "clusters" or networks in regional areas, to bring together relevant players, raise awareness and maximize tourism benefits. South Africa also has identified sports tourism as a growth sector.

Implementation

Successful implementation of a national strategy will require a concerted and coordinated effort from a range of organizations, including governments at all levels (Commonwealth, State/Territory and local), the tourism industry, the sports sector including national and state/ territory sporting organizations and researchers.

At the State/Territory level, State departments and events corporations take on much of the responsibility for building these links. At the local level, there may be a greater need for development of networks or clusters focusing on sports tourism development. At the national level, there may also be a need for better coordination.

Conclusion

Clearly, sports tourism in Australia has enormous potential. A number of factors, including strong inbound tourism growth, a sporting culture, good sporting and tourism infrastructure, and the catalytic effect of the Sydney 2000 Olympic Games, are combining to make this a key growth area. The challenge is to maximize that growth in a manner that can provide genuine economic and social benefits for Australia and Australians.

This draft Strategy poses a number of questions, with the aim of identifying key measures which would need to be implemented to facilitate growth of the sports tourism industry.

Background

The development of the National Sports Tourism Strategy has its genesis in the National Action Plan for Tourism. The Plan, released in 1998, provides a policy framework for the future growth of the tourism industry in Australia. It identifies the development of a range of niche tourism products as one of the avenues which will promote strong future growth and diversification of the industry, and identifies sports tourism as one of the sectors showing enormous potential for further development.

In November 1999 the Federal Minister for Sport and Tourism, the Hon Jackie Kelly MP, announced the Government's intention to develop a National Sports Tourism Strategy in recognition of the need for a planned and consistent approach to building a larger sustainable base for the sports tourism sector. The development of the Strategy to date has involved extensive consultation with a wide range of stakeholders; desk research; the production of a preliminary discussion paper; and the organization of a series of focus group workshops around Australia.

Why Develop a National Sports Tourism Strategy?

In the past decade tourism has been firmly established as a major industry in Australia, economically, socially and as a job provider for Australians. In 1996-97, tourism directly accounted for 5.8% of expenditure on Gross Domestic Product (GDP). Growth in the tourism industry is forecast to continue well into the next decade, especially for international tourism, with the Tourism Forecasting Council predicting that international visitor arrivals will grow at an average annual rate of 7.3 per cent to 2008 when we will welcome 8.4 million visitors.

In 1999, international tourism to Australia generated export earnings of $17 billion and accounted for 14.9% of Australia's total export earnings. Expenditure derived from domestic tourism was $44.8 billion in 1998-99.

Sport has always been an integral part of Australian life and it is increasingly being recognized that sporting events and activities have the potential to be a major tourism drawcard. Australia has something of a natural advantage in this niche market given our strong international image as a sporting nation. This reputation is largely based on the achievements of our sports men and women and images from international events held here. It also forms part of the Australian "lifestyle", an experience which is consistently rated as a major motivating factor in bringing international visitors to Australia.

The popularity of sports events, which constitute a significant proportion of all events held in Australia, guarantees that they are a major component of tourism agencies' strategies for destination development. For the Australian Tourist Commission (ATC), the promotion of Australia as a destination for a holiday featuring sports activity is a logical development of Australia's strong sporting image and the ATC has incorporated a "sports" theme in its overseas marketing.

Sports tourism, or tourism which is associated with sporting activity, therefore has the potential to develop into a highly significant niche sector which provides Australia with economic and social benefits.

The hosting of the Olympic Games in Sydney in 2000 was undeniably a definitive moment for sports tourism in Australia and it brought significant benefits to the Australian tourism sector. While mega-events of this ilk are definitely not the "bread and butter" of sports tourism, the Olympics provided many lessons in organizing, running and capitalizing on the tourism benefits of sporting events.

Strategy to Promote Sport Tourism

The aim of the strategy is to facilitate viable and internationally competitive sports tourism industry and to ensure that the benefits of this niche market are maximized and spread widely throughout Australia. This objective has been identified because of the perception that the tourism benefits which sporting activities and events can provide are not currently being maximized. The strategy identifies opportunities for the development of the sports tourism sector as well as identifying and addressing impediments to the growth of the industry.

The key elements of the strategy are a range of possible actions which can help to:

- Improve the coordination and competitiveness of the sports tourism industry ....
- Identify and address education and training issues for the industry ....
- Minimize the impact of regulatory issues (e.g. visas, customs) on the industry ....
- Identify and address the infrastructure requirements of the industry ....
- Identify and address the research and data collection requirements of the industry ....
- Improve the means of evaluation of the economic benefits of sports tourism.......
- Coordinate the implementation of the strategy ......

What is Sports Tourism?

Sports tourism is a niche market which can be broadly described as a tourism activity generated by participation in sporting activity. That activity can be a sporting event or competition, a tour of a sporting facility, or a training camp. Participation might involve being a competitor/participant, official, or spectator.

The Australian definitions of international and domestic tourism are well understood and accepted and are used as the basis for the definitions of sports tourism adopted for the development of this Strategy. These are:

- Domestic sports tourism: any sports-related trip of over 40 kms and involving a stay of at least one night away from home; and
- International sports tourism: any trip to Australia a prime purpose of which is to participate in a sporting activity, either as a spectator, participant or official.

As to what constitutes a sporting activity in this context some decisions need to be made in relation to activities that could be seen more as recreational (e.g fishing, golf, skiing, horseracing) and also to adventure activities (e.g sky surfing, para-sailing, rock-climbing, etc.). All of these activities require skill and also offer potential for competition, however they are also frequently pursued by individuals in an unstructured way and maybe entirely incidental to their main reason for travelling. While this may not matter in some respects, structured, organised sports events, tours, camps and so on arguably offer more potential for industry and governments to target with a view to increasing the tourism potential, than do leisure and adventure activities – important though they are in their own right. It is therefore those activities which can be targeted for further development which are included within the ambit of this strategy.

Tourism and Sport-The World Market

Tourism and travel make up one of the world's largest industries. In 1999 the World Travel and Tourism Council (WTTC) also reports that across the global economy, travel and tourism generates, directly and indirectly:

- 11% of GDP;
- 200 million jobs;
- 8% of total employment; and
- 5.5 million new jobs per year until 2010.

World Tourism Organization (WTO) data for 1999 show that 663 million people spent at least one night in a foreign country, up 4.1 per cent over the previous year. Spending on international tourism reached US$453 billion — a growth rate of nearly 3 per cent over 1998. These results are in line with WTO's long-term growth forecast Tourism: 2020 Vision which predicts that the tourism sector will expand by an average of 4.1 per cent a year over the next two decades.

Annual international arrivals are expected to surpass one billion by the year 2010 and reach 1.6 billion by the year 2020. Reasons for this sustained growth include greater disposable income in tourism generating countries, and, especially in some of the emerging economies of Asia, more leisure time, earlier retirement, improvements in infrastructure and transport (particularly air transport), and changes in consumer spending preferences.

Sport and active recreation have become very large and successful industries worldwide. A 1994 European Commission Report on the European Community and Sport estimated that the sports industry is responsible for 2.5 per cent of world trade. The factors influencing the growth of sport and recreation are similar to those influencing tourism growth-notably increased disposable income, greater availability of leisure time and changing consumer preferences. An increased awareness of the benefits for all ages of greater physical activity has also been important. In addition, the role of the media in promoting sports has been critical. A number of factors have contributed to this greater international media attention on sport and recreation, especially in western economies:

- increased demand for sports programming from television broadcasters to meet consumer demand, the advent of dedicated sports channels (e.g. Fox Sports, ESPN, C7 Sports), and the availability of satellite technology allowing live coverage;
- increased prominence of professional sportspersons across a range of sports, e.g. golf, tennis, basketball, baseball, surfing, rugby and soccer;
- large amounts of money being spent by corporations directly and indirectly sponsoring events, teams and individuals for commercial advantage;
- sports associations becoming more like large-scale business enterprises;
- growth of merchandise associated with particular sports, sporting activities and sporting teams;
- significant advertising, promotion, and activity associated with high-profile international sporting events, e.g. the Olympic Games, soccer World Cups, Grand Slam tennis, Formula One Grand Prix, and national sporting competitions;
- increasing opportunities for participation, especially in western economies, through changing leisure patterns, ageing of the population, increased disposable income, and increased awareness of the benefits of physical activity.

Sports Tourism

Having regard to the trends emerging in both the tourism and sports sectors, it is not surprising that significant growth is also occurring in travel for sports related purposes. In fact, this growth is also linked to another trend – that of travelling for specific "niche" purposes, of which sporting activity is one.

The British Tourist Authority and English Tourism Board claim as many as 20 per cent of tourists trips are for the prime purpose of sports participation, whilst up to 50 per cent of holidays include incidental sports participation. This level of activity is broadly consistent with Canadian data, with the 1998 Canadian Travel Survey finding that 37% of domestic trips that year were for sports-related purposes.

In the case of the United States, the Travel Industry Association of America found that in the past five years, 38 per cent of US adults attended an organised sports event, competition or tournament as either a spectator or participant, while on a trip of 50 miles or more. These figures are based on rather broad definitions of the "sport" in sports tourism.

Significantly, perhaps, the sports market, and hence the sports tourism market, is becoming increasingly internationalised. As previously mentioned, the availability of sports-only TV channels which display sports from numerous countries around the world, as well as increasing coverage of an ever-expanding range of sporting events through more mainstream media outlets, means there is an increasing awareness of the range of sporting activities being pursued around the world, including in countries such as Australia.

Tourism and Sport-The Australian Market

Tourism

Tourism has grown to be one of Australia's most significant industries. While a small player in terms of world arrivals, Australia is a major tourism destination in terms of tourism receipts, ranking 12th in the world for 1999. In 1996-97, tourism accounted directly for 5.8% of expenditure on Gross Domestic Product (GDP), and was directly responsible for the employment of over 670 000 persons and indirectly for a further 290 000. This accounts for 11.5% of total Australian employment. In 1998/99, expenditure derived from domestic tourism was $44.8 billion. In 1999, international tourism to Australia generated exports of $17 billion and accounted for 14.9% of Australia's total export earnings.

Tourism is destined to continue playing a vital role in Australia's economic and social development. The Tourism Forecasting Council (TFC) predicts that international visitor arrivals will grow at an annual average rate of 7.3 per cent to 2008 and generate nearly $32 billion in export earnings in 2008. This means international visitor number in excess of 8.4 million in 2008-almost double the current level of tourist visitation to Australia. Much higher levels of growth are predicted from emerging Asian markets including China (21.1 per cent), South Korea (23.7 per cent) and Thailand (18.3 per cent). On the domestic front growth is anticipated to be steady with an average annual growth rate of 1.6 per cent for the period 1998-99 to 2008-09.

Sport

Australia has long been regarded as a sporting nation. Significant interest by the Australian public in sports of one type or another across wide demographic boundaries ensures that the sport industry in Australia assumes a significant economic, social and even political profile.

Involvement in sport and sporting activity not only benefits both the health and general wellbeing of our nation, it also makes a sizeable contribution to the Australian economy. Precise figures are extremely difficult to find – a problem for sports tourism also, and one which is discussed later in this strategy. What is clear is that the sports sector generates many billions of dollars within the economy and provides employment for tens of thousands of people.

Despite its size and significance, many sectors of the industry are not highly commercialized, although some, such as the businesses supplying goods and services which support sporting activities, are very commercially focused. There is a large "not-for-profit" segment of the sports sector, exemplified by the number of volunteers working within it. In 1994/95 there were 112,877 volunteers working in the sports industries which was almost double the formal employment in sports industries at that time. The majority of these volunteers (89 per cent) worked within the sports or in the provision of services to sports, sectors.

Structurally, the sports sector is very decentralised. An important part of the sector is the local sporting club-bodies dedicated to the development of single sports run by and for its members. These clubs often affiliate with regional and state associations which, in turn, unite to form National Sporting Organizations (NSOs). Volunteers administer sport at all levels-particularly the club level. At state and national levels professional administrators begin to play a role, although even here volunteers may still make a significant contribution.

Professional clubs also exist in parallel with this system in the major sports like the football codes, basketball, cricket and baseball. They belong to state or national leagues and are managed predominantly by full-time professional administrators and coaches. Special purpose associations exist to promote particular interests such as sports medicine, coaching, school and university competition, physical education, legal issues and professional development for sports workers. These usually affiliate with an umbrella body which operates at the national level.

Government involvement in sport occurs at each of the three levels of government-local, state and national, through the various departments dealing with sport and recreation, the Australian Sports Commission, the Australian Institute of Sport, and the State Institutes of Sports and Academies.

There are also a range of non-government organizations which administer, coordinate and promote particular interests at both state and national levels. Within the government sector, there are a number of vehicles for seeking to discuss and coordinate issues relating to sport industry development. The Sport and Recreation Ministers Council (SRMC) is the peak body for discussion between the Commonwealth and State and Territory Governments for issues concerning sport and recreation needs across Australia. It is supported by the Standing Committee on Recreation and Sport (SCORS), whose members are senior officials in the sports departments of each State and Territory.

The Commonwealth Government has also given recognition to the many commercial businesses which service Australian participation in sport, through the development of a strategic plan to facilitate the growth of the commercial sports and leisure services sector.

Sports Tourism

Both the tourism industry and the sports industry in Australia come together in the sports tourism sector. Those involved include:

- sport and tourism departments.
- major events corporations.
- sporting bodies.
- facilities managers.
- event organisers.
- promoters.
- tour operators.
- accommodation providers.
- transport operators.
- retailers.
- the full range of organizations providing goods and services to both sporting and tourism operators.

However, not all of these groups necessarily perceive themselves as being part of a broader sports tourism industry, resulting in potential lost opportunities associated with the staging of Australia's many and various sporting events.

While it is difficult to establish the size of the industry, some efforts have been made to quantify its value to the Australian economy.

For example, during the focus group process forming part of the development of this draft strategy, a number of participants suggested that the sector accounts for about 5% of the total tourism market, based on the relatively narrow definition proposed in the Strategy.

If this is the case across both international and domestic tourism, sports tourism in Australia would account for annual expenditure of about $3 billion per annum. This estimate is consistent with analysis undertaken by the Bureau of Tourism Research and published in the recent paper Sports Tourism: An Australian Perspective, which found that 6 percent of day trips and 5 per cent of overnight trips taken by Australians in Australia, were taken with sport as the primary motivation.

This corresponds to expenditure of $1847 million by domestic sports tourists, of which $461 million was on day trips and the remaining $1386 million was spent on overnight trips.

Australian domestic sports tourists appear to generate a higher dollar yield than other domestic travellers, with 31% staying in hotel, resort, motel or motor inn accommodation on their sports trip compared with 23% for all domestic travellers. Consequently, their estimated average daily expenditure of $130 is higher than the $112 estimated for other domestic travellers.

Opportunities for Australia at The International, National and Regional Levels

Australia has many competitive advantages in the sports tourism marketplace, including a climate conducive to outdoor activities, a diverse range of sporting activities, access to quality sports facilities, well developed tourism infrastructure and an internationally renowned image as a sporting nation and tourism destination.

Even the fact that our seasons are the reverse of those in the major tourism source markets of the Northern Hemisphere provides a range of opportunities in areas such as pre-season training camps. Similarly, our expertise in areas such as sports science and sports medicine, as well as leading edge facilities such as the Australian Institute of Sport, help to encourage international sporting teams and individuals to travel to Australia.

These assets form the basis for an internationally competitive tourism product. However they have to be managed in a way that delivers the maximum benefits for the country as a whole. While there are numerous opportunities within the broader sports tourism fields, some sectors and some markets appear to have particular potential for Australia to exploit.

International Opportunities

The Olympics

The sport mega-event is the most widely recognized example of sports tourism. And, with mega-events such as the Olympic Games and the World Cup Football it is not surprising that they involve the largest volumes of spectators and the largest revenues of all special events and festivals.

The value of hosting an Olympic Games has been the subject of much research with wide ranging views on the benefits and costs of such an event. A significant increase in tourism is not a guaranteed certainty with many impacts dependent upon the organization and marketing of the Olympic Games. Regardless, the staging of an Olympic Games is recognized as being a unique opportunity for the host city and country to engage in high-profile promotion their tourism products at a worldwide level.

Development of international standard sporting facilities and the upgrading of facilities required for pre-Games training, is both an obvious and tangible legacy.

High quality facilities combined with a successful hosting of the Olympics have given Australia a head start in bidding for major sporting events in the years immediately following the Games. It is also in these years that the Tourism Forecasting Council predict Australia will receive a major tourism benefit from the Olympic Games with additional international visitor numbers of 342 000 in 2000, 335 000 in 2001 and 350 000 in 2002.

If these numbers are realized, and they may well be, Australia will have received an immediate and major dividend from the hosting of the Games. Many of those additional visitors will no doubt participate in sporting activities while in Australia.Just as importantly perhaps, the lessons that have been learned by governments, sporting bodies and business will play a major role in the further development of the sports tourism sector.

The Olympics will also expose Australia's sporting and tourism assets to vast new audiences and markets, providing significant opportunities in the sports tourism field.

Australia's traditional international "sports tourism" markets have been North America, Europe and New Zealand. Rugby tests in particular, but also rugby league, cricket and to a lesser extent netball, generate significant trans-Tasman traffic flows.

More recently, however there appears to be considerable emerging growth potential from upper middle and high income Asian economies, including Japan, Korea and Taiwan. Other emerging markets (e.g. India, Latin America and South Africa) offer similar promise where the distribution of wealth is changing and there is an expanding middle class with an increasing level of disposable income.

National Opportunities

Masters Games

Masters Games provide sports tourism opportunities at the international, national and regional level. They may well prove to be the greatest potential growth area in sports tourism over the next decade. A relatively recent phenomenon, these games have already grown to occupy a central place among sports tourism activities and are keenly fought over and bid for by potential hosts, because of the sheer numbers of participants involved and their demographic profile – i.e. Masters– which generally equates to high levels of disposable income.

At the top of the Masters Games tree – which comprises local, interstate, national and international events – is the World Masters Games. Recognized as the world's biggest multisport festival, the World Masters Games are considered the premier international event for Masters competitors, allowing them to compete regardless of ability, gender, race or religion. In terms of competition, they are twice as big as the Olympic Games. Held every four years, the World Masters Games are participant focused, with competitors only being required to meet each sports age qualification.

In Australia, the first sanctioned Masters Games were held in 1986 in Alice Springs. The first Australian (i.e. national) Masters Games were held in Tasmania in 1987. Since then the Australian Masters Games have been held in Adelaide (1989), Brisbane (1991), Perth (1993), Melbourne (1995), Canberra (1997) and Adelaide (1999). The eighth

Australian Masters Games will be held in Newcastle and the Hunter region in 2001.

The overall philosophy of the Australian Masters Games is to provide an incentive for mature age persons to begin, or continue active participation in sport. It aims to provide a focus for individual sports to develop their own mature age sport events and to maintain mature sports as a continuing aspect of their programs and focus. There is a definite aim of the Games to promote community interest and participation in mature age sport and to thereby contribute to the health of its citizens and the nation.

The organisers of the 2001 Australian Masters Games in Newcastle have also identified the potential for the Games to have a significant impact on tourism, sport and culture in the Newcastle and Hunter region and to increase both tourism and brand awareness of the area at a domestic and business level.

"Manufactured" Events

Over the past twenty years or so the interest in sport, especially elite sporting events, has grown at a phenomenal rate. Sport is no longer just about playing the game, it is now perceived to have an obligation to provide public entertainment.

This growth has been in parallel with advances in technology and the evolution of the digital age. People now expect to be entertained by worldwide sporting events telecast live direct to their television sets-or perhaps on their home computer. According to a survey conducted by the Australian Bureau of Statistics in November 1997, sporting programs were the most commonly watched on television after news and current affairs, and were viewed regularly by over half of all Australians aged over 18 (55%).

A relatively recent concept is the "manufacture" of sporting events for television – events such as the "One Summer" sporting festival of beach related sporting events is a case in point of what is almost exclusively a television event. There can be a number of tourism-related benefits, including marketing benefits, from events such as these.

Another variation on the "manufactured" event theme is an event which is designed from the outset to promote tourism, rather than being designed as a purely sporting event with the tourism aspect an added extra. The main emphasis in events of this nature, of which there are still relatively few, is on the promotion of tourism to the region where the event is being held, rather than just on the event itself.

An excellent example is the Jacobs Creek Tour Down Under in South Australia, which sees cyclists racing through regional South Australia, receiving national and international media coverage and by careful planning and route selection, promoting the region to potential tourists. One of the major benefits of this type of event is that they can be designed using existing locations, and to suit the capabilities of the region.

Examples include cycle races, triathlons, road races, "challenges" such as the Omeo challenge, etc. Critically, these events can be introduced to even out peaks and troughs in tourism activity, and can be tailored to fit into a regional tourism package of events, attractions and activities.

They can also spread the accommodation load across a region if necessary. Given that the region which created the event then "owns" the event, they can be conducted on an annual basis which in the longer term reduces the costs associated with their staging.

Regional and Local Opportunities

Masters Games and "manufactured" events can have significant impact at the regional and local level, as well as nationally. Indeed, there are numerous market sectors within sports tourism which lend themselves to regional areas and the lower level of facilities and infrastructure which these areas generally possess.

A key issue for regional areas is to identify the range and level of resources and infrastructure which they do possess, and to use this information as the basis for identifying and pursuing suitable sports tourism opportunities. Some examples of events which might well lend themselves to hosting by regional or local areas include:

- Schools and underage championships, which can vary in size from quite small to very large (e.g Albury has been very active in pursuing this part of the market);

- National or indeed international events in "lesser" sports (e.g Corowa has hosted a world parachuting championship recently while Manilla is a world-renowned paragliding centre);
- Regional championships in a variety of sports; and
- Sports which can be held at a number of locations throughout a region.

Marketing Opportunities

Sports tourism events at the international, national and regional levels have a double-barrelled effect – the direct effect of the attendance of the competitors and/or spectators and accompanying persons, and the indirect effect of the marketing of the destination which will lead to subsequent tourism flows.

This indirect effect can be very large – most of the tourism benefits of the Olympics are expected to be of this nature. Even for non-mega events, for example events like the Gold Coast Indy Car Race, the Australian Formula 1 and 500cc Motor Cycle Grand Prix and even events such as the Australian Surf Life Saving Championships, this impact can be very significant.

There is a marketing effect through the word-of-mouth recommendation of attendees at the event, (such as with Masters competitions) but potentially a much greater effect if the event attracts widespread media interest – especially live television coverage. The marketing spin-offs from sports tourism events can vary enormously depending on a range of factors, including whether the tourism aspects were considered as an integral part of the event and were "built-in" to the development process.

For example, the Gold Coast Indy Car race is deliberately designed to showcase Australia's premier beach destination – the Gold Coast – with parts of the track running right beside Surfers Paradise beach. Given Australia's status as a relatively little known tourism destination in world terms, the marketing benefits from events, particularly from mega-events such as the Olympics, may be greater than for countries which are already well known tourist destinations. This presents a genuine opportunity for better showcasing Australia's tourism assets through sporting events.

Industry Coordination

It is clear that major sports events can play a significant role in generating tourism activity on a national and international scale. Such events can have positive economic and social benefits, and have in recent years been increasingly recognized by both national and State governments as a legitimate focus for tourism and general economic development strategies.

One manifestation of governments' support of events-based strategies is the provision of funding for events and infrastructure by Commonwealth, State and Territory sport departments, and the creation in most states of dedicated events corporations. As this investment in events increases, Governments are being increasingly required to justify their expenditure in these areas, with the attendant challenge being how to enhance sporting events as tourism products so as to maximize returns on investment.

Developing a Strategic Approach

The Commonwealth government developed Strategic National Plan for the Sport and Leisure Services Industry. The plan articulated a vision for the industry and ways for the industry to become world class in the provision of sport and leisure goods and services.

Success in realising this vision required advanced business networks and better relationships between business, governments, sporting organizations and consumers of leisure activities. A similar challenge faces the sports tourism sector.

The sports tourism focus group discussions identified the need for the sports tourism sector to identify itself as a discrete industry group and to establish the linkages necessary to capture commercial opportunities.

The current lack of an identity and cohesiveness was identified as one of the major impediments to the growth of the sports tourism sector. In addition, the lack of recognition by both government and the private sector of the economic potential of sports tourism has led to many opportunities being overlooked. Some of the key issues which need to be addressed to encourage and enable the growth of sports tourism include:

> *Establishing linkages to enable the raising of awareness of the mutual benefits and advantages of establishing alliances; coordinating planning and the sharing of resources and information; and identifying opportunities and mechanisms for maximizing the tourism benefits of sporting activities.*

Establishing Linkages

The fact that most events are organised by sporting bodies as sporting events first and foremost with tourism almost an optional extra, represents a failure of the market. Sporting bodies arguably have little incentive to pursue the tourism benefits which can flow from sporting activities, especially sporting events, because they themselves cannot directly capture many of those benefits.

The great majority of those benefits accrue to other parties – tour operators, accommodation providers, transport operators, retail outlets, restaurants and so on. And yet many of these people may not even perceive that they stand to benefit significantly from tourism activity associated with sporting events.

To some extent, States and Territories have moved to address this by establishing major events corporations, to bring together the sports and tourism players and to bid for events.

This works very well for some events – most notably the larger, higher profile events on which the events corporations generally focus. However, the needs of second-tier or regional events are not necessarily adequately met through this process. At a regional level, governments could play a role in facilitating the establishment of "cluster" groups comprising the full range of stakeholders in the sports tourism process.

A useful model could be the cluster formed in Cairns following the focus group conducted there – "Sports Tropical North Queensland". Significantly, the Cairns group is being coordinated by the economic development corporation, reflecting the broad benefit which sports tourism events can provide throughout the regional economy.

Sharing of Resources and Information

At the regional level, clusters or networks can play a number of roles to help coordinate activities, assist in the sharing of physical resources and encourage information sharing. For smaller sporting bodies, the level of resources required (e.g. signage, barriers, marquees) may be a deterrent to running events, as can be the lack of knowledge for first time organisers.

Simply sharing these resources can assist in the planning and running of successful events, with regionwide benefits for both sporting and tourism groups. At a national level, the Commonwealth could play a role which would largely be one of the provision of information, including providing links and referrals to the enormous range of information already available, much of which has been produced by States and Territories, but which is currently not being accessed by event organisers or tourism groups.

Maximising the Tourism Benefits

There are a number of ways to maximize the returns from investment in events. These include:

- improving the yield from existing events;
- staging more events;
- targeting and supporting events that offer the biggest potential returns in terms of tourism;
- spreading the benefits of new and existing events to more regions, rather than just the major metropolitan centres; and
- better coordination of sporting events with other tourism related activities to maximize visitor stay and yield.

Success in each of these areas relies on the establishment of alliances between sport and tourism bodies at all levels-national, state/territory and regional-and greater emphasis on cooperative planning and coordination. This emerged as the top priority in almost every focus group discussion held around Australia. Recent international experience such as that in the UK has illustrated that simply bringing the sport and tourism sectors together is not sufficient to encourage the development of working alliances.

It will therefore be important to demonstrate clearly to both the sport and tourism sectors the practical advantages of creating and encouraging alliances. While sporting events continue to be organised purely as sporting events with tourism a secondary consideration, progress towards fully capturing the business opportunities associated with sports tourism will remain difficult.

What is required is for events or activities to be seen as sports tourism opportunities and for organisers to give equal weight to the requirement to run a technically and administratively successful sporting event and the opportunity to maximize the visitation and yield by producing an appropriate tourism package.

Possible Commonwealth Facilitation Role

One of the key suggestions arising from the focus group discussions is for the Commonwealth government to play a facilitation role for the development of sports tourism in Australia. In doing so, the Commonwealth government could help address a perceived general lack of coordination between private sector, government, and sport and tourism bodies, and rectify the absence of an effective and appropriate mechanism for the dissemination of information throughout the sports tourism sector.

This facilitation role could focus primarily on the provision and dissemination of information, referral to appropriate agencies, and the encouragement of better communication between key sports and tourism players.

Project Facilitation

The Commonwealth government could also play a role in the facilitation of major projects – the so-called mega events – which impact on national interests as well as individual State/Territory interests. A possible model could be the approach adopted for the Olympics, where a coordination unit brought together the many Commonwealth agencies necessary to make the event a success. This role would be undertaken on an "as needs" basis, when events of this magnitude are being considered or planned.

Network Facilitation

More generally, as already mentioned, there is a need to help facilitate the establishment of sports tourism networks or clusters, especially at a regional level, to ensure opportunities are not lost and are indeed maximized. There are existing models in other industries. By way of example, as part of the Furnishing Industry Action Agenda, which aims to improve the competitiveness of the furnishing industry, the Commonwealth Government has recently announced the establishment of a Furnishing Industry Unit within the Department of Industry, Science and Resources. This unit will act as a focal point within the Commonwealth for issues of concern to the sector, and will aim to improve networking and statistical data collection.

A similar mechanism could be established for sports tourism and might play a similar role, although broader, to that being undertaken by Soar International in Canada. Soar International is a sports information and event management company contracted by the Canadian Tourism Commission to facilitate the development of sports tourism networks in regional areas.

5

Education and Training

There is widespread recognition that a high level of business expertise and management skill is critical if the sports tourism sector is to successfully meet the needs of the increasingly discerning sports tourism consumer.

The focus group discussions highlighted the demand for appropriate and accessible education and training, particularly in the area of management, where many not-for-profit sporting organizations rely on part-time staff or volunteers. Equally, tourism organizations would benefit from greater awareness of sports tourism opportunities and some education and training to enable them to maximize the tourism potential of sporting events and activities.

Sport and Recreation

Sport and recreation industry specific education and training is provided through a combination of graduate/post graduate university education, vocational education and training (VET), on the job training (sometimes with a VET component), industry based training and accreditation and a range of short courses. The most common VET providers are the technical and further education (TAFE) institutions, although some sectors, for example the fitness industry, mainly use private training providers. Other training providers include community based organizations, individual businesses and some secondary schools.

A national industry training advisory body, Sport and Recreation Training Australia, which is jointly funded by industry and government with employer and employee representation, provides advice on the range of industry training needs. A National Sport Industry Training package became available in 1999. Some areas of the industry have introduced training and accreditation systems for instructors, primarily as a result of the threat of litigation in an area of high risk of injury to participants. Employment in these areas is generally dependent on possession of an industry qualification in addition to specific industry skills.

Tourism

As in the sport and recreation sector, the tourism industry has access to industry specific education and training from a combination of graduate/post graduate university education, vocational education and training (VET), on the job training, industry based training and accreditation and a range of short courses.

A national industry training advisory body, Tourism Training Australia (TTA) develops and delivers integrated tourism packages for the tourism industry. Many forms of management and staff training are available, including in-house or on the job training, self paced and distance learning packages, and formal courses offered by TAFE colleges, universities and private tourism training enterprises.

Among the priority areas identified by TTA for future skills development are management and business skills for medium and small enterprises, marketing skills and specific management and operational skills for the meetings, conferences, exhibitions and events sector.

The Sports Tourism Sector

Despite the education and training opportunities available in the sport and recreation and tourism industries, there remains a continuing need for improving work force and management skills. This is particularly so in areas characterized by volunteers or low wage employees or where there is a predominance of part time jobs and high staff turnover. In particular, organizations relying on government funding find it difficult to attract and retain skilled employees.

In terms of higher education, new courses focusing specifically on sports tourism are starting to emerge. For example, Southern Cross University recently introduced a degree course in Sports Tourism.

However, more generally, as was suggested at the focus group discussions, a more comprehensive range of education and training opportunities is needed if the sports tourism sector is to fully realize its growth potential.

This could be achieved through the development of an industry training package that identifies the skill requirements for qualifications in various occupations, and the appropriate training courses to acquire these skills. Development of such a package would require input from industry associations, government sport and tourism bodies, industry training bodies and universities and TAFE institutions. A range of accreditation opportunities could be also developed to enhance professional development opportunities for employees, trainees, and volunteers.

Improved access and take-up of management courses would also assist businesses improve their performance. This is particularly so for many not-for-profit sporting organizations whose personnel may have a high degree of technical knowledge about their sport but are less skilled in business management. Volunteers can also pose particular challenges in the take up of management training due to time and resource constraints.

One means of improving management training could be to augment generic management courses with elements tailored to the sports tourism sector, for example, on strategic planning and development of an event calendar, how to create and maintain linkages between sport and tourism organizations, and ways to prepare an appropriate tourism package for a particular sporting market.

One suggestion made in the focus group discussions was for agencies responsible for funding sporting bodies to provide greater recognition for sporting organizations whose executive hold relevant qualifications or undertake appropriate courses or participate in the existing volunteer and management improvement programs. Another suggestion was for State and Territory funding agencies or regional organizations to arrange mobile "in-service" training for regional areas.

Specific sports tourism development courses could also assist in the formation and development of sports tourism clusters, such as the one established in Cairns. There could be a role for regional development and tourism associations to develop and make available 'value adding' packages to regional tourism and sporting organizations that include, for example, checklists and guidelines for organizing committees. Such packages could include tourism product marketing material for sporting organisers and information about the event participants for tourism agencies and businesses.

Regulatory Issues

Governments at all levels can and do impose requirements which impact on sports tourism events and activities. These can be broad requirements such the need for international competitors or spectators to sporting events to obtain a visa or electronic travel authority to enter Australia or they can be specific to a particular event, for example, the closure of roads for the holding of a fun run or triathlon.

Dealing with Commonwealth, State/Territory and Local government departments and agencies can be a daunting prospect for event organisers. This can be especially so for organisers who may be tackling the task of organizing their event for the first time or for volunteers in sporting organizations who have neither experience in dealing with regulatory requirements or the time available to deal with these. During the focus group discussions, the issue of government regulatory requirements was frequently raised as a significant barrier to the successful organization of sporting events and activities, and the maximisation of tourism opportunities from those activities.

It was suggested on numerous occasions that governments could play a role by providing event organisers with a mechanism to help deal with complex regulatory requirements. A number of State and Territory governments have already developed assistance packages that go some way towards providing just such a service. For example, the Canberra Tourism and Events Corporation (CTEC) has developed a publication entitled Assistance for Special Events – Information Handbook for Event Organisers, which contains a section on Government liaison with relevant contact details for organizations such as police, emergency services, roads and traffic bodies, venue hire, litter disposal and so on. The Handbook provides a how-to guide for organizing an event, covering issues such as budgeting, sponsorship, media relations, general organization tips, and evaluating the outcome of the event.

This kind of assistance is not available in all States and Territories. Even where advice is available through Events Corporations, this may not always be available at the local or regional level – i.e. contact details may not be available for all local government agencies with whom event organisers in regional areas might have to deal. Further, the CTEC publication does not deal with liaison with Commonwealth agencies such as Customs, Immigration and Quarantine for events where there may be international competitors involved. There is therefore a clear information gap for event organisers in dealing effectively with government agencies – at the local, Commonwealth, and in some instances at least, State/Territory level. There may be a need for Commonwealth, State/Territory and local governments to cooperate more fully in the provision of information to help fill this gap.

Commonwealth Agencies

At the Commonwealth level, a number of agencies oversee regulatory requirements which impact on event organisers, in particular where there are international competitors, spectators or other participants involved.

Visas

Visitors to Australia are required to obtain a visa to enter the country. In the case of most visitors travelling as tourists, this takes the form of an Electronic Travel Authority (ETA) which is, in effect, an "invisible visa".

There are different categories of visas, including business visas and sport visas. The latter are often used by professional sports people who will be staying for some time in Australia pursuing their sporting interests. Depending on the nature and duration of the sporting activity being undertaken, people travelling to Australia who will be participating in some form of sports tourism activity may choose to travel under all of these different visa types.

Two recent innovations by the Department of Immigration and Multicultural Affairs (DIMA) which administers Australia's visa system, will assist organisers and international participants in sporting events in Australia. These are the International Event Coordinator Network (IECN), and Streamlined Short Term Business Entry. The IECN is a network of immigration officers located within the DIMA Business Centre in each State and Territory capital city. The role of these officers is to alert event organisers of immigration requirements and to advise Australian posts overseas of details of forthcoming events. The network is potentially of great benefit to event organisers, including organisers of sporting events, who appear not to have utilized its services greatly to this point.

Customs

The Australian Customs Service maintains Australia's border integrity by ensuring that prohibited goods are not brought into Australia and that other goods brought in either permanently or temporarily, pay the appropriate rate of duty or tax. This may include sporting goods brought in by international visitors for use in competition.

Quarantine

The Australian Quarantine Inspection Service (AQIS) seeks to protect Australia against the introduction of exotic plant and animal matter which could pose a disease risk for Australia's unique environment and its agricultural industries. For this reason, AQIS inspects goods entering Australia, including sporting equipment, food supplements, and therapeutic substances.

Where horses are brought to Australia to compete in races or in equestrian events, a period of quarantine is required. Early contact with AQIS helps minimize any quarantine difficulties which might otherwise impact on a sporting event. AQIS also anticipate that the knowledge and experience gained from the Olympics will help them to adopt best practice approaches to future major sporting events.

Infrastructure

The ability of cities or regions to host successful sports tourism activities and events depends on there being adequate infrastructure in place. This includes sporting facilities, accommodation, air, road and rail transport networks both to and within the region, and other tourism related facilities such as restaurants, retail outlets and entertainment venues.

While the focus of event organisers tends to be on the actual sporting infrastructure, the existence of adequate sporting facilities does not necessarily mean that an event can be held at that location. If accommodation and transport requirements cannot be met or are inadequate, even small regional events will be difficult to host. Accordingly, a strategic approach which considers the adequacy and availability of all relevant infrastructure needs to be adopted when planning sporting events and activities.

Sporting facilities are expensive to provide. For this reason, their funding has almost always been the domain of governments – local, State and Territory and Commonwealth. This can lead to distortions in the provision of facilities, with priorities sometimes influenced by factors other than the perceived benefits to a community. Arguably, this has led to an over-investment in sporting facilities in some areas, and consequent excess capacity. This excess capacity represents a genuine opportunity for sports tourism development – significant benefits can be gained through better facilities utilization, without the need for further costly investment. The relationship between facilities and the hosting of events is complex. Investment in facilities can rarely be justified on the basis of being used only for major sporting events. Also, it cannot be assumed that the mere provision of high quality sporting facilities will guarantee a region or a state a flow of major sports tourism opportunities. It is ultimately then incumbent upon a region itself to attract facilities funding, possibly through the hosting of a "catalytic" event, and thereafter to "sell" those facilities effectively to event organisers to help ensure their sustainable use.

Cost-effectiveness is a key consideration in attracting facilities funding. It may be that the costs associated with the construction and maintenance of national or international standard facilities simply cannot be justified for community use alone or even taking into consideration increased use associated with the hosting of national or international events. The commercial viability of facilities can be further reduced when accompanying accommodation and transport infrastructure is inadequate for the hosting of major events.

More recently there has been a trend towards the construction of multipurpose facilities which can be utilized for a variety of community and entertainment functions as well as the holding of a variety of sporting activities and events. This kind of facility can prove more cost effective than traditional facilities dedicated to a narrow focus on a particular sport or range of sports.

When considering facilities investment, it is also important-both for governments and private investors-to consider the regional facilities environment so as to avoid duplication and maximize the synergies with complementary facilities in nearby regions. The development of regional sporting "hubs" for particular sports can also help reduce the risk of constructing sports specific facilities which are economically unsustainable.

More generally, a strategy by governments and sporting organizations of "sharing" State or national events around regional Australia would help justify the financial investment in regional facilities as well as help ensure a more even distribution of the economic benefits associated with sporting events.

State/Regional Facilities and Asset Audits

Facilities investment and prioritization of facilities funding would also be enhanced by improved information about the supply and demand for regional sporting infrastructure. This would also help address the difficulties faced by event promoters, organisers or prospective organisers who often lack awareness of just what facilities and of what standard, are available in various regions.

Currently, the Commonwealth is working with the State and Territory governments on undertaking a facilities audit of state, national and international standard facilities. To complement this work regions could benefit if similar audits were conducted at the regional level.

Frequently, events may be organised with little knowledge of, or regard to, other events planned for the same time. This can have serious ramifications for all events staged at that time, with multiple demands on infrastructure and services, which may well exceed the capacity of the region to manage. Data on the utilization of sporting facilities is therefore important, particularly where there may be strong seasonal variations. In this way, sports tourism activities, along with other events-based tourism activity, can be targeted at low or shoulder season times, to help minimize peaks and troughs.

Accommodation Infrastructure

One of the key issues for maximizing the tourism benefits of sporting activity and events is the availability of a range of accessible accommodation, covering the budget to the luxury markets. As part of each region's asset audit, an accommodation directory should be produced detailing the bed numbers in each sector of the market. By identifying the range of accommodation available, local sports tourism organisers can more effectively target particular events, knowing that suitable accommodation for the specific market is available. For example, under age championships may well have quite different accommodation needs from a masters competition. As part of this accommodation audit, consideration could be given to utilising or upgrading existing facilities such as school dormitories, barracks etc., which may well provide adequate accommodation for the lower end of the market.

A vital part of encouraging the development of sports tourism in a region is identifying the benefits which can accrue to the whole community. In particular the businesses directly involved in the provision of services should be made aware of the importance of catering for the needs of their guests to ensure they have a good experience. In the case of accommodation providers, they need to address the particular needs of athletes including bed lengths and adequate and appropriate catering.

Transport Infrastructure

A key issue emerging from the focus group discussions is high cost of transportation in many areas of regional Australia – both to and within regions. An associated issue was lack of transport capacity – the inability to move large numbers of participants in and out of many regions in a short space of time.

Ongoing reforms and deregulation in the transport sector, especially domestic aviation, have the potential to deliver significant benefits to regional Australia, and to help encourage the development of sports tourism and other events based tourism in regional Australia.

Research and Data Collection

Sports tourism is a relatively new area of study given its recent rise as a significant niche sector for the Australian tourism industry. A number of Australian researchers have begun to specialize in this field but the current information base available to the industry is still relatively small and a range of research needs to be conducted.

A major inhibitor to more and better quality research is the current lack of data available. While some data is collected in relation to individual events, there is no widespread or systematic data series across all sports tourism activities at a state or national level.

The International Visitor Survey (IVS) and National Visitor Survey (NVS) produced by the Bureau of Tourism Research (BTR) currently include limited questions regarding activities undertaken by visitors while travelling throughout Australia. The NVS includes the categories of Sport-Participant or Spectator under Main Purpose of Visit in its survey form.

In the IVS 'to participate in or watch an organised sporting event' is a response to a question regarding factors that influenced the decision to visit Australia. This data provides at best a very partial picture of the level of sports tourism activity in Australia. To improve the available data, there may be some scope to expand the range of questions regarding sports related activities within these surveys or to initiate a stand-alone sports tourism baseline study.

The BTR have also undertaken initial research profiling Australian 'sports tourists'. (Tourism Research Report 3rd edition – Sports Tourism: An Australian Perspective) This research extends the definition of sports tourism further than that adopted for this Strategy to include day trips, i.e. a round trip of at least 50 kilometres, where the traveller stays away from home for at least 4 hours but does not spend a night away from home as part of that travel.

The Survey results showed that 6 per cent of day trips and 5 per cent of overnight trips taken by Australians in Australia, were taken with sport as the primary motivation. (It could be anticipated that a significant further number of trips were undertaken with sport as a secondary motivation.) The paper found that Australians who travelled to take part in sports, either as spectators, officials or participants (day and overnight) are likely to be:

- male aged between 15 and 24 years;
- from an upper income household (earning more than $78 000 per year);
- and that they generate higher yield per night.

The slightly different definition employed in the BTR study suggests what should probably be the first step in data collection for the sports tourism sector-the establishment of a uniform set of standard definitions for sports tourism. The adoption of standard definitions provides the opportunity for various researchers to produce data which has comparability across the sports tourism sector. An extensive range of agreed definitions should be developed, allowing researchers to choose those required for specific data sets while retaining commonality. The definition adopted in this Strategy might provide the basis for discussion towards such agreement.

Data types which might provide the basis for a range of research in the sports tourism field include (for both domestic and international visitors):

- expenditure on trips involving sporting activities (including expenditure on total trip and on the "sports" component);
- more detailed questions on motivation for travel, especially for domestic travellers;
- satisfaction information;
- length of stay data (including length of stay for total trip and for the "sports" component);
- demographic information (age, gender, income, occupation);
- type of accommodation used while travelling for sports related purposes; and
- type of transport used while travelling for sports related purposes.

Areas of research which may be useful to the industry include:

- appraisal of potential and proposed sport events;
- estimation of market for new or proposed sport tours;

- identification of infrastructure needed for sports tourism;
- specification of new tourism uses for existing sports infrastructure;
- recommendations for modifications to existing sports infrastructure to enhance tourism value; and
- profiling of sports tourism segments (e.g training camps, tours of facilities).

Other possible areas of research could be:

- measuring the economic impact of sport events at a regional, State/Territory and national level;
- measuring the economic impact of sporting infrastructure;
- measuring the social impact of sports tourism; and
- assessment of the environmental impacts of sport infrastructure and sports tourists.

Work by government bodies such as the Bureau of Tourism Research and the Australian Bureau of Statistics can often provide useful broader contexts for specific research and in the case of BTR often more targeted baseline data. Specific research needs can also be met through academic and industry collaboration. For example, the Cooperative Research Centre for Sustainable Tourism has an events sub-program which potentially can address some of the research and data needs, especially if its activities are focused towards sports events and activities at the non-micro level. The CRC has also recently established a sports tourism "node", located at the University of Canberra, to provide a focus for its research into the sports tourism market.

There is considerable scope for cooperation between industry and research bodies in improving the information available to the sports tourism sector. There is also scope for industry to address its own information needs in terms of local environments and of its specific marketing and development requirements.

Evaluation of Events

Ongoing public sector reform and rationalisation have placed public tourism authorities and sporting organizations under increasing pressure to operate cost-effectively. Government agencies have to be more accountable for policies, programs and funding decisions and this includes funding for sporting events. Governments lend their support to events on the basis of decisions made regarding benefits and costs ranging from financial to social and cultural. Such events may have the capacity to create income and employment in the short term and generate increased visitation and related investment in the longer term.

Determining the value of sporting events has been a perennially difficult issue for governments to resolve. There are no standard criteria for evaluating the economic significance of staging events. There also appears to be an absence of rigorous and comprehensive criteria for evaluating publicly funded tourism events, with great disparity between States, regions and research companies in their approach, both to the assessment of economic impact and to less tangible cultural and social impacts.

These differing approaches have made it difficult for governments not only to justify expenditure on events, but also to compare the economic success of various events. It is imperative for the credibility of the industry that sound methodologies are used to measure the return on the investment, and that these methodologies are widely accepted.

Development of a commonly accepted framework for evaluation would allow event organisers to compare and predict outcomes for their events with similar sized events. The ability to establish these areas of comparability (as well as differences) is important in gaining an overall view of sports tourism events in Australia and making assessments about the size and characteristics of this industry. This would also facilitate national and international comparisons.

Given the limited budgets of organizations expected to undertake evaluations of events and the often complex methodology, a framework for evaluation is essential for smaller/regional organizations. Several of the State events bodies have developed basic evaluation models which are appropriate but more importantly are financially accessible to the smaller sporting and tourism organizations. It may be appropriate to develop a national standard model for events of this size and nature, possibly based on one of the existing models. Mega-events such as the 2000 Sydney Olympics Games stand alone in terms of developing methodology to assess their impact-the impact is felt at regional, state and national levels.

Much preparatory work has already been completed by researchers in this area leading up to the Games and this will continue post-Games. Notable in this regard is the Federal Government publication The Olympic Effect which assesses the likely tourism impact of the Games. A particular challenge will be to ensure that some of the innovative modelling approaches and methodologies developed for, and implemented during, the Games, can filter down to evaluation for smaller events.

Implementation

The proposals contained in this strategy will require the concerted efforts of a range of organizations if they are to be successfully implemented and if the sports tourism sector is to achieve its full potential. Those organizations include governments at all levels (Commonwealth, State/Territory and local), the tourism industry, the sports sector including national and state/territory sporting organizations and researchers.

A key theme of the strategy is the need for better coordination between what is a very diverse range of stakeholders involved in the sports tourism sector. Lack of communication and coordination, especially between sporting groups and the tourism sector, has been identified as a major impediment to maximizing the tourism potential of sporting activities and events.At the state/territory level, events corporations take on much of the responsibility for building these links. At the local level, there is arguably a greater need for development of networks or "clusters" focusing on sports tourism development. At the national level, there may also be a role for an overarching coordination mechanism of this nature.

Such a national-level group, which could be similar to the Canadian Sports Tourism Coalition, could be comprised of representatives of key stakeholders across industry and government, and could play a significant role in:

- raising the level of awareness about the sports tourism sector within both industry and government;

- identifying and pursuing specific research needs and priorities;
- identifying and overseeing the role of any facilitation unit which might be established following the release of this strategy; and
- overseeing and reporting on progress in implementing the strategy, sports tourism development
    1. Promote network of sport and tourism organizations to improve communication and coordination.
    2. Develop industry profile-establish peak body.

International Case Studies

Britain

In 1992 the creation of the Department of National Heritage (DNH) pulled together under one roof the leisure sectors of sport, tourism, and the arts. For the first time there appeared to be a formal connection between sport and tourism which might lead to some development of the sports tourism sector. Unfortunately this turned out not to be the case, and for all practical purposes, no significant relationship between sport and tourism was established at either the policy or operational level. In fact, rather than further integrate sport and tourism, the subsequent policies of the DNH tended to reverse previous policies that allowed greater integration e.g. reduction of English Tourist Board core funding and a narrower focus for the Sports.

However, the historical difficulties of linking sport and tourism in Britain may be a thing of the past. The Department of Culture, Media and Sport (formerly DNH) announced in February 1999 the Government's intention to develop innovative niche markets such as sports tourism. The announcement forms part of a 15 point plan for tourism to unlock the full potential of Britain's unique cultural and natural heritage. UK Sport has also created an economic impact "guidance document" to assist with the undertaking of impact studies to determine the value of sports events. (Dept of Culture, Media & Sport; English Tourism Council)

Furthermore, the British Tourist Authority has recently developed a sports tourism marketing strategy which is backed up by three staff in England and a recently appointed staff member in their Sydney office. This innovative move to place a dedicated sports tourism officer in a key source market may place the UK at the forefront of international sport tourism development. While it is very early in the process, the appointment of a dedicated officer in this role may open up a range of opportunities for sports tourism in the UK. There may be lessons for Australia and in particular marketing body the Australian Tourist Commission, should the UK's approach prove to be successful.

Canada

In 1998, 37% of Canada's 73.7 million domestic trips were for sports tourism purposes. In Canada, sport tourists are defined as individuals who travelled and in doing so participated in or attended a sport event during the reference period. Sport tourists account for between 2.5 and 5 million individuals from June to September, July and August being the most popular months for sport tourist activities (15% and 18%). (Statistics Canada-1998 Canadian Travel Survey) (Note that this does not mean that 37% of tourism activity was sports tourism – rather that 37% of travellers travelled at least once for sports purposes).

Since 1996 the Canadian Tourism Commission (CTC) has been involved in a program designed to promote community and tourism industry interest in development of sports tourism as a viable contributor to the economic wellbeing of local communities.

The Canadian Sports Tourism Initiative is a program designed to increase the quality and quantity of sports events hosted in Canada and has a number of objectives:

- To create a viable sports tourism industry in Canada;
- To organize Canadian communities to pursue sports tourism by providing them with assistance in organizing the appropriate local resources and infrastructures to be effective;
- To assist communities in developing sports tourism commissions, appropriately organised to recruit sports events;
- To create linkages with the Canadian national, provincial and local sports system and event hosts to assist in the development of the sports tourism industry;
- To create new revenue streams and resources for local event organisers, sports friendly businesses and sport in general;

- To provide effective communication channels to facilitate business to business relationship marketing opportunities between event rights holders and potential host cities; and
- To create an industry-led, Canadian Sports Tourism Coalition to provide a forum for education, market intelligence and sports tourism marketing for communities and sports involved in the sports tourism business.

Based on positive support demonstrated by communities across Canada, in 1997, a partnership between the CTC, client communities and sport/tourism industry was borne. Soar International, a Vancouver based sports information and event management company was contracted to manage the process.

Communities that have decided to be part of the Sports Tourism Initiative's community planning program participated in a comprehensive planning process. To start the process, a Soar International facilitator presents a half day session to a broad constituency of local sports, tourism and community leaders, covering such topics as what is sports tourism, who are sports tourists, how are sports events organised, where are the opportunities to work together and how a sports tourism commission can be developed. Secondly, using a local project coordinator and a planning tool kit adapted to fit the local community process, data on which to base a sports tourism marketing strategy is gathered.

With this data, Soar International facilitates a workshop which provides sufficient information to prepare a strategic business plan. Using a locally facilitated process, this plan is presented to all the key groups in the community with an interest to ensuring its successful implementation. Soar International then assists the community to refine and implement the strategic plan on an ongoing basis. By the end of 1999 the regions of Kelowna, Cranbrook, Edmonton, London, Kingston, Hamilton, Moncton, St. John's, Gatineau and Newfoundland/ Cornerbrook had all undertaken the sports tourism planning process.

South Africa

In May 1996 the South African Department of Environmental Affairs and Tourism released a white paper on the development and promotion of tourism in South Africa. The sports tourism sector was specifically identified within this policy document. The intent was both to encourage the development of sports tourism and to encourage the provision of facilities, training, marketing and promotion to give emphasis to the development of this segment of the industry.

Following the release of the white paper, and in order to capitalize on South Africa's sporting successes and re-entry into the world tourism scene, South Africa Sports Tourism (SAST) was launched jointly by the Ministry of Environmental Affairs and Tourism, and the Ministry of Sport and Recreation in October 1997.

The success of SAST in developing the international market for sport tourism in South Africa is yet to be established. As can be seen in the graph below, Satour figures suggest that Sports Tourism (spectator and participant) makes up four per cent of the domestic tourism market.

Careers in Tourism, and the associated fields of sports, hospitality and events, are vital to the economies of many countries. In Australia alone, tourism and related sectors are worth $70 billion to the economy, with Queensland as the foremost tourism state.

The Bachelor of International Hotel and Tourism

Management at St. Lucia and the Bachelor of Business at Ipswich focus on the business principles at work in the travel and tourism industry.

Graduates are well prepared to work within hotels and resorts; conference and convention centres; travel and transportation companies; state regional and local tourism organizations; and hospitality or tourism training and consultancy firms in a variety of managerial and coordination roles.

The School of Tourism's Executive Shadowing Program is a unique work placement program that is competitively offered to students enrolled in the final year Professional Development course. Under this program students spend quality time 'shadowing' a senior manager in business or government in their industry of interest.

The Faculty of Business, Economics and Law's Employment Services team organize opportunities for students to network with potential employers in a range of areas.

Possible jobs

To begin with, most graduates can expect to work in assistant type positions as experience "on the ground" is often a requirement of higher-level roles.

However, with a qualification, skills and industry knowledge acquired during degree studies, graduates can rise quickly to higher-level positions. Event Management can be a complex and involved task depending on the type and size of the event. Event management includes organizing the supply of equipment, materials and services well ahead of time and then coordinating the activities during the event.

Recent event management graduates have found work in the following roles:

- Event Coordinator – Singapore Tourism Board.
- Project Coordinator – AMB Exhibitions.
- Event Coordinator – Event Planners Australia.
- Events Assistant – Brisbane Exhibition & Convention Centre.
- Events Assistant – Major Sports Facility Authority Queensland.

Sport and Recreation Management focuses on various leisure industry operation and management issues including sport and fitness, adventure and outdoor tourism, wilderness and natural park recreation and community recreation. UQ sport and leisure graduates have gained employment as:

- Relationship Manager – Riverlife Adventure Centre.
- Sponsorship & Event Manager – Queensland Rugby.
- Parks Manager – National Parks Board Singapore.
- Duty Manager – North Brisbane Sporting Association.

Travel and Tourism Management explores tourism and travel from both a national and international perspective, gaining an understanding of the operation and functions of this industry, including transportation, tour operations, tourism advisory, and travel consultancy.

- Groups and Tours Coordinator – Hilton.
- Travel Consultant – Tourism Queensland.
- Tour guide – Cascade Brewery.

- Flight Attendant – Singapore Airlines.
- Travel Agent – Travelscene.
- Programs & Travel Advisor – Overseas Working Holidays.

Hotel Management deals with the management processes and strategies of hotels and resorts. This includes food and catering management, gaming and service delivery. Many graduates start their careers with hotel management trainee programs, such as those offered by the Accor Group. Other recent graduates have gone into roles such as:

- Function and Events Supervisor – Bretts Wharf.
- Reservation Sales Agent – Marriott Hotel.
- Business Development Assistant – Mirvac Resorts and Hotels.
- Catering Sales Manager – Swissotel Merchant Court Singapore.
- Corporate Management Trainee – Intercontinental Hotel Group.
- Guest Service Agent – Sofitel.

Graduate profile:

Kristie Gillman: Kristie Gillman used her experience in UQ's School of Tourism Executive Shadowing Program to land a job in the engine room of the Queensland Government. Kristie, who graduated in 2008 with a major in event management, completed an executive shadowing placement with the Department of Premier Cabinet in 2008; she was then offered a graduate position once she finished uni.

"Having a real experience on placement made a real difference to me; it allowed me to see theory in practice and to develop my networks," Kristie said. "The Executive Shadowing Program was invaluable." The Executive Shadowing Program is a unique work placement initiative run by the School of Tourism that gives students the opportunity to work with a senior industry figure and to observe organizational functions from a strategic level.

Programs that will get you there:

- Bachelor of Business.
- Bachelor of International Hotel and Tourism Management.

6

Research Into Action: Getting into the Game

Introduction

The term sport tourism has only recently been widely adopted to describe sport-related leisure travel. Several constraints that have arisen in sport tourism research are just beginning to be addressed. Much of the research is localized and not focused on an international perspective. Dividing academia and professional practice are continuing concern and ongoing debate over what sport tourism is. The literature suggests that there are three macro behaviours: participating, watching, and visiting.

Impact of this Research

The active sport tourist is involved in one of three types of vacations: the pure sport holiday, sport as a secondary purpose, and informal sports holiday. Each is characterized by type of involvement, level of involvement, skill level, commitment, and investment. The three types of active sport tourists, however, provide important market segment information to organizations that might be targeting particular types of sport tourists. A major concern for sport tourism is the reported lack of coordination between tourism agencies and sports agencies.

Most sport tourists are between the ages of 18 and 44. Seniors, however, are defying the traditional perspective of declining activity, and are continuing to participate in active sport tourism.

Event sport tourism evokes similar — yet different — motivators among participants, many of whom report that such tourism provides the opportunity to be present, and nothing is better than being at the event. Much of the work in event sport tourism is focused not on the tourist but on the economic impact. Understanding and correctly implementing the methodology of economic impact is difficult for many organizations. Those engaging in event sport tourism must realize both the positive and negative impact of such tourism on the local community. Where active community involvement has been encouraged, feedback has been positive; major tax-dollar investment has inspired negative feedback.

Nostalgia sport tourism is the least researched or understood of the three areas. Much work needs to be done here as the number of such facilities and attractions continues to grow.

How to Use this Research

As parks and recreation departments become more involved in sport tourism, they must recognize that:

- Three distinct and separate market segments exist.
- Motivation for participation varies within each market segment, and opportunities to participate, spectate, and engage in nostalgia will attract different individuals for different reasons.
- Age is becoming less important.
- Providers of sports events must listen to participants and spectators as part of an ongoing assessment program.
- The community's perceived benefits and negative impacts of sports events must be understood and carefully weighed when such events are anticipated or planned.

Special Case Study

Sport tourism in Nepal

Nepal is also popular for Sport tourism such as golfing in Kathmandu, paraglading in Pokhara and Marathon Sky Race in the mountain region, Mountain Bike and Motor cycle tours, Everest Marathon Race, Elephant Polo, International Elephent Race Comptition, White Water Rafting Comptition, Canoing Comptition etc. Adventure Silk Road Inc has been in tourism business since more then two decades specializing in Nature, Culture and Adventure Sports Tourism in Nepal. With the thrills of outdoor activities Nepal also offers city fun for its visitors. While visitors enjoy the rustic by simply beholding spectacular sights and partaking in the activities of exotic cultures, in cities like Kathmandu and Pokhara some entertainment is on par with western world.

Sport Tourism Nepal

Nepal is also popular for Sport tourism such as golfing in Kathmandu, paraglading in Pokhara and Marathon Sky Race in the mountain region, Mountain Bike and Motor cycle tours, Everest Marathon Race, Elephant Polo, International Elephent Race Comptition, White Water Rafting Comptition, Canoing Comptition etc. Adventure Silk Road Inc has been in tourism business since more then two decades specializing in Nature, Culture and Adventure Sports Tourism in Nepal.

With the thrills of outdoor activities Nepal also offers city fun for its visitors. While visitors enjoy the rustic by simply beholding spectacular sights and partaking in the activities of exotic cultures, in cities like Kathmandu and Pokhara some entertainment is on par with western world.

Visitors have a choice from a potpourri of amusements. They can: partake in cultural shows that include theatre and local art; wine and dine at premier hotels that provide excellent service; enjoy music and dance at newly-opened discotheques; try a luck at rummy or blackjack at one of our casinos; or just watch a movie as cozy twosome in one of our movie theatres.

Kathmandu, which is generally a quiet city after twilight bustles with life till the wee hours of morning in the narrow alleys of Thamel and other selected places. Bars and pubs, many of which feature live music stay open till late night while discotheques function to keep boredom at bay for the young Nepali crowd and tourists out for the night.

A taste of Nepali culture is still sought by tourists. Visitors are fascinated by ethnic ambience in local restaurants that serve authentic Nepali food. Art galleries and museums of the Valley exhibiting cultural treasures are also among preferred tourist choices.

Health clubs and gymnasium are available for sports lovers. While latest Nepali and Hindi movies run in most movie theatres, a theatre in Kathmandu also runs good English movies. Video and DVD stores offer wider range of choices.

Tenzing-hillarry Everest marathon Nepal

Inspired and encouraged by the grand success of Everest Marathon held on May 19, 2003 to commemorate Golden Jubilee Celebration of ascent on Mt. Everest by Late Tenzing Norgay Sherpa and Sir Edmund Hillary, Himalaya Expeditions have taken a step further by giving a lifeline to this marathon by organizing it annually on May 29. The support and suggestion provided by the grandson of Late Tenzing Norgay Sherpa has motivated us to organize this marathon under the banner of Tenzing-Hillary Everest Marathon in the everlasting memory of the two legendary figures.

5th Tenzing Hillary Everest Marathon is slated to organize on May 29, 2007, 54th anniversary of ascent on Mt. Everest by Tenzing Sherpa and Edmund Hillary. Since the name of Tenzing and Hillary has been associated with Mt. Everest, marathon will be a most befitting tribute to these great souls who climbed Mt. Everest for the first time in the history of human civilization.

The start line of the Tenzing Hillary Everest Marathon is at Everest Base camp 5356m (17,149 feet) in Nepal. The marathon finish at the Sherpa town of Namche Bazaar at 3446m (11,300 feet) and the course is a measured 42.195 km (26.2 miles) over rough mountain trails. Everest Marathon is the world's most spectacular race to be held in 2005 for the third time.

For acclimatizing to the high altitude all runners of the Everest Marathon are requested to be in Nepal three weeks prior to the race. This three week holiday combines sightseeing in the capital, Kathmandu, a 15 day trek to the start under medical supervision, an ascent of Kala Pattar (5623m) for the best views of Everest. Although the course of the Everest Marathon is basically down hill, there are two steep uphill sections.

There may be snow and ice on the upper part and there is considerable exposure along much of the route of the marathon.

Experience of rough terrain is essential for Everest Marathon and road marathon experience is not sufficient to run Everest Marathon.

The Everest region is understandably one of the most popular and spectacular destinations for trekking, and it offers some of the most fascinating and enjoyable trekking. Your acclimization trek begins with a sweeping scenic flight to Lukla. The trek starts from Lukla following many farm villages enroute with beautiful views of the high snow capped peaks of the world, and to the highest spot at Kalapatar for the outstanding breathtaking view panorama of peaks and its glacier including Mt. Everest at a stone throw distance.

During your trekking period upto Everest Basecamp, you will pass through the Everest National Park crossing through Namche Bazaar, Khumbu's Sherpa capital and Buddhist monasteries of Pangboche, one of the oldest in the area, and at Thyangboche, one of the newest as it was re-built after being burnt to the ground. A visit to Kala Patthar (5545m) will be rewarded with unmatched views of Nuptse, Everest, Lhotse. This marathon itself is a part of trekking.

Outline Itinerary

- Day 01: (May 14, 2007): Arrival Of Participants.
- Day 02: (May 15, 2007): Today Will Be A Sightseeing.
- Day 03: (May 16, 2007): Departure Of Group To Lukla.
- Day 04: (May 17, 2007): Lukla To Phakding (9,321 Ft.).
- Day 05—07: (May 18, 19 & 20, 2007): Phankding To Namche Bazaar.
- Day 08: (May 21, 2007): Trek To Thyangboche Monastery (12,683 Ft).
- Day 09: (May 22, 2007): Trek To Dingboche (1 4,464 Ft.).
- Day 10: (May 23, 2007): Acclimatization Day In Dingboche.
- Day 11: (May 24, 2007): Trek To Lobuche (16,105 Ft.).
- Day 12: (May 25, 2007): Trek To Gorak Shep (16,859 Ft.)- Lobuche (16,105 Ft.).
- Day 13: (May 26, 2007): Trek To Gorak Shep (16,859 Ft.).
- Day 14: (May 27, 2007: Trek To Everest Base Camp (17,593 Ft).

- Day 15: (May 28, 2007): Rest Day At Everest Base Camp (17.593 Ft.).
- Day 16: (May 29, 2007): Race Day-Race Will Commence At 7am.
    * 1st Check Point-Gorak Shep.
    * 2nd Check Point-Periche.
    * 3rd Check Point-Phunge Thanga After Thyangboche.
    * 4th And Final Check-Namche Bazaar-Finish Line.
- Day 17: (May 30, 2007): Trek Back Down To Lukla.
- Day 18: (May 31, 2007): Flight Back To Kathmandu.
- Day 19: (June 01, 2007): Free Day In Kathmandu.
- Day 20: (June 02, 2007): Departure For Home.
- Date: May 14-June 2, 2007.
- Race Date: May 29, 2007.
    * Cost for Runners: US $2085: Kathmandu to Kathmandu.
    * Cost for Non-Runners: US $ 1,885 pp USD.
    * Single supplement: US $ 220 pp.

Price Does Not Include:

- Airport transfers on private vehicle.
- Twin sharing accommodation in Kathmandu on Bed & Breakfast basis.
- An English speaking tour guide for city sightseeing.
- An English speaking trekking guide for the trekking with necessary crew.
- All meals included during the trek
- Wages of guide and other members of the team.
- National park fees, Govt. taxes and other applicable fees.
- Domestic airfare as mentioned in the above itinerary.

Price Does Not Include:

- Entry Visa for Nepal. ($30 US D, can be paid upon arrival to Nepal).
- International flight Ticket.

- Meals while in Kathmandu. (4 lunches and dinners).
- Expenses of personal nature & gratitude.
- Personal clothing.
- International travel, cancellation & medical insurance.
- Emergency evacuation or medical costs.
- Airport taxes upon departure from Kathmandu.
- Extra expenses incurred due to leaving the trip early.
- Venue: Everest Base Camp (5,364m) to Namche Bazaar (3446m).
- Event: 26.2-mile marathon.
- Maximum number of applicants: Select Numbers.
- Closing date for applications is, May 1st, 2007.

Tenzing Hillary Everest Marathon 2007 event is open to all athletes, runners, extreme sport lovers and high altitude running enthusiasts regardless of caste, creed, country or religion. To take part, participants do not necessarily have to be runners or athletes. Even non-runners can do so. Friends and family of people taking part in the race can also apply, as non-runners.

Qualifications for runners and athletes to participate in the Tenzing Hillary Everest Marathon 2007 event:

Runners must be physically fit and mentally sound. A medical certificate from a doctor is necessary, stating that the runners are healthy, free of injury and therefore fit to take part in this racing event. Health certificates should be faxed or mailed with your entry form. See sign up procedure.

Qualifications for non-runners: Non-runners should be in good health and physical fitness. All non-runners must have previous hiking experience on varied mountainous terrain.

Flight Arrangements

Our arrangement starts only from Nepal, so make sure that you have organized your flight to Nepal using one of your close by local flight centres or travel agents.If your flight date to Kathmandu differs with our arrival / departure dates, we can organize your hotel for such forced stay days in Kathmandu. The cost for such extra stay nights would be US $25 per night (sharing twin in a double room).

Arrivals and Departures

Everyone will be met at the airport in Kathmandu by one of our Representative and taken you to the Kathmandu Guest House. Please provide us your flight details;

Nepal Visa

Your can get your Nepal entry visa upon arrival at Kathmandu Airport. Entry Visa costs US $ 30. Please organize small note bills for the visa and few passport size photographs, because visa officer will not have change to give you back if you are paying him by bigger bills.

Alternatively you can also get Nepal entry visa from the Nepalese embassy or Nepalese Consulates different country.

International Elephant Race Competition Nepal

Elephant Polo Tournament Nepal-14 Days

The World Elephant Polo Association (WEPA) was formed in 1982 at Tiger Tops Jungle Lodge in the Royal Chitwan National Park in south west Nepal. The first games were played on a grass airfield in Meghauly which is located just on the edge of the National Park. The co-founders, James Manclark, a Scottish landowner and former Olympic tobogganer and Jim Edwards, owner of Tiger Tops Jungle Lodge and Chairman of the Tiger Mountain Group, came up with the idea in a bar in St. Moritz, Switzerland, where they are both members of the Cresta Club.

Elephant polo was first played in India around the turn of the 20th century, by members of the Maharaja's Harem (Zenena) – to keep them busy. WEPA is the first paramount organization in the modern times to host and create elephant polo as a game with organized competitions.

The first games were played with a soccer ball, but after finding that the elephants like to smash the balls, the soccer ball was replaced with a standard polo ball. The sticks are made of bamboo and have a standard polo mallet on the end. The length of the stick depends on the size of the elephant-anywhere from 5 to 12 feet.

Most of the rules of the games are based on horse polo, but the pitch is 3/4 length (because of the slower speed of the elephants) and there are some necessary additions-for instance, it is a penalty for an elephant to lie down in front of the goal line. Players are secured in rope harnesses, with a rope across their thighs and rope stirrups. The game will stop if a player's harness becomes too loose and there is a danger of the player falling off. Players have fallen off elephants only a few times in WEPA's 20-year history.

The primary difference between horse and elephant polo, besides the substitution of an elephant for a horse, is that the elephants are "driven" by their trainers, called "mahouts." The mahouts have generally worked with the elephant for many years and the elephants respond quickly to the mahout's signals and commands.

The mahout communicates with the elephant with verbal commands and by applying pressure to the back of the elephant's ears with their feet. The player's responsibility is to let the mahout know where to go, how fast, when to stop, etc. Most of the mahouts and all of the elephants only understand Nepali, so the communication is difficult at times. The professional players tend to learn some basics Nepali to help with the communication on the pitch.

The WEPA tournament has been hosted by Tiger Tops at Meghauly each December since 1982. It is an invitational event and has in the past included teams representing a wide variety of countries and sponsors

Outline Itinerary

- Please Visit Following Links to Find Nepal Treks, Tours & Many Different Types of Holiday Package Itinerary.
- Trekking in Nepal Tours in Nepal Mountain Expedition in Nepal Trekking Peak Climbing in Nepal.
- Domestic Flight Nepal Rent A Car Nepal Hindu Pilgrimage Tours Nepal Hotel Reservation Nepal.
- Botanical Tour in Nepal Eco Tour in Nepal Mountain Biking Tour in Nepal White Water Rafting in Nepal.
- Fishing Tour in Nepal Sport Tourism Nepal Butterfly Tour in Nepal Honeymoon Tour Nepal in Nepal.

- Golf Tour in Nepal Hunting Tour in Nepal Buddhist Circuit Nepal & India Heli Skiing in Nepal.
- Yoga, Meditation Nepal Child Adoption Nepal Filming Tourism in Nepal Bird Watching Nepal in Nepal.
- Village Tourism Nepal MICE Tour in Nepal Helicopter Tour Nepal Traditional Wedding in Nepal.
- Visit for Tours & Treks to China Tibet, Bhutan, India, Pakistan, Sri Lanka, Thailand, Myanmar, Mongolia & Vietnam.
- Bhutan Tours & Treks Pakistan Tours & Treks China Tibet Tours & Treks Mongolia Tours & Treks.
- About Us India Tours & Treks Sri Lanka Tours & Treks Thailand Tours & Treks.
- Contact Us General Information Myanmar Tour & Treks Vietnam Tours & Treks.

Trekking in Nepal

Nepal offers excellent trekking options to visitors. It is a unique destination for trekking as it offers the unbeatable combination of natural beauty and cultural diversities from the easy walking excursions to the strenuous climb of the snowy peaks. The most rewarding way to experience Nepal's natural embellishment and cultural assortment is to walk through the length, breadth and the altitudes of the country. You can trek up to the foot of the great Himalayan ranges, such as Mt. Everest, Langtang and Annapurna or make a circuit of the highest mountains. You can also get beyond the mountains in Tibet — like arid landscape with ancient culture such as upper Dolpa and Mustang.

This is why trekking in Nepal is considered as a big part of the ultimate Himalayan adventure and is a trekker's paradise. Nepal is gateway to the adventure in Tibet and Bhutan. Adventure Silk Road with its professionally managed operations based in Nepal offers the excellent experiences for the trekkers in Nepal. Come, Join Us on any of our trekking adventures in the Himalayan destinations!

Langtang Gosainkunda Helambhu Trekking

The Langtang-Gosainkunda region is a collection of Sherpa valleys north of Kathmandu, close to the Tibetan border. The rough road now reaches as far as Dunche, only a day's drive from Kathmandu. Yet, despite this, Langtang remains a relatively less trekked area. Bill tillman, a famous explorer and climbing partner of Eric Shipton, described Langtang as one of the world's most beautiful valleys. We exit by passing the holy lake of Gosainkunda and crossing the Laurebina La (4100 m.). Here, you will have excellent view into Tibet and meet Hindu pilgrims before gradually dropping down the ridges and driving back to Kathmandu.

The Langtang valley is aptly called " the valley of glaciers". Here the mountain–scape is spectacular. On either side of valley, mountains rise, soaring into the sky. The valley offers pine forest, slow moving rivers and swift mountain streams, rugged rock and snow–capped peaks, grassy downs and meadows strewn with daisies and wild primulas. In the upper part of valley there are snow bridges spanning angry torrents, high passes enveloped in mist, tiny lakes with icebergs floating on them and water of crystalline brightness. There are also high mountains of solid ice.

Starts with an overland journey to Dunche, the main trading post of the area. From here we spend four days hiking up through this beautiful alpine valley to Kyangjin where we rest for a day for some exploration of the high mountains and glacial systems. Here, mountains rise soaring towards the sky. The landscapes we cross are extremely varied; rice-terraces, gigantic rhododendron, pine forest, and in the highest parts, a rock and shrub wilderness with the fascinating backdrop of snow capped peaks. This trek also provides a chance to observe one of a holy site of Hindu and Buddhist the sacred Gosainkunda Lake. We cross the Laurebina pass (4600 meters) and drop into the lush Helambu region and different cultural experiences eventually finishing the trek an hours drive from Kathmandu. This trek offers fascinating views of Langtang range, Ganesh Himal, Dorje Lakap, Nayakanga, and Langshisa etc.

Outline Itinerary

- Day 01: Arrive In Kathmandu.
- Day 02: Kathmandu City Tour.
- Day 03: Kathmandu-Dhunce.

- Day 04: Dhunche-Bharku-Syabrubesi.
- Day 05: Syabrubesi-Khanjung-Syarpagaon.
- Day 06: Syarpagaon-Lamahotel-Langtang Valley.
- Day 07: Langtang Valley-Kyangjing Gompa.
- Day 08: Kyangjing Gompa-Yalacheese Factory-Ghora Tabala.
- Day 09: Ghora Tabala-Syabrugaon.
- Day 10: Syabru-Sing Gompa (3254m).
- Day 11: Sing Gompa-Gosainkunda (4300m).
- Day 12: Gosainkunda-Thare Pati (2360m).
- Day 13: Thare Pati-Gul Bhanyjang (2130m).
- Day 14: Gul Bhanjyang-Chisopani (2194m).
- Day 15: Chisapani-Nagarkot-2300m.
- Day 16: Nagarkot-Kathmandu.
- Day 17: Free Day In Kathmandu.
- Day 18: Departure.
- Trip Cost Based on Camping Arrangements.
- Deluxe Hotels Option Standard Hotels Option Economy Hotels Option.
- Group Size Cost in US$.
- Per Person Group Size Cost in US$.
- Per Person Group Size Cost in US$.

Per Person

- 01-Person 000.00 01-Person 000.00 01-Person 000.00,
- 02-Person 000.00 02-Person 000.00 02-Person 000.00,
- 03-05 Person 000.00 03-05 Person 000.00 03-05 Person 000.00,
- 06-09 Person 000.00 06-09 Person 000.00 06-09 Person 000.00,
- 10-14 Person 000.00 10-14 Person 000.00 10-14 Person 000.00,
- 15 & Above 000.00 15 & Above 000.00 15 & Above 000.00,

Trip Cost includes:

1. Airport transfers on private vehicle.

2. Twin sharing accommodation in Kathmandu as per the category of package trip taken on Bed & Breakfast basis.
3. An English speaking tour guide for city sightseeing.
4. An English speaking trekking guide for the trekking with necessary Cook & porters.
5. All meals included during the trek prepared by Adventure Silk Road's cook in aid of kitchen boy and other helpers.
6. Wages of guide and other members of the team.
7. National park fees, Govt. taxes and other applicable fees.
8. Domestic airfare as mentioned in the above itinerary.

Trip cost does not include:

1. International Airfare.
2. Nepalese Visa fee and airport departure tax.
3. Lunch & dinner in Kathmandu.
4. Personal / Travel / Medical insurance and any other insurance for the members.
5. Expenses of personal nature viz. tips, laundry, phone calls, alcoholic beverages, bottled drinks etc.
6. Emergency evacuations.

Any other cost, which is not mentioned in cost inclusive field above.

Preferred Hotels for the Different Packages

- Deluxe Trip Standard Trip Economy Trip.
- Kathmandu 5-Star: Shangri-La or Similar 4-Star: Vaishali or Similar Hotel Nature or Similar.
- Trip Cost Based on Mountain Lodges (Tea Houses).
- Deluxe Hotels Option Standard Hotels Option Economy Hotels Option.
- Group Size Cost in US$.
- Per Person Group Size Cost in US$.
- Per Person Group Size Cost in US$.

Per Person

- 01-Person 000.00 01-Person 000.00 01-Person 000.00,
- 02-Person 000.00 02-Person 000.00 02-Person 000.00,
- 03-05 Person 000.00 03-05 Person 000.00 03-05 Person 000.00,
- 06-09 Person 000.00 06-09 Person 000.00 06-09 Person 000.00,
- 10-14 Person 000.00 10-14 Person 000.00 10-14 Person 000.00,
- 15 & Above 000.00 15 & Above 000.00 15 & Above 000.00,

Trip Cost includes:

1. Airport transfers on private vehicle.
2. Twin sharing accommodation in Kathmandu as per the category of package trip taken on Bed & Breakfast basis.
3. 3 meal (breakfast, Lunch & Dinner) in local restaurants along the trekking trail.
4. Accommodation in guesthouses (Tea House) on trekking trail.
5. An English speaking tour guide for city sightseeing.
6. An English speaking trekking guide for the trekking with necessary porters.
7. Wages of guide and other members.
8. National park fees, Govt. taxes and other applicable fees.
9. Domestic airfare as mentioned in the above itinerary.

Trip cost does not include:

1. International Airfare.
2. Nepalese Visa fee and international airport departure tax.
3. Lunch & dinner in Kathmandu.
4. Personal / Travel / Medical insurance and any other insurance for the members.
5. Hot water for shower during the trek.
6. Expenses of personal nature viz. tips, laundry, phone calls, alcoholic beverages, bottled drinks etc.
7. Any other cost, which is not mentioned in cost inclusive field above.

Preferred Hotels For The Different Packages

Deluxe Trip Standard Trip Economy Trip

- Kathmandu 5-Star: Shangri-La or Similar 4-Star: Vaishali or Similar Hotel Nature or Similar.
- Please Visit Following Links to Find Nepal Treks, Tours & Many Different Types of Holiday Package Itinerary.
- Trekking in Nepal Tours in Nepal Mountain Expedition in Nepal Trekking Peak Climbing in Nepal.
- Domestic Flight Nepal Rent A Car Nepal Hindu Pilgrimage Tours Nepal Hotel Reservation Nepal.
- Botanical Tour in Nepal Eco Tour in Nepal Mountain Biking Tour in Nepal White Water Rafting in Nepal.
- Fishing Tour in Nepal Sport Tourism Nepal Butterfly Tour in Nepal Honeymoon Tour Nepal in Nepal.
- Golf Tour in Nepal Hunting Tour in Nepal Buddhist Circuit Nepal & India Heli Skiing in Nepal.
- Yoga, Meditation Nepal Child Adoption Nepal Filming Tourism in Nepal Bird Watching Nepal in Nepal.
- Village Tourism Nepal MICE Tour in Nepal Helicopter Tour Nepal Traditional Wedding in Nepal.
- Visit for Tours & Treks to China Tibet, Bhutan, India, Pakistan, Sri Lanka, Thailand, Myanmar, Mongolia & Vietnam.
- Bhutan Tours & Treks Pakistan Tours & Treks China Tibet Tours & Treks Mongolia Tours & Treks.
- About Us India Tours & Treks Sri Lanka Tours & Treks Thailand Tours & Treks.
- Contact Us General Information Myanmar Tour & Treks Vietnam Tours & Treks.

Helambu Trekking Nepal-14 Days

This trek is ideal for people with less time who do not wish to travel too far from the Kathmandu Valley. Helambu is a lush region to the North of Kathmandu inhabited by Sherpas and Tamang people although the Sherpas of this region differ in their practices from their cousins in the Everest region. The trek passes through some beautiful forests and very interesting villages on route.

The Helambu region is a relatively low altitude trek and one of the most convenient of the short trek close to Kathmandu but crowd less. For a spectrum of Nepali people and the Himalayas, the Helambu trek is unrivalled. The trek passes through some beautiful forests and very interesting villages on route.

As the journey progresses you visit the homes of Brahmins, Tamangs and Sherpa people of Nepal. This place has scenic grandeur and pleasant climate as well as a long history of Buddhism, culture and ancient tradition of Tamang and Sherpas.

In Helambu region the Sherpa are quite distinct from the Sherpas of Solu khumbu (Everest region) both in language and customs. The people in Helambu where carefully exploited to a lower cast because of a Nepali king who was afraid they could give rebellion as they live all around the city regions. To this result, they still live in backward civilization. The ranges of mountains that rise above us match the diversity of the people we meet. From low altitudes we have excellent views of mountains that include Langtang, the Annapurnas, Manaslu and even Everest on a clear day. This is a pleasant and exciting journey, a time to relax and become immersed in the beauty of the Himalayas.

- Outline Itinerary.
- Day 01: Arrive In Kathmandu.
- Day 02: Kathmandu City Tour.
- Day 03: Kahmandu-Sundarijal-Chisapani.
- Day 04: Chisapani-Kutugsang.
- Day 05: Kutugsang-Tharepati.
- Day 06: Tharepati-Melamche.
- Day 07: Melamche-Sermanthang.
- Day 08: Sermanthang-Melamchepul-Kathmandu.
- Day 09: Kathmandu-Rafting-Chitwan.
- Day 10: Royal Chitwan National Park.
- Day 11: Royal Chitwan National Park-Pokhara.

- Day 12: Pokhara City Tour.
- Day 13: Pokhara-Kathmandu.
- Day 14: Departure.

Trip Cost Based on Camping Arrangements.

Deluxe Hotels Option Standard Hotels Option Economy Hotels Option;

- Group Size Cost in US$.
- Per Person Group Size Cost in US$.
- Per Person Group Size Cost in US$.

Per Person

- 01-Person 000.00 01-Person 000.00 01-Person 000.00,
- 02-Person 000.00 02-Person 000.00 02-Person 000.00,
- 03-05 Person 000.00 03-05 Person 000.00 03-05 Person 000.00,
- 06-09 Person 000.00 06-09 Person 000.00 06-09 Person 000.00,
- 10-14 Person 000.00 10-14 Person 000.00 10-14 Person 000.00,
- 15 & Above 000.00 15 & Above 000.00 15 & Above 000.00,

Trip Cost includes:

1. Airport transfers on private vehicle.
2. Twin sharing accommodation in Kathmandu as per the category of package trip taken on Bed & Breakfast basis.
3. An English speaking tour guide for city sightseeing.
4. An English speaking trekking guide for the trekking with necessary Cook & porters.
5. All meals included during the trek prepared by Adventure Silk Road's cook in aid of kitchen boy and other helpers.
6. Wages of guide and other members of the team.
7. National park fees, Govt. taxes and other applicable fees.
8. Domestic airfare as mentioned in the above itinerary.

Trip cost does not include:

1. International Airfare.
2. Nepalese Visa fee and airport departure tax.
3. Lunch & dinner in Kathmandu.
4. Personal / Travel / Medical insurance and any other insurance for the members.
5. Expenses of personal nature viz. tips, laundry, phone calls, alcoholic beverages, bottled drinks etc.
6. Emergency evacuations.
7. Any other cost, which is not mentioned in cost inclusive field above.

Preferred Hotels For The Different Packages:

- Deluxe Tour Standard Tour Economy Tour,
- Kathmandu 5-Star: Shangri-La or Similar 4-Star: Vaishali or Similar Hotel Nature or Similar,
- Chitwan Island J. Resort or similar Jungle Safari Lodge or similar Rhino Lodge or similar,
- Vehicle All Vehicle with A/C All Vehicle non A/C All Regular Vehicle,
- Trip Cost Based on Mountain Lodges (Tea Houses),
- Deluxe Hotels Option Standard Hotels Option Economy Hotels Option,
- Group Size Cost in US$,
- Per Person Group Size Cost in US$,
- Per Person Group Size Cost in US$.

Per Person

- 01-Person 000.00 01-Person 000.00 01-Person 000.00,
- 02-Person 000.00 02-Person 000.00 02-Person 000.00,
- 03-05 Person 000.00 03-05 Person 000.00 03-05 Person 000.00,
- 06-09 Person 000.00 06-09 Person 000.00 06-09 Person 000.00,

- 10-14 Person 000.00 10-14 Person 000.00 10-14 Person 000.00,
- 15 & Above 000.00 15 & Above 000.00 15 & Above 000.00,

Trip Cost includes:

1. Airport transfers on private vehicle.
2. Twin sharing accommodation in Kathmandu as per the category of package trip taken on Bed & Breakfast basis.
3. 3 meal (breakfast, Lunch & Dinner) in local restaurants along the trekking trail.
4. Accommodation in guesthouses (Tea House) on trekking trail.
5. An English speaking tour guide for city sightseeing.
6. An English speaking trekking guide for the trekking with necessary porters.
7. Wages of guide and other members.
8. National park fees, Govt. taxes and other applicable fees.
9. Domestic airfare as mentioned in the above itinerary.

Trip cost does not include:

1. International Airfare.
2. Nepalese Visa fee and international airport departure tax.
3. Lunch & dinner in Kathmandu.
4. Personal / Travel / Medical insurance and any other insurance for the members.
5. Hot water for shower during the trek.
6. Expenses of personal nature viz. tips, laundry, phone calls, alcoholic beverages, bottled drinks etc.
7. Any other cost, which is not mentioned in cost inclusive field above.

Langtang Gosaikunda Trekking Nepal-15 Days

Langtang Gosaikunda trek combines the remote and spectacular valley of Langtang, with the high mountain lakes at Gosainkunda. Visit the beautiful Langtang National park and then trek to the end of the valley to view the wonderful mountains views.

Following the Trisuli River north out of Kathmandu, we travel through Trisuli Bazaar and Dhunche to Syabrubensi, a Sherpa village located at the very edge of the Langtang National Park. We then swing east into the Langtang valley, crossing the river several times as we travel up along a gorge-like, lower section of the valley. We pass through oak and rhododendron forests and even cross glacial moraine on our way to the Tamang village of Langtang. A little further up the valley is Kyangin Gompa, where we stop overnight and sample the local yak cheese.

We pass through Nubamatang, nestled in a hidden valley, on our way up to view the glaciers, which mark the gateway into Tibet. Backtracking, we travel through Syabru and Sing Gompa to a high plateau, where the sacred lake Gosainkunda is located. Crossing the Llaurebena Pass (4610m), we continue south, leaving the Langtang region behind us as we travel through the Helambu valley to Gul Bhanjyang.

The Langtang Himal is a region north part of Kathmandu vally and it lies just south of Tibetan border. The langtang valley is surrounded by high peaks of great appeal. It has become famous ever since the British mountaineer Bill Tilman described it as the most beautiful valley in the world. The highest peak in this area is Shisapangma or Gosaithan 8027m in Tibet. The course from the Langtang valley to Gosaikund is full of diversity and it is attracting many tourists. The langtang valley is also know as the treasure house of Alpine plants. The whole valley is cover with flowers during the summer. This high and isolated region is inhabited by Tamangs whose religious practices, language and dress are much more similar to Tibetan.

Outline Itinerary

- Day 01: Arrive In Kathmandu.
- Day 02: Kathmandu City Tour.
- Day 03: Kathmandu-Dhunce.
- Day 04: Dhunche-Bharku-Syabrubesi.
- Day 05: Syabrubesi-Khanjung-Syarpagaon.
- Day 06: Syarpagaon-Lamahotel-Langtang Valley.
- Day 07: Langtang Valley-Kyangjing Gompa.

- Day 08: Kyangjing Gompa-Yalacheese Factory-Ghora Tabala
- Day 09: Ghora Tabala-Syabrugaon.
- Day 10: Syabrugaon-Dhunche.
- Day 11: Dhunche-Kathmandu.
- Day 12: Kathmandu-Rafting-Royal Chitwan National Park.
- Day 13: Royal Chitwan National Park.
- Day 14: Royal Chitwan National Park / Kathmandu.
- Day 15: Departure.

Trip Cost Based on Camping Arrangements:

Deluxe Hotels Option Standard Hotels Option Economy Hotels Option

- Group Size Cost in US$.
- Per Person Group Size Cost in US$.
- Per Person Group Size Cost in US$.

Per Person

- 01-Person 000.00 01-Person 000.00 01-Person 000.00,
- 02-Person 000.00 02-Person 000.00 02-Person 000.00,
- 03-05 Person 000.00 03-05 Person 000.00 03-05 Person 000.00,
- 06-09 Person 000.00 06-09 Person 000.00 06-09 Person 000.00,
- 10-14 Person 000.00 10-14 Person 000.00 10-14 Person 000.00,
- 15 & Above 000.00 15 & Above 000.00 15 & Above 000.00,

Trip Cost includes:

1. Airport transfers on private vehicle.
2. Twin sharing accommodation in Kathmandu as per the category of package trip taken on Bed & Breakfast basis.
3. An English speaking tour guide for city sightseeing.
4. An English speaking trekking guide for the trekking with necessary Cook & porters.

5. All meals included during the trek prepared by Adventure Silk Road's cook in aid of kitchen boy and other helpers.
6. Wages of guide and other members of the team.
7. National park fees, Govt. taxes and other applicable fees.
8. Domestic airfare as mentioned in the above itinerary.

Trip cost does not include:

1. International Airfare.
2. Nepalese Visa fee and airport departure tax.
3. Lunch & dinner in Kathmandu.
4. Personal / Travel / Medical insurance and any other insurance for the members.
5. Expenses of personal nature viz. tips, laundry, phone calls, alcoholic beverages, bottled drinks etc.
6. Emergency evacuations.
7. Any other cost, which is not mentioned in cost inclusive field above.

Trip Cost Based on Mountain Lodges (Tea Houses);

Deluxe Hotels Option Standard Hotels Option Economy Hotels Option;

- Group Size Cost in US$,
- Per Person Group Size Cost in US$,
- Per Person Group Size Cost in US$,

Per Person

- 01-Person 000.00 01-Person 000.00 01-Person 000.00,
- 02-Person 000.00 02-Person 000.00 02-Person 000.00,
- 03-05 Person 000.00 03-05 Person 000.00 03-05 Person 000.00,
- 06-09 Person 000.00 06-09 Person 000.00 06-09 Person 000.00,
- 10-14 Person 000.00 10-14 Person 000.00 10-14 Person 000.00,
- 15 & Above 000.00 15 & Above 000.00 15 & Above 000.00,

Trip Cost includes:

1. Airport transfers on private vehicle.

2. Twin sharing accommodation in Kathmandu as per the category of package trip taken on Bed & Breakfast basis.
3. 3 meal (breakfast, Lunch & Dinner) in local restaurants along the trekking trail.
4. Accommodation in guesthouses (Tea House) on trekking trail.
5. An English speaking tour guide for city sightseeing.
6. An English speaking trekking guide for the trekking with necessary porters.
7. Wages of guide and other members.
8. National park fees, Govt. taxes and other applicable fees.
9. Domestic airfare as mentioned in the above itinerary.

Trip cost does not include:

1. International Airfare.
2. Nepalese Visa fee and international airport departure tax.
3. Lunch & dinner in Kathmandu.
4. Personal / Travel / Medical insurance and any other insurance for the members.
5. Hot water for shower during the trek.
6. Expenses of personal nature viz. tips, laundry, phone calls, alcoholic beverages, bottled drinks etc.
7. Any other cost, which is not mentioned in cost inclusive field above.

Helambu Gosainkunda Trekking Nepal-14 Days

This is the most easily accessible of all areas from Kathmandu. It lies about 70k.m north of Kathmandu valley, is an area inhabited by sherpas. The language, culture and dress of the Helambu sherpas are very different from those of Solu khumbu sherpas. Gosaikunda is one of the Hindu holy place and is considered to be made by Lord Shiva.

The Buddhist Tamang that live nearby also revere it as their holy place. Every August on full moon night lake is thronged with pilgrims for a big festival. On other days the lake sits in a tranquil atmosphere.

During the trek you will see spectacular views of Langtang (7245m), Ganesh Himal (7405m), Dorje Lhakpa (6990m) and other small mountains of Langtang Himalayan range. This trek takes you to the complex topography and geology, together with the varied climatic conditions of Langtang National Park, giving a wide spectrum of vegetation types (including a sub-tropical forest). Langtang and Gosainkunda area covered with 108 holy Lakes. Culturally the area is mixed; the home of several groups including Tamang, Sherpa, Cherti and Brahaman people.

This is one of the most popular short and medium range treks in Nepal with many attractions: scenic grandeur, glimpse of Sherpa & Tamang life, rhododendron forest, lakes, glaciers & snow mountains. The trek begins from Dhunche and the trail leads up to Kyanchin Gompa and passes the sacred lake, Gosainkunda (4602m.). Exploring colourful Helambu region with delightful Sherpa villages, the trek ends in Kathmandu. A stunningly picturesque region affords superb panoramic views of Himalayas stretching from the Annapurnas to Mt. Everest and is really an ideal destination for short trek.

Outline Itinerary

- Day 01: Arrive In Kathmandu.
- Day 02: Kathmandu City Tour.
- Day 03: Kathmandu City Tour.
- Day 04: Kahmandu-Sundarijal-Chisapani.
- Day 05: Chisapani-Kutugsang.
- Day 06: Kutugsang-Tharepati.
- Day 07: Tharepati-Gosainkunda Phedi.
- Day 08: Phedi-Gosainkunda.
- Day 09: Gosainkunda-Dhunche.
- Day 10: Dhunche-Kathmandu.
- Day 11: Kahmandu-Rafting-Royal Chitwan National Park.
- Day 12: Royal Chitwan National Park.
- Day 13: Royal Chitwan National Park / Kathmandu.
- Day 14: Departure.

Trip Cost Based on Camping Arrangements;

Deluxe Hotels Option Standard Hotels Option Economy Hotels Option;

- Group Size Cost in US$.
- Per Person Group Size Cost in US$.
- Per Person Group Size Cost in US$.

Per Person

- 01-Person 000.00 01-Person 000.00 01-Person 000.00,
- 02-Person 000.00 02-Person 000.00 02-Person 000.00,
- 03-05 Person 000.00 03-05 Person 000.00 03-05 Person 000.00,
- 06-09 Person 000.00 06-09 Person 000.00 06-09 Person 000.00,
- 10-14 Person 000.00 10-14 Person 000.00 10-14 Person 000.00,
- 15 & Above 000.00 15 & Above 000.00 15 & Above 000.00,

Trip Cost includes:

1. Airport transfers on private vehicle.
2. Twin sharing accommodation in Kathmandu as per the category of package trip taken on Bed & Breakfast basis.
3. An English speaking tour guide for city sightseeing.
4. An English speaking trekking guide for the trekking with necessary Cook & porters.
5. All meals included during the trek prepared by Adventure Silk Road's cook in aid of kitchen boy and other helpers.
6. Wages of guide and other members of the team.
7. National park fees, Govt. taxes and other applicable fees.
8. Domestic airfare as mentioned in the above itinerary.

Trip cost does not include:

1. International Airfare.
2. Nepalese Visa fee and airport departure tax.
3. Lunch & dinner in Kathmandu.
4. Personal / Travel / Medical insurance and any other insurance for the members.

5. Expenses of personal nature viz. tips, laundry, phone calls, alcoholic beverages, bottled drinks etc.
6. Emergency evacuations.
7. Any other cost, which is not mentioned in cost inclusive field above.

Trip Cost Based on Mountain Lodges (Tea Houses);

Deluxe Hotels Option Standard Hotels Option Economy Hotels Option;

- Group Size Cost in US$.
- Per Person Group Size Cost in US$.
- Per Person Group Size Cost in US$.

Per Person

- 01-Person 000.00 01-Person 000.00 01-Person 000.00,
- 02-Person 000.00 02-Person 000.00 02-Person 000.00,
- 03-05 Person 000.00 03-05 Person 000.00 03-05 Person 000.00,
- 06-09 Person 000.00 06-09 Person 000.00 06-09 Person 000.00,
- 10-14 Person 000.00 10-14 Person 000.00 10-14 Person 000.00,
- 15 & Above 000.00 15 & Above 000.00 15 & Above 000.00.

Trip Cost includes:

1. Airport transfers on private vehicle.
2. Twin sharing accommodation in Kathmandu as per the category of package trip taken on Bed & Breakfast basis.
3. 3 meal (breakfast, Lunch & Dinner) in local restaurants along the trekking trail.
4. Accommodation in guesthouses (Tea House) on trekking trail.
5. An English speaking tour guide for city sightseeing.
6. An English speaking trekking guide for the trekking with necessary porters.
7. Wages of guide and other members.
8. National park fees, Govt. taxes and other applicable fees.
9. Domestic airfare as mentioned in the above itinerary.

Trip cost does not include:

1. International Airfare.
2. Nepalese Visa fee and international airport departure tax.
3. Lunch & dinner in Kathmandu.
4. Personal / Travel / Medical insurance and any other insurance for the members.
5. Hot water for shower during the trek.
6. Expenses of personal nature viz. tips, laundry, phone calls, alcoholic beverages, bottled drinks etc.
7. Any other cost, which is not mentioned in cost inclusive field above.

Everest Classic Trekking Nepal-22 Days

Probably the most famous mountain of the world, Mount Everest's grandiose stature continues to amaze many travellers. This ascent to the 5,300m base camp of the world's highest peak will take you to the heart of the Sherpa nation and through awe-inspiring, barren ice-capped landscapes.

Trek in the footsteps of legends as we ascend from 9,200 feet to 18,190 feet in elevation, where verdant forested valleys fall away before the icebound drama of the world's highest mountains. Trekking at a moderate pace allows time to acclimatize and to learn about the rich Sherpa culture of the Solu Khumbu region. Explore brilliantly decorated temples and monasteries. Traverse the lower slopes of Tawoche, a 21,463' collection of bare rock, glaciers and towering ice spires. On Kala Patar, skirt car-sized boulders to reach its 18,190' summit at sunset and enjoy one of the best light shows on earth! Your friendly Sherpa staff provides surprisingly tasty meals while lending support and companionship. Begin and end this epic journey in exotic Kathmandu.

Mt. Everest is famous not only for its proximity to the world's highest mountain (8,848 m) but also for its Sherpa Villages and Monasteries. It takes three weeks to start the trekking from Jiri and fly back from Lukla. Walking to and from Everest Base Camp takes at least one month to complete the trekking. Many trekkers find the walk to Everest better then the destination itself. The Everest trekking areas offer a visit to the homeland of the Sherpas, a chance to get close to the highest mountain in the world, as well as the feeling in one that of surrounded by peaks. This trek starts as following:

Outline Itinerary

- Day 01: Arrive In Kathmandu.
- Day 02: Kathmandu City Tour.
- Day 03: Kathmandu-Jiri.
- Day 04: Jiri-Deurali.
- Day 05: Deurali-Sete.
- Day 06: Sete-Junbesi.
- Day 07: Junbesi-Nunthala.
- Day 08: Nunthala-Khari Khola.
- Day 09: Khari Khoila-Puiyan.
- Day 10: Puiyan-Phakding.
- Day 11: Phakding-Namche Bazaar.
- Day 12: Namche Bazaar-Khumjung.
- Day 13: Khunjung-Tengboche.
- Day 14: Tengboche-Dingboche.
- Day 15: Dingboche-Lobuche.
- Day 16-17: Lobuche-Kalapatter-Gorkshep-Ebc-Lobuche.
- Day 18: Loboche-Tengbuche.
- Day 19: Tengboche-Monjo.
- Day 20: Monjo-Lukla.
- Day 21: Lukla-Kathmandu.
- Day 22: Departure.

Trip Cost Based on Camping Arrangements;

Deluxe Hotels Option Standard Hotels Option Economy Hotels Option;

- Group Size Cost in US$.
- Per Person Group Size Cost in US$.
- Per Person Group Size Cost in US$.

Per Person

- 01-Person 000.00 01-Person 000.00 01-Person 000.00,
- 02-Person 000.00 02-Person 000.00 02-Person 000.00,
- 03-05 Person 000.00 03-05 Person 000.00 03-05 Person 000.00,
- 06-09 Person 000.00 06-09 Person 000.00 06-09 Person 000.00,
- 10-14 Person 000.00 10-14 Person 000.00 10-14 Person 000.00,
- 15 & Above 000.00 15 & Above 000.00 15 & Above 000.00,

Trip Cost includes:

1. Airport transfers on private vehicle.
2. Twin sharing accommodation in Kathmandu as per the category of package trip taken on Bed & Breakfast basis.
3. An English speaking tour guide for city sightseeing.
4. An English speaking trekking guide for the trekking with necessary Cook & porters.
5. All meals included during the trek prepared by Adventure Silk Road's cook in aid of kitchen boy and other helpers.
6. Wages of guide and other members of the team.
7. National park fees, Govt. taxes and other applicable fees.
8. Domestic airfare as mentioned in the above itinerary.

Trip cost does not include:

1. international Airfare.
2. Nepalese Visa fee and airport departure tax.
3. Lunch & dinner in Kathmandu.
4. Personal / Travel / Medical insurance and any other insurance for the members.
5. Expenses of personal nature viz. tips, laundry, phone calls, alcoholic beverages, bottled drinks etc.
6. Emergency evacuations.
7. Any other cost, which is not mentioned in cost inclusive field above.

    - Preferred Hotels For The Different Packages,

- Deluxe Trip Standard Trip Economy Trip,
- Kathmandu 5-Star: Shangri-La or Similar 4-Star: Vaishali or Similar Hotel Nature or Similar,
- Trip Cost Based on Mountain Lodges (Tea Houses),
- Deluxe Hotels Option Standard Hotels Option Economy Hotels Option,
- Group Size Cost in US$,
- Per Person Group Size Cost in US$,
- Per Person Group Size Cost in US$.

Per Person

- 01-Person 000.00 01-Person 000.00 01-Person 000.00,
- 02-Person 000.00 02-Person 000.00 02-Person 000.00,
- 03-05 Person 000.00 03-05 Person 000.00 03-05 Person 000.00,
- 06-09 Person 000.00 06-09 Person 000.00 06-09 Person 000.00,
- 10-14 Person 000.00 10-14 Person 000.00 10-14 Person 000.00,
- 15 & Above 000.00 15 & Above 000.00 15 & Above 000.00,

Trip Cost includes:

1. Airport transfers on private vehicle.
2. Twin sharing accommodation in Kathmandu as per the category of package trip taken on Bed & Breakfast basis.
3. 3 meal (breakfast, Lunch & Dinner) in local restaurants along the trekking trail.
4. Accommodation in guesthouses (Tea House) on trekking trail.
5. An English speaking tour guide for city sightseeing.
6. An English speaking trekking guide for the trekking with necessary porters.
7. Wages of guide and other members.
8. National park fees, Govt. taxes and other applicable fees.
9. Domestic airfare as mentioned in the above itinerary.

Trip cost does not include:

1. International Airfare.

2. Nepalese Visa fee and international airport departure tax.
3. Lunch & dinner in Kathmandu.
4. Personal / Travel / Medical insurance and any other insurance for the members.
5. Hot water for shower during the trek.
6. Expenses of personal nature viz. tips, laundry, phone calls, alcoholic beverages, bottled drinks etc.
7. Any other cost, which is not mentioned in cost inclusive field above.

Everest Base Camp Trekking Nepal-18 Days

The trek to Everest Base Camp is without doubt one of the most famous in the world. It takes you into the heart of the Nepalese Himalaya, with awe-inspiring views of many of the world's highest and most beautiful mountains. The name "EVEREST" is magic in itself. Everest (8848m.) is called "*Sagarmatha*" in Nepali – "*Higher than the Sky*" and "*Chhomolungma*" in Tibetan – "*Mother Goddess of the Earth*". The quickest and easiest way to reach this region is by flight to Lukla at 2827 m.

The Mount Everest or Solu Khumbu region is the second most popular trekking area in Nepal. It would probably be the most popular destination, but it is more expensive and difficult to get to Solu Khumbu than to the Annapurna area. To get near Everest, you must either walk for a week or fly to Lukla, a remote mountain airstrip. Solu Khumbu is justifiably famous, not only for its proximity to the world's highest mountain (8848m.), but also for its Sherpa villages and monasteries. The nominal goal of an Everest trek is the Everest base camp at an elevation of about 5340m. You cannot see Everest from the base camp, so most trekkers climb Kala Patthar, a 5545m bump on the southern flank of Pumori (7145m.). From Kala Patthar there is a dramatic view of Everest.

Outline Itinerary

- Day 01: Arrive In Kathmandu.
- Day 02: Kathmandu City Tour.
- Day 03: Kathmandu-Lukla-Phakding.

- Day 04: Phakding-Namche Bazaar.
- Day 05: Acclimatise Day In Namche Bazaar.
- Day 06: Namche Bazaar-Khumjung.
- Day 07: Khunjung-Tengboche (Thyangboche).
- Day 08: Tengboche-Dingboche.
- Day 09: Acclimatisation Day In Dingboche.
- Day 10: Dingboche-Lobuche.
- Day 11-12: Lobuche-Kalapatter-Gorkshep-Ebc-Lobuche.
- Day 13: Loboche-Tengbuche.
- Day 14: Tengboche-Monjo.
- Day 15: Monjo-Lukla.
- Day 16: Lukla-Kathmandu.
- Day 17: Free Day In Kathmandu.
- Day 18: Departure.

Trip Cost Based on Camping Arrangements;

Deluxe Hotels Option Standard Hotels Option Economy Hotels Option;

- Group Size Cost in US$.
- Per Person Group Size Cost in US$.
- Per Person Group Size Cost in US$.

Per Person

- 01-Person 000.00 01-Person 000.00 01-Person 000.00,
- 02-Person 000.00 02-Person 000.00 02-Person 000.00,
- 03-05 Person 000.00 03-05 Person 000.00 03-05 Person 000.00,
- 06-09 Person 000.00 06-09 Person 000.00 06-09 Person 000.00,
- 10-14 Person 000.00 10-14 Person 000.00 10-14 Person 000.00,
- 15 & Above 000.00 15 & Above 000.00 15 & Above 000.00,

Trip Cost includes:

1. Airport transfers on private vehicle.
2. Twin sharing accommodation in Kathmandu as per the category of package trip taken on Bed & Breakfast basis.

3. An English speaking tour guide for city sightseeing.
4. An English speaking trekking guide for the trekking with necessary Cook & porters.
5. All meals included during the trek prepared by Adventure Silk Road's cook in aid of kitchen boy and other helpers.
6. Wages of guide and other members of the team.
7. National park fees, Govt. taxes and other applicable fees.
8. Domestic airfare as mentioned in the above itinerary.

Trip cost does not include:

1. International Airfare.
2. Nepalese Visa fee and airport departure tax.
3. Lunch & dinner in Kathmandu.
4. Personal / Travel / Medical insurance and any other insurance for the members.
5. Expenses of personal nature viz...tips, laundry, phone calls, alcoholic beverages, bottled drinks etc.
6. Emergency evacuations.
7. Any other cost, which is not mentioned in cost inclusive field above.

Trip Cost Based on Mountain Lodges (Tea Houses);

Deluxe Hotels Option Standard Hotels Option Economy Hotels Option;

- Group Size Cost in US$,
- Per Person Group Size Cost in US$,
- Per Person Group Size Cost in US$.

Per Person

- 01-Person 000.00 01-Person 000.00 01-Person 000.00,
- 02-Person 000.00 02-Person 000.00 02-Person 000.00,
- 03-05 Person 000.00 03-05 Person 000.00 03-05 Person 000.00,
- 06-09 Person 000.00 06-09 Person 000.00 06-09 Person 000.00,
- 10-14 Person 000.00 10-14 Person 000.00 10-14 Person 000.00,
- 15 & Above 000.00 15 & Above 000.00 15 & Above 000.00.

Trip Cost includes:

1. Airport transfers on private vehicle.
2. Twin sharing accommodation in Kathmandu as per the category of package trip taken on Bed & Breakfast basis.
3. 3 meal (breakfast, Lunch & Dinner) in local restaurants along the trekking trail.
4. Accommodation in guesthouses (Tea House) on trekking trail.
5. An English speaking tour guide for city sightseeing.
6. An English speaking trekking guide for the trekking with necessary porters
7. Wages of guide and other members.
8. National park fees, Govt. taxes and other applicable fees.
9. Domestic airfare as mentioned in the above itinerary.

Trip cost does not include:

1. International Airfare.
2. Nepalese Visa fee and international airport departure tax.
3. Lunch & dinner in Kathmandu.
4. Personal / Travel / Medical insurance and any other insurance for the members.
5. Hot water for shower during the trek.
6. Expenses of personal nature viz. tips, laundry, phone calls, alcoholic beverages, bottled drinks etc.
7. Any other cost, which is not mentioned in cost inclusive field above.

Gokyo & Everest Base Camp Trekking-21 Days

This trek is a combination of the Gokyo Lake and the Everest Base Camp. A visit to Gokyo Ri offers magnificent view of Cho Oyu, Everest, Lhotse, Nuptse and Amadablam. We then cross over the Cho Lo pass and visit the Everest Base Camp. This trek also offers a walk through the most dramatic landscape and magnificent views of the mountain range in the region.

With eight of the worlds ten highest peaks, Nepal is loaded with spectacular mountains vistas. Everest trek in justifiably famous, not only for its proximity to the world's highest mountain (8848m) but also for its friendly Sherpa people, picturesque villages great variety of cultures and traditions, colourful festivals and monasteries. The flora and fauna are other ornaments of the Sagarmatha National Park. The story of the yeti is still a mystery to the world from the Kahumbu region.

Everest Base Camp trek has everything: the incredible mountain views from Chukung, Kala Pattar and Gokyo Ri. Popularly known as "The Ultimate Trek," it includes all that the Khumbu has to offer including the fascinating villages and Tibetan Buddhist monasteries and the culture and hospitality of the Sherpa people, who will surely win your hearts. After starting with a flight to Lukla (2,805m/9,200ft) we trek up to Kala Pattar view point (5,550m/18,200ft) trek up the Khumbu Glacier to Everest Base camp set under the awesome Khumbu Icefall. Then we veer off the main trail to cross the Cho La pass (5,422m/17,783ft) into the Gokyo Valley. To top off this unique trek we climb Gokyo Ri (5,488m/18,000ft) for a panoramic view of the greatest mountain scenery in the world-including five 8000+m/26,000+ft giants and myriad other peaks of the Khumbu Himal.

Outline Itinerary

- Day 01: Arrive In Kathmandu.
- Day 02: Kathmandu City Tour.
- Day 03: Kathmandu-Lukla-Phakding.
- Day 04: Phakding-Namche Bazaar.
- Day 05: Acclimatise Day In Namche Bazaar.
- Day 06: Namche Bazaar-Khumjung.
- Day 07: Khumjung-Phortse Thanghka.
- Day 08: Phortse Thanghka-Dole.
- Day 09: Dole-Machhermo.
- Day 10: Machhermo-Gokyo.
- Day 11: Gokyo.
- Day 12-13: Gokyo-Chhugyuma-Dzogla-Lobuche.
- Day 14-15: Lobuche-Kalapatter-Gorkshep-Ebc-Lobuche.

- Day 16: Loboche-Tengbuche.
- Day 17: Tengboche-Monjo.
- Day 18: Monjo-Lukla.
- Day 19: Lukla – Kathmandu.
- Day 20: Free Day In Kathmandu.
- Day 21: Departure.

Trip Cost Based on Camping Arrangements;

Deluxe Hotels Option Standard Hotels Option Economy Hotels Option;

- Group Size Cost in US$,
- Per Person Group Size Cost in US$,
- Per Person Group Size Cost in US$.

Per Person

- 01-Person 000.00 01-Person 000.00 01-Person 000.00,
- 02-Person 000.00 02-Person 000.00 02-Person 000.00,
- 03-05 Person 000.00 03-05 Person 000.00 03-05 Person 000.00,
- 06-09 Person 000.00 06-09 Person 000.00 06-09 Person 000.00,
- 10-14 Person 000.00 10-14 Person 000.00 10-14 Person 000.00,
- 15 & Above 000.00 15 & Above 000.00 15 & Above 000.00.

Trip Cost includes:

1. Airport transfers on private vehicle.
2. Twin sharing accommodation in Kathmandu as per the category of package trip taken on Bed & Breakfast basis.
3. An English speaking tour guide for city sightseeing.
4. An English speaking trekking guide for the trekking with necessary Cook & porters.
5. All meals included during the trek prepared by Adventure Silk Road's cook in aid of kitchen boy and other helpers.
6. Wages of guide and other members of the team.
7. National park fees, Govt. taxes and other applicable fees.
8. Domestic airfare as mentioned in the above itinerary.

Trip cost does not include:

1. International Airfare.
2. Nepalese Visa fee and airport departure tax.
3. Lunch & dinner in Kathmandu.
4. Personal / Travel / Medical insurance and any other insurance for the members.
5. Expenses of personal nature viz. tips, laundry, phone calls, alcoholic beverages, bottled drinks etc.
6. Emergency evacuations.
7. Any other cost, which is not mentioned in cost inclusive field above.

Trip Cost Based on Mountain Lodges (Tea Houses);

Deluxe Hotels Option Standard Hotels Option Economy Hotels Option;

- Group Size Cost in US$,
- Per Person Group Size Cost in US$,
- Per Person Group Size Cost in US$.

Per Person

- 01-Person 000.00 01-Person 000.00 01-Person 000.00,
- 02-Person 000.00 02-Person 000.00 02-Person 000.00,
- 03-05 Person 000.00 03-05 Person 000.00 03-05 Person 000.00,
- 06-09 Person 000.00 06-09 Person 000.00 06-09 Person 000.00,
- 10-14 Person 000.00 10-14 Person 000.00 10-14 Person 000.00,
- 15 & Above 000.00 15 & Above 000.00 15 & Above 000.00.

Trip Cost includes:

1. Airport transfers on private vehicle.
2. Twin sharing accommodation in Kathmandu as per the category of package trip taken on Bed & Breakfast basis.
3. 3 meal (breakfast, Lunch & Dinner) in local restaurants along the trekking trail.
4. Accommodation in guesthouses (Tea House) on trekking trail.

5. An English speaking tour guide for city sightseeing.
6. An English speaking trekking guide for the trekking with necessary porters.
7. Wages of guide and other members.
8. National park fees, Govt. taxes and other applicable fees.
9. Domestic airfare as mentioned in the above itinerary.

Trip cost does not include:

1. International Airfare.
2. Nepalese Visa fee and international airport departure tax.
3. Lunch & dinner in Kathmandu.
4. Personal / Travel / Medical insurance and any other insurance for the members.
5. Hot water for shower during the trek.
6. Expenses of personal nature viz. tips, laundry, phone calls, alcoholic beverages, bottled drinks etc.
7. Any other cost, which is not mentioned in cost inclusive field above.

Everest Yeiland Trekking Nepal-15 Days

With eight of the world's ten highest peaks, Nepal is loaded with spectacular mountains vistas. Everest trek in justifiably famous, not only for its proximity to the world's highest mountain (8848m) but also for its friendly Sherpa people, picturesque villages great variety of cultures and traditions, colourful festivals and monasteries. The flora and fauna are other ornaments of the Sagarmatha National Park. The story of the yeti is still a mystery to the world from the Kahumbu region. It will give us enormous pleasure to introduce you to an astounding view of the world's highest peak. Perhaps in viewing Everest in this way, you will be fulfilling a long held desire. Certainly you will never be quite the same again. Ever since the days of early climbing expeditions, this 8,848m mountain has had a lure of its own, drawing climbers to scale it and trekkers to gaze on its icy faces. It easy to see why the trek to the base camp of Mount Everest has become one of the most popular routes in Nepal.

We start our trek from Lukla after a 30 minute flight from Kathmandu. When we land at that tiny airstrip, the adventure really begins. During trekking, we spend several days moving through the homelands of the Sherpa people, and will see Buddhist monasteries and close up views of Mt. Everest and neighbouring Ama Dablam, considered by many to be among the most beautiful mountains in Nepal. We spend 2 nights at Namche Bazaar, the bustling market town in the heart of Sherpa country, and at Pheriche see a cluster of houses set among the high summer grazing pastures of the region. We spend the time in Namche Bazaar exploring and acclimatizing, which is an important factor in your enjoyment of the trek.

People who have fully acclimatized may trek to the Everest Base Camp but without doubt, for many people the main highlight will be the magnificent views which unfold from the summit of Kalapathar-the extradinary ice sculptures of the Khumbu Glacier, Nuptse and the southwest face of Everest itself.

Outline Itinerary

- Day 01: Arrive In Kathmandu.
- Day 02: Kathmandu-Nagarkot.
- Day 03: Kathmandu-Lukla / Phakding.
- Day 04: Phakding-Namche Bazaar.
- Day 05: Namche Bazaar-Khumjung.
- Day 06: Khunjung-Tengboche (Thyangboche).
- Day 07: Tengboche-Dingboche.
- Day 08: Dingboche-Lobuche.
- Day 09-10: Lobuche-Kalapatter-Gorkshep-Ebc-Lobuche.
- Day 11: Lobuche-Tengboche.
- Day 12: Tengboche-Monjo.
- Day 13: Monjo-Lukla.
- Day 14: Lukla-Kathmandu.
- Day 15: Departure.

Trip Cost includes:

1. Airport transfers on private vehicle.

2. Twin sharing accommodation in Kathmandu as per the category of package trip taken on Bed & Breakfast basis.
3. An English speaking tour guide for city sightseeing.
4. An English speaking trekking guide for the trekking with necessary Cook & porters.
5. All meals included during the trek prepared by Adventure Silk Road's cook in aid of kitchen boy and other helpers.
6. Wages of guide and other members of the team.
7. National park fees, Govt. taxes and other applicable fees.
8. Domestic airfare as mentioned in the above itinerary.

Trip cost does not include:

1. International Airfare.
2. Nepalese Visa fee and airport departure tax.
3. Lunch & dinner in Kathmandu.
4. Personal / Travel / Medical insurance and any other insurance for the members.
5. Expenses of personal nature viz. tips, laundry, phone calls, alcoholic beverages, bottled drinks etc.
6. Emergency evacuations.
7. Any other cost, which is not mentioned in cost inclusive field above.

Trip Cost includes:

1. Airport transfers on private vehicle.
2. Twin sharing accommodation in Kathmandu as per the category of package trip taken on Bed & Breakfast basis.
3. 3 meal (breakfast, Lunch & Dinner) in local restaurants along the trekking trail.
4. Accommodation in guesthouses (Tea House) on trekking trail.
5. An English speaking tour guide for city sightseeing.
6. An English speaking trekking guide for the trekking with necessary porters.
7. Wages of guide and other members.

8. National park fees, Govt. taxes and other applicable fees.
9. Domestic airfare as mentioned in the above itinerary.

Trip cost does not include:

1. International Airfare.
2. Nepalese Visa fee and international airport departure tax.
3. Lunch & dinner in Kathmandu.
4. Personal / Travel / Medical insurance and any other insurance for the members.
5. Hot water for shower during the trek.
6. Expenses of personal nature viz. tips, laundry, phone calls, alcoholic beverages, bottled drinks etc.
7. Any other cost, which is not mentioned in cost inclusive field above.

Lower Dolpa Trekking Nepal-28 Days

Dolpo is located inside the Shy – Phoksundo National Park of mid–western Nepal, behind the Dhaulagiri massif, towards the Tibetan Plateau. Cut off by a series of very high passes, closed by snow most of the year, Dolpo remains a truly isolated corner of Nepal. Time has stood still here for centuries as the inhabitants of Tibetan stock continue to live, cultivate and trade the way they have done since time immemorial. The finally preserved Ecosystem encompasses a wild and wonderful variety of plants and wildlife, including the blue sheep and leopard. A trek through Dolpo is an experience not easily forgotten.

Dolpa offers a wonderful chance to experience a landscape and culture far different from seen in other parts of country, it is located in the central west of the country. The focal point of the area is Shey Phokundo National park. This remote and rugged protected area is both scenically and culturally attractive. It is the habitat of various rare and endangered plant and wildlife species many of which can be seen nowhere else in the country. Animal species of particular interest in the national park are populations of snow leopard, grey wolf and blue sheep.

The most obvious group of people seen in the northern parts of the area. Particularly in Dopa, are of Tibetan origin. Similar to Tibetans and Sherpas they rely on eking out a living on the high pastures and supplementing this with trade both to the north and the south. For years, their salt caravans have been a common site along the mountain passes. Their religion is a mixture of Tibetan Buddhism and the ancient, pre Buddhist, Bon religion, a largely animistic faith. Strangely, their language is based on the Tibetan dialect spoken in Kham, a province of old Tibet located many hundreds of kilometres to the east.

Lower down the people are a mixture of ethnic groups, such as the Magar, Gurung and hill people of Hindu caste origin. Of particular interest are the Thakuri, the royal family caste. Again they are quite different in culture and language to their cousins further east.

Outline Itinerary

- Day 01: Arrive In Kathmandu.
- Day 02: Kathmandu City Tour.
- Day 03: Kathmandu-Nepalgunj.
- Day 04: Nepalgunj-Ghotichour.
- Day 05: Ghotichaur-Napukhona.
- Day 06: Napakuna-Chaurikot.
- Day 07: Charikot-Veri Side.
- Day 08: Very River Side-Garpung Khola.
- Day 09-11: Garpung Khola-Kagmara Peak And Pass.
- Day 12: Pungmo.
- Day 13: Pungmo-Phoksundo Lake.
- Day 14: Phoksundo Lake.
- Day 15: Phoksundo Lake-Bagala Pass.
- Day 16: Bagala Pass-Numla Pass Base Camp.
- Day 17: Numla Pass Base Camp-Dho Tarap.
- Day 18: Dho Tarap.
- Day 19: Dho Tarap-Cave.
- Day 20: To Lahani.
- Day 21: Lahani-Tarakot.

- Day 22: Tarakot-Dunaii.
- Day 23: Dunai-Jhupal.
- Day 24: Jhupal-Nepalgunj.
- Day 25: Nepalgunj-Kathmandu.
- Day 26-27: Free Day In Kathmandu.
- Day 28: Departure.

Trip Cost Based on Camping Arrangements;

Deluxe Hotels Option Standard Hotels Option Economy Hotels Option;

- Group Size Cost in US$,
- Per Person Group Size Cost in US$,
- Per Person Group Size Cost in US$.

Per Person

- 01-Person 000.00 01-Person 000.00 01-Person 000.00,
- 02-Person 000.00 02-Person 000.00 02-Person 000.00,
- 03-05 Person 000.00 03-05 Person 000.00 03-05 Person 000.00,
- 06-09 Person 000.00 06-09 Person 000.00 06-09 Person 000.00,
- 10-14 Person 000.00 10-14 Person 000.00 10-14 Person 000.00,
- 15 & Above 000.00 15 & Above 000.00 15 & Above 000.00.

Trip Cost includes:

1. Airport transfers on private vehicle.
2. Twin sharing accommodation in Kathmandu as per the category of package trip taken on Bed & Breakfast basis.
3. An English speaking tour guide for city sightseeing.
4. An English speaking trekking guide for the trekking with necessary Cook & porters.
5. All meals included during the trek prepared by Adventure Silk Road's cook in aid of kitchen boy and other helpers.
6. Wages of guide and other members of the team.
7. National park fees, Govt. taxes and other applicable fees.
8. Domestic airfare as mentioned in the above itinerary.

Trip cost does not include:

1. International Airfare.
2. Nepalese Visa fee and airport departure tax.
3. Lunch & dinner in Kathmandu.
4. Personal / Travel / Medical insurance and any other insurance for the members.
5. Expenses of personal nature viz. tips, laundry, phone calls, alcoholic beverages, bottled drinks etc.
6. Emergency evacuations.
7. Any other cost, which is not mentioned in cost inclusive field above.

Preferred Hotels For The Different Packages;

- Deluxe Trip Standard Trip Economy Trip.
- Kathmandu 5-Star: Shangri-La or Similar 4-Star: Vaishali or Similar Hotel Nature or Similar.
- Trip Cost Based on Mountain Lodges (Tea Houses).
- Deluxe Hotels Option Standard Hotels Option Economy Hotels Option.
- Group Size Cost in US$.
- Per Person Group Size Cost in US$.
- Per Person Group Size Cost in US$.

Per Person

- 01-Person 000.00 01-Person 000.00 01-Person 000.00,
- 02-Person 000.00 02-Person 000.00 02-Person 000.00,
- 03-05 Person 000.00 03-05 Person 000.00 03-05 Person 000.00,
- 06-09 Person 000.00 06-09 Person 000.00 06-09 Person 000.00,
- 10-14 Person 000.00 10-14 Person 000.00 10-14 Person 000.00,
- 15 & Above 000.00 15 & Above 000.00 15 & Above 000.00.

Trip Cost includes:

1. Airport transfers on private vehicle.
2. Twin sharing accommodation in Kathmandu as per the category of package trip taken on Bed & Breakfast basis.

3. 3 meal (breakfast, Lunch & Dinner) in local restaurants along the trekking trail.
4. Accommodation in guesthouses (Tea House) on trekking trail.
5. An English speaking tour guide for city sightseeing.
6. An English speaking trekking guide for the trekking with necessary porters.
7. Wages of guide and other members.
8. National park fees, Govt. taxes and other applicable fees.
9. Domestic airfare as mentioned in the above itinerary.

Trip cost does not include:

1. International Airfare.
2. Nepalese Visa fee and international airport departure tax.
3. Lunch & dinner in Kathmandu.
4. Personal / Travel / Medical insurance and any other insurance for the members.
5. Hot water for shower during the trek.
6. Expenses of personal nature viz. tips, laundry, phone calls, alcoholic beverages, bottled drinks etc.
7. Any other cost, which is not mentioned in cost inclusive field above.

Kanchanjunga Trekking Nepal-30 Days

We invite you to trek in one of the most remote and beautiful areas in Nepal which still lies shrounded in mystery: Kanchenjunga.

The area is abundant with wildlife, as inhabitation consists of only scattered villages. There are musk deer, blue sheep and, for the believer, the Yeti! Magnificent views of Everest, Makalu and Kanchanjunga massif will make the trip worth your while.

Mount Kanchanjunga (8586 M.) is the third highest mountain in the world and the second highest peak in Nepal. It is located in the extreme northeast corner of Nepal bordering Sikkim (an Indian State) to the east and China to the north. This trek is the most adventurous of all the routes offered. This trek begins at Tumlingtar or Taplejung accessible by air, or Ilam or Basantpur accessible by road. Soaring peaks, the Yalung Glacier and a wide variety of natural vegetation and agricultural areas can be seen in this region

Outline Itinerary

- Day 01: Arrive In Kathmandu.
- Day 02: Kathmandu City Tour.
- Day 03: Kathmandu-Hille.
- Day 04: Hille-Shidua.
- Day 05: Shidua-Door Pani.
- Day 06: Door Pani-Gupa Pokhari.
- Day 07: Gupa Pokhara-Nesum.
- Day 08: Nesum-Taplejung.
- Day 09: Taplejung-Chirwa.
- Day 10: Chirwa-Sakathum).
- Day 11: Sakathum-Amjilassa.
- Day 12: Amjilassa-Kyapar.
- Day 13: Kyapar-Ghunsa.
- Day 14: Khambachan.
- Day 15: Khambachan.
- Day 16: Khambachan-Lhonak.
- Day 17: Day Trip To Pangpema.
- Day 18: Khambachen-Tha Passes.
- Day 19: High Camp.
- Day 20: High Camp-Ramche.
- Day 21: Ramche-Tseram.
- Day 22: Tseram-Torontan.
- Day 23: Torantan-Yamphudin.
- Day 24: Yamphudin-Ponphe.
- Day 25: Ponphe-Pha Khola.
- Day 26: Pha Khola-Taplejung.
- Day 27: Taplejung-Kahmandu.

- Day 28-29: Free Day In Kathmandu.
- Day 30: Departure.

Trip Cost Based on Camping Arrangements;

Deluxe Hotels Option Standard Hotels Option Economy Hotels Option;

- Group Size Cost in US$,
- Per Person Group Size Cost in US$,
- Per Person Group Size Cost in US$,

Per Person

- 01-Person 000.00 01-Person 000.00 01-Person 000.00,
- 02-Person 000.00 02-Person 000.00 02-Person 000.00,
- 03-05 Person 000.00 03-05 Person 000.00 03-05 Person 000.00,
- 06-09 Person 000.00 06-09 Person 000.00 06-09 Person 000.00,
- 10-14 Person 000.00 10-14 Person 000.00 10-14 Person 000.00,
- 15 & Above 000.00 15 & Above 000.00 15 & Above 000.00,

Trip Cost includes:

1. Airport transfers on private vehicle.
2. Twin sharing accommodation in Kathmandu as per the category of package trip taken on Bed & Breakfast basis.
3. An English speaking tour guide for city sightseeing.
4. An English speaking trekking guide for the trekking with necessary Cook & porters.
5. All meals included during the trek prepared by Adventure Silk Road's cook in aid of kitchen boy and other helpers.
6. Wages of guide and other members of the team.
7. National park fees, Govt. taxes and other applicable fees.
8. Domestic airfare as mentioned in the above itinerary.

Trip cost does not include:

1. International Airfare.
2. Nepalese Visa fee and airport departure tax.
3. Lunch & dinner in Kathmandu.

4. Personal / Travel / Medical insurance and any other insurance for the members.
5. Expenses of personal nature viz. tips, laundry, phone calls, alcoholic beverages, bottled drinks etc.
6. Emergency evacuations.
7. Any other cost, which is not mentioned in cost inclusive field above.

Trip Cost Based on Mountain Lodges (Tea Houses);

Deluxe Hotels Option Standard Hotels Option Economy Hotels Option;

- Group Size Cost in US$,
- Per Person Group Size Cost in US$,
- Per Person Group Size Cost in US$.

Per Person

- 01-Person 000.00 01-Person 000.00 01-Person 000.00,
- 02-Person 000.00 02-Person 000.00 02-Person 000.00,
- 03-05 Person 000.00 03-05 Person 000.00 03-05 Person 000.00,
- 06-09 Person 000.00 06-09 Person 000.00 06-09 Person 000.00,
- 10-14 Person 000.00 10-14 Person 000.00 10-14 Person 000.00,
- 15 & Above 000.00 15 & Above 000.00 15 & Above 000.00,

Trip Cost includes:

1. Airport transfers on private vehicle.
2. Twin sharing accommodation in Kathmandu as per the category of package trip taken on Bed & Breakfast basis.
3. 3 meal (breakfast, Lunch & Dinner) in local restaurants along the trekking trail.
4. Accommodation in guesthouses (Tea House) on trekking trail.
5. An English speaking tour guide for city sightseeing.
6. An English speaking trekking guide for the trekking with necessary porters
7. Wages of guide and other members.

8. National park fees, Govt. taxes and other applicable fees.
9. Domestic airfare as mentioned in the above itinerary.

Trip cost does not include:

1. International Airfare.
2. Nepalese Visa fee and international airport departure tax.
3. Lunch & dinner in Kathmandu.
4. Personal / Travel / Medical insurance and any other insurance for the members.
5. Hot water for shower during the trek.
6. Expenses of personal nature viz. tips, laundry, phone calls, alcoholic beverages, bottled drinks etc.
7. Any other cost, which is not mentioned in cost inclusive field above.

Rolwaling Trekking Nepal-18 Days

Rolwaling meaning 'the furrow left by the plough' is a quiet mountain and steep-walled valley as its name suggest. It is rugged yet beautiful area rarely visited unlike its neighbouring Himalayas of Khumbu and offers lots of mountaineering challenges to the adventurer. The trek to Rolwaling involves crossing of high pass Trashi Labtsa (5,755m) and the climbing of Parcharmo (6,273m) and it is a must to equip oneself with mountaineering gear (to be brought by the trekkers).

The trail starts from Charikote, which is a day's drive away from Kathmandu then it leads up along the Tamba Kosi river banks under the shadow of Mt. Gauri Shanker (7,145m), the holy mountain to Bhote Kosi river. From Simigaon, the trail turns right along Rolwaling Khola running deeply below ahead and parting from the old trade route to Tibet. Views of Melungtse (7,181m) appear proceeding further through the village of Beding (3,690m) with its monastery. From the village of Na (4,183m) the trail ascends through grass-covered valley to Tso Rolpa then traversing the moraine on the north side of the valley onto the snout of the Tram Bau Glacier, which feeds the Rolwaling river. The route up Prachormo is highly crevasseous. After assault, the trail drops to Thame, from where the route along Bhote Kosi river leads to Namche Bazaar and onto Lukla for flight to Kathmandu.

Outline Itinerary

- Day 01: Arrive In Kathmandu.
- Day 02: Kathmandu City Tour.
- Day 03: Kathmandu-Barabesi-Gorthali.
- Day 04: Gorthali-Dolangsa.
- Day 05: Dolangsa-Ruptahang.
- Day 06: Ruptanhang-Chilanka.
- Day 07: Chilanka-Laduk.
- Day 08: Laduk-Manthala.
- Day 09: Manthale-Simigaon.
- Day 10: Simigaon-Gyalche.
- Day 11: Gyalche-Bedding.
- Day 12: Bedding-Ngaon.
- Day 13: Ngaon-Bedding.
- Day 14: Bedding Simigaon.
- Day 15: Simigaon-Manthala.
- Day 16: Manthala-Chatre.
- Day 17: Charte-Charikot-Kathmandu.
- Day 18: Departure.

Trip Cost Based on Camping Arrangements;

Deluxe Hotels Option Standard Hotels Option Economy Hotels Option;

- Group Size Cost in US$,
- Per Person Group Size Cost in US$,
- Per Person Group Size Cost in US$.

Per Person

- 01-Person 000.00 01-Person 000.00 01-Person 000.00,
- 02-Person 000.00 02-Person 000.00 02-Person 000.00,
- 03-05 Person 000.00 03-05 Person 000.00 03-05 Person 000.00,
- 06-09 Person 000.00 06-09 Person 000.00 06-09 Person 000.00,

- 10-14 Person 000.00 10-14 Person 000.00 10-14 Person 000.00,
- 15 & Above 000.00 15 & Above 000.00 15 & Above 000.00.

Trip Cost includes:

1. Airport transfers on private vehicle.
2. Twin sharing accommodation in Kathmandu as per the category of package trip taken on Bed & Breakfast basis.
3. An English speaking tour guide for city sightseeing.
4. An English speaking trekking guide for the trekking with necessary Cook & porters.
5. All meals included during the trek prepared by Adventure Silk Road's cook in aid of kitchen boy and other helpers.
6. Wages of guide and other members of the team.
7. National park fees, Govt. taxes and other applicable fees.
8. Domestic airfare as mentioned in the above itinerary.

Trip cost does not include:

1. International Airfare.
2. Nepalese Visa fee and airport departure tax.
3. Lunch & dinner in Kathmandu.
4. Personal / Travel / Medical insurance and any other insurance for the members.
5. Expenses of personal nature viz. tips, laundry, phone calls, alcoholic beverages, bottled drinks etc.
6. Emergency evacuations.
7. Any other cost, which is not mentioned in cost inclusive field above.

Trip Cost Based on Mountain Lodges (Tea Houses);

Deluxe Hotels Option Standard Hotels Option Economy Hotels Option;

- Group Size Cost in US$,
- Per Person Group Size Cost in US$,
- Per Person Group Size Cost in US$.

Per Person

- 01-Person 000.00 01-Person 000.00 01-Person 000.00,
- 02-Person 000.00 02-Person 000.00 02-Person 000.00,
- 03-05 Person 000.00 03-05 Person 000.00 03-05 Person 000.00,
- 06-09 Person 000.00 06-09 Person 000.00 06-09 Person 000.00,
- 10-14 Person 000.00 10-14 Person 000.00 10-14 Person 000.00,
- 15 & Above 000.00 15 & Above 000.00 15 & Above 000.00,

Trip Cost includes:

1. Airport transfers on private vehicle.
2. Twin sharing accommodation in Kathmandu as per the category of package trip taken on Bed & Breakfast basis.
3. 3 meal (breakfast, Lunch & Dinner) in local restaurants along the trekking trail.
4. Accommodation in guesthouses (Tea House) on trekking trail.
5. An English speaking tour guide for city sightseeing.
6. An English speaking trekking guide for the trekking with necessary porters.
7. Wages of guide and other members.
8. National park fees, Govt. taxes and other applicable fees.
9. Domestic airfare as mentioned in the above itinerary.

Trip cost does not include:

1. International Airfare.
2. Nepalese Visa fee and international airport departure tax.
3. Lunch & dinner in Kathmandu.
4. Personal / Travel / Medical insurance and any other insurance for the members.
5. Hot water for shower during the trek.
6. Expenses of personal nature viz. tips, laundry, phone calls, alcoholic beverages, bottled drinks etc.
7. Any other cost, which is not mentioned in cost inclusive field above.

Jumla Rara Trekking Nepal-15 Days

Jumla & Rara lie in the remote Karnali region, northwest of Kathmandu. The region is made-up of long ridges covered with temperate forests and alpine pastures enclosing high valleys. Summer rainfall is low, but winter snow can be heavy and persistent. Since the region is fairly high and free from monsoon thunder-storms, the summer season is ideal for trekking. Winters are cold, but the autumn seasons trekking is rewarded with a profusion of alpine flowers. In the western part of the country, Jumla & Rara lie in the remote Karnali region, northwest of Kathmandu. The Rara region is made-up of long ridges covered with temperate forests and alpine pastures enclosing high valleys. Summer rainfall is low, but winter snow can be heavy and persistent.

Since the region is fairly high and free from monsoon thunderstorms, the summer season is ideal for trekking. Winters are cold, but the autumn seasons trekking is rewarded with a profusion of alpine flowers. The trail is very much "off the beaten path" and affords glimpses of culture and scenery very different from those in the rest of the country. The centrepiece of the park is the biggest lake of Nepal.

Along mountain paths and a series of picturesque villages, one reaches the magnificent banks of Rara Lake. The park includes Trans-Himalayan valley with high ridges covered with forest and alpine pastures. Being among the local people with their distinctive culture and traditions gives the visitor a unique experience and makes for a wonderful holiday. The primitive people give the trekker a look backward and a chance to reflect on his own modern society and development.

The great high mountains scenery enchants and fascinate as always. Like most of Nepal, Rara National Park is a naturalist's dream. Animals like the gaur, serow, musk deer, yellow-throated martin and a wide variety of birds such as the impeyan pheasant, Kalij and dove are ever present.

Outline Itinerary

- Day 01: Arrive In Kathmandu.
- Day 02: Kathmandu City Tour.
- Day 03: Kathmandu-Nepalgunj.
- Day 04: Nepalgunj-Jumla.

- Day 05: Jumla-Danphelanga.
- Day 06: Danphelanga-Chautha.
- Day 07: Chautha-Dhotu.
- Day 08: Dhotu-Rara Lake.
- Day 09: Rara Lake.
- Day 10: Rara/Ghorasain.
- Day 11: Ghorasain-Sinja.
- Day 12: Sinja-Jaljala Chaur.
- Day 13: Chere Chaur-Jumla.
- Day 14: Jumla Nepalgunj-Kathamdnu.
- Day 15: Departure.

Trip Cost Based on Camping Arrangements;

Deluxe Hotels Option Standard Hotels Option Economy Hotels Option;

- Group Size Cost in US$,
- Per Person Group Size Cost in US$,
- Per Person Group Size Cost in US$.

Per Person

- 01-Person 000.00 01-Person 000.00 01-Person 000.00,
- 02-Person 000.00 02-Person 000.00 02-Person 000.00,
- 03-05 Person 000.00 03-05 Person 000.00 03-05 Person 000.00,
- 06-09 Person 000.00 06-09 Person 000.00 06-09 Person 000.00,
- 10-14 Person 000.00 10-14 Person 000.00 10-14 Person 000.00,
- 15 & Above 000.00 15 & Above 000.00 15 & Above 000.00.

Trip Cost includes:

1. Airport transfers on private vehicle.
2. Twin sharing accommodation in Kathmandu as per the category of package trip taken on Bed & Breakfast basis.
3. An English speaking tour guide for city sightseeing.
4. An English speaking trekking guide for the trekking with necessary Cook & porters.

5. All meals included during the trek prepared by Adventure Silk Road's cook in aid of kitchen boy and other helpers.
6. Wages of guide and other members of the team.
7. National park fees, Govt. taxes and other applicable fees.
8. Domestic airfare as mentioned in the above itinerary.

Trip cost does not include:

1. International Airfare.
2. Nepalese Visa fee and airport departure tax.
3. Lunch & dinner in Kathmandu.
4. Personal / Travel / Medical insurance and any other insurance for the members.
5. Expenses of personal nature viz. tips, laundry, phone calls, alcoholic beverages, bottled drinks etc.
6. Emergency evacuations.
7. Any other cost, which is not mentioned in cost inclusive field above.

Trip Cost Based on Mountain Lodges (Tea Houses);

Deluxe Hotels Option Standard Hotels Option Economy Hotels Option;

- Group Size Cost in US$,
- Per Person Group Size Cost in US$,
- Per Person Group Size Cost in US$.

Per-Person

- 01-Person 000.00 01-Person 000.00 01-Person 000.00,
- 02-Person 000.00 02-Person 000.00 02-Person 000.00,
- 03-05 Person 000.00 03-05 Person 000.00 03-05 Person 000.00,
- 06-09 Person 000.00 06-09 Person 000.00 06-09 Person 000.00,
- 10-14 Person 000.00 10-14 Person 000.00 10-14 Person 000.00,
- 15 & Above 000.00 15 & Above 000.00 15 & Above 000.00.

Trip Cost includes:

1. Airport transfers on private vehicle.

2. Twin sharing accommodation in Kathmandu as per the category of package trip taken on Bed & Breakfast basis.
3. 3 meal (breakfast, Lunch & Dinner) in local restaurants along the trekking trail.
4. Accommodation in guesthouses (Tea House) on trekking trail.
5. An English speaking tour guide for city sightseeing.
6. An English speaking trekking guide for the trekking with necessary porters.
7. Wages of guide and other members.
8. National park fees, Govt. taxes and other applicable fees.
9. Domestic airfare as mentioned in the above itinerary.

Trip cost does not include:

1. International Airfare.
2. Nepalese Visa fee and international airport departure tax.
3. Lunch & dinner in Kathmandu.
4. Personal / Travel / Medical insurance and any other insurance for the members.
5. Hot water for shower during the trek.
6. Expenses of personal nature viz. tips, laundry, phone calls, alcoholic beverages, bottled drinks etc.
7. Any other cost, which is not mentioned in cost inclusive field above.

Dolpa Trekking & Expedition Nepal-30 Days

Dolpo is located inside the Shy – Phoksundo National Park of mid–western Nepal, behind the Dhaulagiri massif, towards the Tibetan Plateau. Cut off by a series of very high passes, closed by snow most of the year, Dolpo remains a truly isolated corner of Nepal. Time has stood still here for centuries as the inhabitants of Tibetan stock continue to live, cultivate and trade the way they have done since time immemorial. The finally preserved Ecosystem encompasses a wild and wonderful variety of plants and wildlife, including the blue sheep and leopard. A trek through Dolpo is an experience not easily forgotten.

Dolpo trekking is opened to trekking in 1989, the Dolpo region is hard to match for it's pristine beauty and rugged charm, where one can still have opportunity to meet the nomadic people and their life style almost untouched and unexplored. The Himalayas offer an endless variety of landscapes, cultures and great people. This unbounded diversity makes it a destination you can visit over and over again. It even becomes more interesting and fascinating with every time you return.

Lying in the rain shadow area of the Himalayas, the landscape resembles that of the Tibetan Plateau instead of the lush, green, monsoon watered hills, elsewhere in Nepal, at comparative altitudes. The people, very pleasant by nature, are of Tibetan descent who follow the pre-Buddhist Bon religion. Their language is closely related to Tibetan. The elevation of the trails is from 1650 meters (5,412ft) to 5136 meters (16,846ft) above sea level.

Outline Itinerary

- Day 01: Arrive In Kathmandu.
- Day 02: Kathmandu City Tour.
- Day 03: Kathmandu-Baglung.
- Day 04: Baglung-Tatopani.
- Day 05: Tatopani-Babichour.
- Day 06: Babichour-Takum.
- Day 07: Takum-Lulang.
- Day 08: Lulang-Jaljala La.
- Day 09: Jaljala La-Dhorpatan.
- Day 10: Dhorpatan-Tankor.
- Day 11: Tanko-Pelma.
- Day 12: Pelma-Dhule.
- Day 13: Dhule-Sengkhola.
- Day 14: Sengkhola-Purbang.
- Day 15: Purbang-Tarakot.
- Day 16: Tarakot-Dunai.
- Day 17: Dunai-Hanke.
- Day 18: Hanke-Reggi.
- Day 19: Reggi-Phoksundo Lake.

- Day 20: Phoksundo Lake.
- Day 21: Phoksundo Lake-Bagala Pass.
- Day 22: Bagala Pass-Numla Pass Base Camp.
- Day 23: Numla Pass Base Camp-Dho Tarap.
- Day 24: Dho Tarap-Lahani.
- Day 25: Lhani-Tarakot.
- Day 26-27: Tarakot-Dunai-Jhuphal.
- Day 28: Jhuphal-Nepalgunj-Kathmandu.
- Day 29: Free Day In Kathmandu.
- Day 30: Departure.

Trip Cost Based on Camping Arrangements;

Deluxe Hotels Option Standard Hotels Option Economy Hotels Option;

- Group Size Cost in US$,
- Per Person Group Size Cost in US$,
- Per Person Group Size Cost in US$.

Per Person

- 01-Person 000.00 01-Person 000.00 01-Person 000.00,
- 02-Person 000.00 02-Person 000.00 02-Person 000.00,
- 03-05 Person 000.00 03-05 Person 000.00 03-05 Person 000.00,
- 06-09 Person 000.00 06-09 Person 000.00 06-09 Person 000.00,
- 10-14 Person 000.00 10-14 Person 000.00 10-14 Person 000.00,
- 15 & Above 000.00 15 & Above 000.00 15 & Above 000.00.

Trip Cost includes:

1. Airport transfers on private vehicle.
2. Twin sharing accommodation in Kathmandu as per the category of package trip taken on Bed & Breakfast basis.
3. An English speaking tour guide for city sightseeing.
4. An English speaking trekking guide for the trekking with necessary Cook & porters.
5. All meals included during the trek prepared by Adventure Silk Road's cook in aid of kitchen boy and other helpers.

6. Wages of guide and other members of the team.
7. National park fees, Govt. taxes and other applicable fees.
8. Domestic airfare as mentioned in the above itinerary.

Trip cost does not include:

1. International Airfare.
2. Nepalese Visa fee and airport departure tax.
3. Lunch & dinner in Kathmandu.
4. Personal / Travel / Medical insurance and any other insurance for the members.
5. Expenses of personal nature viz. tips, laundry, phone calls, alcoholic beverages, bottled drinks etc.
6. Emergency evacuations.
7. Any other cost, which is not mentioned in cost inclusive field above.

Trip Cost Based on Mountain Lodges (Tea Houses);

Deluxe Hotels Option Standard Hotels Option Economy Hotels Option;

- Group Size Cost in US$,
- Per Person Group Size Cost in US$,
- Per Person Group Size Cost in US$.

Per Person

- 01-Person 000.00 01-Person 000.00 01-Person 000.00,
- 02-Person 000.00 02-Person 000.00 02-Person 000.00,
- 03-05 Person 000.00 03-05 Person 000.00 03-05 Person 000.00,
- 06-09 Person 000.00 06-09 Person 000.00 06-09 Person 000.00,
- 10-14 Person 000.00 10-14 Person 000.00 10-14 Person 000.00,
- 15 & Above 000.00 15 & Above 000.00 15 & Above 000.00.

Trip Cost includes:

1. Airport transfers on private vehicle.
2. Twin sharing accommodation in Kathmandu as per the category of package trip taken on Bed & Breakfast basis.

3. 3 meal (breakfast, Lunch & Dinner) in local restaurants along the trekking trail.
4. Accommodation in guesthouses (Tea House) on trekking trail.
5. An English speaking tour guide for city sightseeing.
6. An English speaking trekking guide for the trekking with necessary porters.
7. Wages of guide and other members.
8. National park fees, Govt. taxes and other applicable fees.
9. Domestic airfare as mentioned in the above itinerary.

Trip cost does not include:

1. International Airfare.
2. Nepalese Visa fee and international airport departure tax.
3. Lunch & dinner in Kathmandu.
4. Personal / Travel / Medical insurance and any other insurance for the members.
5. Hot water for shower during the trek.
6. Expenses of personal nature viz. tips, laundry, phone calls, alcoholic beverages, bottled drinks etc.
7. Any other cost, which is not mentioned in cost inclusive field above.

Manasalu Trekking Expedition Nepal-25 Days

Pristine mountain views, rich culture and genuine adventure sum up the trek experience to the base of Mt. Manasalu. Opened in 1992, this area offers a combination of rich culture heritage, unsurpassed beauty and biological diversity. Beginning in Gorkha, home of the celebrated Gorkha soldiers, visit the ancient palace of King Prithivi Narayan Shah. Soon after civilisation fades and we glimpse ancient villages, observing the simple agricultural habits of its people.

From here, begin your ascent through the Gandaki River valley, fed by innumerable rivers and waterfalls and plunge into its bathing pools. From here, the strenuous section begins and yaks begin to outnumber people in a rocky landscape. In Samagoan (3450m.), visit the glacial green lake of Birendra, before crossing into mystic Samdo, a mere 15 km from the Tibetan border. Here, Tibetan monks inhabit sacred monasteries.

There, combined with the views of Tibetan plateaux against stark white Himalayas makes this a truly spiritual place. Continuing, more monasteries await you in Larkya Bazaar, along with your biggest challenge- crossing Larkya pass. Snow covered peaks reaching over 6500 mt, demand your utmost respect as you are crossing, quite literally, the top of the world. The relaxing descent will take you through alpine, tropical areas, bursting with ferns, bamboo's, pine, waterfalls and aqua-blue green lakes laced with cotton-white beaches. Finally, the Manasalu will disappear behind you as you descend to Beshishar (832m.). This 3 week's excursion will leave you with a sense of peace and respect for the people of Nepal and its ecological wonders.

Outline Itinerary

- Day 01: Arrive In Kathmandu.
- Day 02: Kathmandu City Tour.
- Day 03: Kathmandu –Gorkha.
- Day 04: Gorkha – Khanchok.
- Day 05: Khanchok – Arughat.
- Day 06: To 09 Arughat – Jagat.
- Day 10: Jagat – Nyak.
- Day 11: Nyak – Gap.
- Day 12: Gap – Cho.
- Day 13: To 15 Cho-Sama Gompa.
- Day 16: Manasalu Base Camp-Yak Kharka.
- Day 17: Yak Kharka – Bimdakothi.
- Day 18: Bimdakothi – Tilje.
- Day 19: Tilje – Chamje.
- Day 20: Chamje-Naya Gaon.
- Day 21: Naya Gaon – Beshishar.
- Day 22: Beshishar – Kathmandu.
- Day 23-24: Free Day In Kathmandu.
- Day 25: Departure.

Trip Cost Based on Camping Arrangements;

Deluxe Hotels Option Standard Hotels Option Economy Hotels Option;

- Group Size Cost in US$,
- Per Person Group Size Cost in US$,
- Per Person Group Size Cost in US$.

Per Person

- 01-Person 000.00 01-Person 000.00 01-Person 000.00,
- 02-Person 000.00 02-Person 000.00 02-Person 000.00,
- 03-05 Person 000.00 03-05 Person 000.00 03-05 Person 000.00,
- 06-09 Person 000.00 06-09 Person 000.00 06-09 Person 000.00,
- 10-14 Person 000.00 10-14 Person 000.00 10-14 Person 000.00,
- 15 & Above 000.00 15 & Above 000.00 15 & Above 000.00.

Trip Cost includes:

1. Airport transfers on private vehicle.
2. Twin sharing accommodation in Kathmandu as per the category of package trip taken on Bed & Breakfast basis.
3. An English speaking tour guide for city sightseeing.
4. An English speaking trekking guide for the trekking with necessary Cook & porters.
5. All meals included during the trek prepared by Adventure Silk Road's cook in aid of kitchen boy and other helpers.
6. Wages of guide and other members of the team.
7. National park fees, Govt. taxes and other applicable fees.
8. Domestic airfare as mentioned in the above itinerary.

Trip cost does not include:

1. International Airfare.
2. Nepalese Visa fee and airport departure tax.
3. Lunch & dinner in Kathmandu.
4. Personal / Travel / Medical insurance and any other insurance for the members.
5. Expenses of personal nature viz. tips, laundry, phone calls, alcoholic beverages, bottled drinks etc.

6. Emergency evacuations.
7. Any other cost, which is not mentioned in cost inclusive field above.

Trip Cost Based on Mountain Lodges (Tea Houses);

Deluxe Hotels Option Standard Hotels Option Economy Hotels Option;

- Group Size Cost in US$,
- Per Person Group Size Cost in US$,
- Per Person Group Size Cost in US$.

Per Person

- 01-Person 000.00 01-Person 000.00 01-Person 000.00,
- 02-Person 000.00 02-Person 000.00 02-Person 000.00,
- 03-05 Person 000.00 03-05 Person 000.00 03-05 Person 000.00,
- 06-09 Person 000.00 06-09 Person 000.00 06-09 Person 000.00,
- 10-14 Person 000.00 10-14 Person 000.00 10-14 Person 000.00,
- 15 & Above 000.00 15 & Above 000.00 15 & Above 000.00.

Trip Cost includes:

1. Airport transfers on private vehicle.
2. Twin sharing accommodation in Kathmandu as per the category of package trip taken on Bed & Breakfast basis.
3. 3 meal (breakfast, Lunch & Dinner) in local restaurants along the trekking trail.
4. Accommodation in guesthouses (Tea House) on trekking trail.
5. An English speaking tour guide for city sightseeing.
6. An English speaking trekking guide for the trekking with necessary porters.
7. Wages of guide and other members.
8. National park fees, Govt. taxes and other applicable fees.
9. Domestic airfare as mentioned in the above itinerary.

Trip cost does not include:

1. International Airfare.

2. Nepalese Visa fee and international airport departure tax.
3. Lunch & dinner in Kathmandu.
4. Personal / Travel / Medical insurance and any other insurance for the members.
5. Hot water for shower during the trek.
6. Expenses of personal nature viz. tips, laundry, phone calls, alcoholic beverages, bottled drinks etc.
7. Any other cost, which is not mentioned in cost inclusive field above.

Bright Future for International Sports Tourism in Asia

Major sports events are not a new phenomenon in Asia; Tokyo and Seoul have both hosted successful Olympic Games, the first Asian Games was held 95 years ago and the South East Asian games has been on the calendar for 50 years. However Asia's travel and tourism industry is witnessing something new after Beijing hosted the Olympic Games in August 2008 – this mega-event was supported by a raft of new events and investment region-wide which are beginning to drive significant tourism volumes.

Abacus President and CEO Robert Bailey said that Beijing has proved to be an inspiration for Asia and the travel industry has begun to see just how powerful a driver of growth that sports tourism can be. "Added to that, certain sports which used to be the preserve of Western countries also see the prospect of growth here in Asia and there is a sort of gold rush as these codes seek greater exposure here," he said. "With a number of countries within the region now boasting first-class facilities and many more developing them, Asia is on track to be the home of the away game."

Mr. Bailey believes mega sporting events can generate more tourist business by spotlighting a host city and there are many opportunities for travel agents to specialise in this emerging high-end niche segment as regional demand grows.

A study of sports tourists by the Sports Business Group found; "They are passionate, high-spending, enjoy new sporting experiences and often stimulate other tourism. Their direct benefit to a destination is cash-their indirect benefit can be years of follow-on tourists."

The Lure of the East

While not every country in Asia is in a position to be able to host an Olympics, the Beijing Olympics has been paralleled by the increasing number of Asian cities injecting themselves on to the international circuit for other sports. Driving the growth of sport tourism has been increased global interest in sporting events on the back of the massive expansion in satellite and digital television coverage over the last 10 years. Sports that have a traditional fan-base in western countries are becoming popular in Asia and, due to the population numbers, governing bodies now view Asia as the new 'frontier' for growth. Formula 1 Grand Prix has moved a number of the races from European or North American cities to cities in Asia and the races are now held in Tokyo, Shanghai, Kuala Lumpur and soon Singapore.

Earlier this year, the English Premier League toyed with a fantastical idea to play one round of the competition, or five matches, in cities outside of England. The preferred choices were cities in North America and Asia. While this was rejected by football's governing body FIFA, it revealed that even the most popular domestic football league sees Asia as a growth area. Two of the world's most powerful rugby union nations, Australia and New Zealand, have agreed to play a first-class match in Hong Kong, in 2008. Robert Bailey said, "The pulling power of sports is such that true fans will overcome their fears of the new and different, to follow their teams in foreign fields. Fan groups such as those seen at the Hong Kong Sevens, Formula 1 and the cricket in Australasia are a taste of things to come."

Investing in the Future

Governments in Asia are already responding to this push from sports codes by investing on an unprecedented level. Singapore, the latest city to join the Formula 1 circuit is a perfect example. As well as transforming the Marina Bay area, and building tourism infrastructure such as a new airport terminal and a range of new attractions, the Singapore Government is pledging a 60% grant to the Formula 1 organisers for each year of the race, estimated to be US$66.8 million a year. The Singapore Grand Prix is expected to attract 80,000 track-side spectators and another 500 million viewers worldwide via the television broadcast, while the Singapore Tourism Board estimates the race will put US$72 million directly back into Singapore's coffers. As well as the hosting the Formula 1 event, Singapore is building a US$1.3 billion Sports Hub, with facilities such as the multipurpose stadium expected to attract a wide variety of international sporting events in future years.

In 2010 the inaugural Youth Olympic Games will be held in Singapore. Over and above the Sin$75 million budget for the Games themselves, the Singapore Tourism Board has indicated it will spend "hundreds of millions" to publicise the event and expects it to generate a minimum of 180,000 visitor nights for Singapore, much of it sustained by overseas visitors. Singapore's Minister for Community Development, Youth and Sports, Dr. Vivian Balakrishnan said that by throwing its support behind the big sporting events the republic is hoping to develop a whole, self-sustaining sport 'ecosystem' that will create 20,000 jobs and contribute US$1.47 billion in GDP by 2015.

The Middle East is doing things on an even grander scale. In its imitable style of mega-developments, Dubai is building a self-contained 50 million square foot 'sports city' within the Dubai Land development to woo sporting events and the accompanying tourists to the emirate.

Dubai Sports City caters for almost every sport imaginable, including four stadia, a golf course designed by Ernie Els, elite training schools including the first Manchester United Soccer School and the ICC Global Cricket Academy, a large gymnasium and an Olympic-length swimming pool. In 2004, the gulf state of Qatar unveiled a US$15 billion tourism development plan that had a strong emphasis on sport. At the time the state had already hosted international tennis, golf event and squash competitions and was preparing to host the 2006 Asian Games. Following that initial investment, Qatar now ranks among the best tourism destinations in the world according to the World Economic Forum and has announced it is bidding for the 2016 Olympic Games and looking to host a Formula 1 race. Research company Euromonitor points out, "This approach dovetails nicely with efforts to promote itself as an international conference and exhibition centre; both strategies represent two key pillars in Qatar's plan to differentiate itself from its neighbours." At the farthest reaches of Asia Pacific, the host of the 2011 Rugby World Cup, New Zealand is simply refurbishing one of its stadiums for the competition, which will bring an estimated 66,000 visitors to the country and US$400 million to the economy. However the nation has created a ministerial position and joint taskforce to oversee the event, and even announced a specific "leveraging and legacy" project to ensure the country squeezes every last benefit out of hosting what is the third most watched sporting event after the Olympics and Football world cup.

Getting in on the Action

Asia may be arriving a little later than the Middle East to the sports tourism 'party' but there is no doubting the commitment of many government and travel industry professionals in the region. According to Abacus' Robert Bailey this all points to the great potential for all industry players that sports tourism presents. "Just as professionalism in sport has created a number of new jobs for players, coaches, officials and even doctors, the increase in sports tourism has created new avenues for travel agencies to grow," he said. One of India's largest travel agencies, Kuoni India, founded its SOTC Sport Abroad division in 2003 just in time for the Cricket World Cup in South Africa and has "never looked back", according to Shyam Kartikeya, the head of SOTC Sport Abroad.

"Year after year we have only grown and have handled all major international events related to Cricket, Soccer, Formula 1, Olympics and more." "As disposable incomes in India grow, people are exploring travel from a different perspective," Mr. Kartikeya added. "Also the visibility of certain sports has grown tremendously in past few years and it is only going to grow more in near future which will only lead to people wanting to enjoy their favourite sport while they travel."

SOTC Sport Abroad has been selected as the official India-region Ticket Partner for the Singapore Formula 1 Grand Prix this year and Mr. Kartikeya said cultivating official relationships with organisers is key for an agency wanting to capitalise on sports tourism.

"As a large agency, experienced in handling sporting events, being appointed the official travel agent for an event is an important first step and we work hard to earn this status from the outset. From there, we prepare – blocking flights, hotels and tickets based on our previous experience in this sector of the industry. It's then down to marketing and connecting with the travellers through our 3,500 travel agents across India," he said. Chief of Thailand's Six Stars Travel agency, Duke Bhornlerts, a self-confessed sports fan, said he was motivated to move into sports tourism after a number of customers expressed a desire to travel overseas specifically to watch a sports game.

Six Star Travel now sends customers to the Australian Open, English Premier League games and Formula 1 Grand Prix races, among other events.

Mr. Bhornlerts believes the demand for sport tourism will only grow in Thailand and across Asia. "If Thailand and the rest of Asia do not want to lose out on this market, they will have to follow the example of other countries like Hong Kong with the Rugby Sevens and Formula 1 Grand Prix hosts Malaysia, China and Japan, and develop their own 'brand' of sports tourism," he said.

Six Stars Travel has responded to these opportunities by adding specialist travel services, including sports tours, to the usual range of travel services it provides such as booking air tickets and accommodation, packages for free and independent travellers and arranging group tours. Abacus' Robert Bailey said that as sports tourism in Asia matures, travel agents themselves will become very important to governments and events organisers because of the distribution reach and complexity that is often involved. "We see travel agents as being a critical element to Asia's success in becoming a sports tourism hot-spot," said Robert Bailey, "and even an exclusive event like the Singapore Formula 1 Grand Prix has called on the services of select, experienced travel agents to help promote the event around the world."

Mr. Bailey said that travel agents who want to get involved in sports tourism need to start getting more aggressive about their knowledge and understanding of events happening in the region, and to seek to be involved as strategic partners well ahead of the event. "Sports tourism has potential for great reward and the level of interest from the corporate sector and also government commitment and investment around the region indicates sports events will continue to be a very strong driver of growth for Asia's travel industry for the foreseeable future," said Robert Bailey. "The extent to which travel agents get involved in sports tourism is really a matter of customer demand and personal preference. Right now, the ball really is in their court."

Sports Tourism

Definition

Sports tourism refers to international trips specifically taken to watch sporting events. Common examples include international events such as world cups (soccer, rugby, cricket, etc.), the Olympics and Formula 1 Grand Prix, regional events (such as the soccer European Champions League), and individual (non-team) participant sports such as tennis, golf and horse racing.

Estimate of Global Market Size

The most popular global sporting events are the soccer FIFA World Cup and the Olympics, followed by the European Football Championships. However other popular sporting events also attract a large number of international visitors. These include the Rugby Union World Cup and Formula 1 Grand Prix.

- The FIFA Football World Cup held in France in 1998 attracted 900,000 international football fans and generated $12.3 billion.
- It is estimated that the 2000 Olympics in Sydney generated 111,000 additional international arrivals to Australia specifically travelling for sports tourism.
- Euro 2004 (the European Football Championships) attracted 500,000 sports tourists to Portugal, generating $320 million for the Portuguese economy.
- The Monaco Grand Prix (which alongside the Indy 500 and Le Mans is one of the most famous motor racing fixtures of the year) attracts 200,000 visitors over its four-day duration.
- The 2007 Cricket World Cup staged in the Caribbean was thought to have generated an additional 100,000 visitors who travelled specifically for the tournament.

Whilst the number of sports tourists fluctuates on an annual basis depending on the events taking place (it is greatest during FIFA World Cup and Olympics years), on average an estimated 12 million international trips are made for the main purpose of watching a sporting event.

Potential for Growth

Increased media exposure of sporting events over the last decade has raised the profile of many sports, and although TV coverage is better than at any time in the past, an increasing number of sports fans want to experience live events. The media also has the ability to make national and international icons of sporting stars, thereby generating greater demand, as fans want to see their sporting idols "in the flesh".

Sporting events themselves are being made increasingly appealing to attend, with greater levels of comfort, and other events – such as festivals-being created around them (such as horse racing weekends, boating regattas, etc.). Low-cost regional airlines (and more affordable long haul flights), are also driving demand for sporting events as flights become more convenient, more regular, and of course more affordable.

Overall, the sports tourism niche market is expected to grow annually at around 6% for the next five years.

Brief Profile of Consumers

Sports tourists are more easily profiled according to the sports they follow. However, in general terms the bulk of the market tends to be young-between 18 and 34 years, and in the C1 and C2 (middle) socioeconomic groups. This would also be the typical profile of a sports tourist following soccer matches. Rugby and cricket followers tend to be slightly older and with greater disposable income. Horse racing has a broad range of followers with no clear demographic structure. Followers of athletics tend to be young, low spenders, whilst those following the Formula 1 Grand Prix circuit tend to be skewed towards males in their 90s with above average disposable income.

Main Competing Destinations

The main competing destinations tend to vary depending on where the large events, such as the FIFA World Cup and Olympics are held. However, those holding key annual tournaments of global sporting interest include:

- United States,
- United Kingdom,
- France,
- Australia,
- Spain.

For specific sports, such as golf, motor racing, or yachting, this list of competing destinations would vary considerably.

7

Major Sports Events-I

Olympic Games

The Olympic Games are a major international event of summer and winter sports, in which thousands of athletes compete in a wide variety of events. The Games are currently held every two years, with Summer and Winter Olympic Games alternating. Originally, the ancient Olympic Games were held in Olympia, Greece, from the 8th century BC to the 5th century AD. In the late 19th century, Baron Pierre de Coubertin was inspired by Olympic festivals to revive the Games. For this purpose, he founded the International Olympic Committee (IOC) in 1894, and two years later, the modern Olympic Games were established in Athens. The IOC has since become the governing body of the Olympic Movement, whose structure and actions are defined by the Olympic Charter.

The evolution of the Olympic Movement during the 20th century forced the IOC to adapt the Games to the world's changing social circumstances. Some of these adjustments included the creation of the Winter Games for ice and snow sports, the Paralympic Games for athletes with physical disabilities, and the Youth Olympic Games for teenage athletes.

The IOC also had to accommodate the Games to the varying economical, political, and technological realities of the 20th century. As a result, the Olympics shifted away from pure amateurism, as envisioned by Coubertin, to allow participation of professional athletes. The growing importance of the mass media created the issue of corporate sponsorship and commercialization of the Games.

The Olympic Movement currently comprises international sports federations (IFs), National Olympic Committees (NOCs), and organizing committees for each specific Olympic Games. As the decision-making body, the IOC is responsible for choosing the host city for each Olympic Games. The host city is responsible for organizing and funding a celebration of the Games consistent with the Olympic Charter. The Olympic program, consisting of the sports to be contested at each Olympic Games, is also determined by the IOC. The celebration of the Games encompasses many rituals and symbols, such as the Olympic flag and torch, as well as the opening and closing ceremonies. There are over 13,000 athletes that compete at the Summer and Winter Olympics in 33 different sports and nearly 400 events. The first, second, and third place finishers in each event receive gold, silver or bronze Olympic medals, respectively.

The Games have grown in scale to the point that nearly every nation is represented. Such growth has created numerous challenges, including boycotts, doping, bribery of officials, and terrorism. Every two years, the Olympics and its media exposure provide unknown athletes with the chance to attain national, and in particular cases, international fame. The Games also constitute a major opportunity for the host city and country to promote and showcase themselves to the world.

Ancient Olympics

The Ancient Olympic Games in series of competitions held between representatives of several city-states from Ancient Greece, which featured mainly athletic but also combat and chariot racing events. The origin of these Olympics is shrouded in mystery and legend. One of the most popular myths identifies Heracles and his father Zeus as the progenitors of the Games. According to legend, it was Heracles who first called the Games "Olympic" and established the custom of holding them every four years. A legend persists that after Heracles completed his twelve labours, he built the Olympic stadium as an honour to Zeus. Following its completion, he walked in a straight line for 200 steps and called this distance a "stadion", which later became a unit of distance. Another myth associates the first Games with the ancient Greek concept of Olympic truce. The most widely accepted date for the inception of the Ancient Olympics is 776 BC; this is based on inscriptions, found at Olympia, of the winners of a footrace held every four years starting in 776 BC. The Ancient Games featured running events, a pentathlon (consisting of a jumping event, discus and javelin throws, a foot race and wrestling), boxing, wrestling, and equestrian events. Tradition has it that Coroebus, a cook from the city of Elis, was the first Olympic champion.

The Olympics were of fundamental religious importance, featuring sporting events alongside ritual sacrifices honouring both Zeus (whose famous statue by Phidias stood in his temple at Olympia) and Pelops, divine hero and mythical king of Olympia. Pelops was famous for his chariot race with King Oenomaus of Pisatis. The winners of the events were admired and immortalized in poems and statues. The Games were held every four years, and this period, known as an Olympiad, was used by Greeks as one of their units of time measurement. The Games were part of a cycle known as the Panhellenic Games, which included the Pythian Games, the Nemean Games, and the Isthmian Games.

The Olympic Games reached their zenith in the 6th and 5th centuries BC, but then gradually declined in importance as the Romans gained power and influence in Greece. There is no consensus on when the Games officially ended, the most common-held date is 393 AD, when the emperor Theodosius I declared that all pagan cults and practices be eliminated. Another date cited is 426 AD, when his successor Theodosius II ordered the destruction of all Greek temples. After the demise of the Olympics, they were not held again until the late 19th century.

Modern Games

Forerunners and Revival

The first significant attempt to emulate the ancient Olympic Games was the *L'Olympiade de la République*, a national Olympic festival held annually from 1796 to 1798 in Revolutionary France. The competition included several disciplines from the ancient Greek Olympics. The 1796 Games also marked the introduction of the metric system into sport. In 1850 an Olympian Class began at Much Wenlock, in Shropshire, England. It was renamed the Wenlock Olympian Games in 1859, and continues today as the Wenlock Olympian Society Annual Games. Dr. Brookes adopted events from the programme of the Olympics held in Athens in 1859 in to future Games. In 1866, a national Olympic Games in Great Britain was organized by Dr. William Penny Brookes at London's Crystal Palace.

Greek interest in reviving the Olympic Games began with the Greek War of Independence from the Ottoman Empire in 1821. It was first proposed by poet and newspaper editor Panagiotis Soutsos in his poem "Dialogue of the Dead", published in 1833. Evangelis Zappas, a wealthy Greek philanthropist, sponsored the first "Olympic Games" in 1859 which was held in an Athens city square. Athletes participated from Greece and the Ottoman Empire. Zappas paid for the restoration of the ancient Panathenaic Stadium so that it could host all future Olympic Games. The Panathenian stadium hosted the first in 1870 and a second in 1875.

In the search for a reason for the French defeat in the Franco-Prussian War (1870–1871), historian Baron Pierre de Coubertin theorized that the soldiers had not received proper physical education. In 1890, after attending the Olympian Games of the Wenlock Olympian Society, Coubertin decided that a large-scale revival of the Olympic Games was achievable. Coubertin built on the ideas of Brookes and Zappas with the aim of internationally rotating the Olympic Games from country to country. He presented these ideas during the first Olympic Congress of the newly created International Olympic Committee (IOC). This meeting was held from June 16 to June 23, 1894, at the Sorbonne University in Paris. On the last day of the Congress, it was decided that the first multinational Olympic Games would take place two years later in Athens. The IOC was fully responsible for the Games' organization, and, for that purpose, elected the Greek writer Demetrius Vikelas as its first president.

Reintroduction

There were fewer than 250 athletes at the first Olympic Games of the modern times. Due to the failure of the Greek government to follow Zappas' explicit instructions the Panathenian Stadium had to be refurbished a second time in preparation for the 1896 Athens Games. These Olympics featured nine sporting disciplines: athletics, cycling, fencing, gymnastics, shooting, swimming, tennis, weightlifting, and wrestling; rowing events were scheduled for competition but had to be cancelled due to bad weather conditions. The fencing events were hosted inside the landmark building called the Zappeion (named after Evangelis Zappas). The Greek officials and public were enthusiastic about the experience of hosting these Games. This feeling was shared by many of the athletes, who even demanded that Athens be the host of the Olympic Games on a permanent basis. The IOC had, however, envisaged these modern Olympics to be an itinerating and truly global event. As such they decided to hold the second Games in Paris.

Changes and Adaptations

Following the success of the 1896 Games, that was organized by a Greek Olympic Committee and that was hosted in a stadium that had already hosted two Olympic Games, the Olympics entered a period of stagnation that threatened their survival. The celebrations in Paris in 1900 and St. Louis in 1904 were overshadowed by the World's Fair exhibitions, held at the same time and location. The St. Louis Games, for example, hosted 650 athletes, but 580 were originally from the United States. The homogeneous nature of this edition was a low point for the Olympic Movement. The Games rebounded when the 1906 Intercalated Games (so-called because they were the second Games held within the third Olympiad) were held in Athens. Another successful Olympic Games organised by a Greek Olympic Committee and hosted in a stadium that had already hosted the Olympics three times. These Games are not officially recognized and no further editions have been held since. These Games attracted a broad international field of participants, and generated great public interest. This marked the beginning of a rise in both the popularity and the size of the Olympics.

Winter Games

The Winter Olympics were created to feature snow and ice sports that were logistically impossible to hold during the Summer Games. Figure skating (in 1908 and 1920) and ice hockey (in 1920) were featured as Olympic events at the Summer Olympics. The IOC desired to expand this list of sports to encompass other winter activities. At the 1921 Olympic Congress, in Lausanne, it was decided to hold a winter version of the Olympic Games. A winter sports week (it was actually 11 days) was held in 1924 in Chamonix, France; this event became the first Winter Olympic Games. The IOC mandated that the Winter Games be celebrated every four years on the same year as their summer counterpart. This tradition was upheld until the 1992 Games in Albertville, France; after that, beginning with the 1994 Games, the Winter Olympics were held on the third year of each Olympiad.

Paralympics

In 1948, Sir Ludwig Guttman, determined to promote the rehabilitation of soldiers after World War II, organized a multisport event between several hospitals to coincide with the 1948 London Olympics. Guttman's event, known then as the Stoke Mandeville Games, became an annual sports festival. Over the next twelve years, Guttman and others continued their efforts to use sports as an avenue to healing. For the 1960 Olympic Games, in Rome, Guttman brought 400 athletes to compete in the "Parallel Olympics", which became known as the first Paralympics. Since then, the Paralympics have been held in every Olympic year. As of the 1988 Summer Olympics in Seoul, South Korea, the host city for the Olympics has also played host to the Paralympics.

Youth Games

Starting in 2010, the Olympic Games will be complemented by Youth Games, where athletes between the ages of 14 and 18 will compete. The Youth Olympic Games were conceived by IOC president Jacques Rogge in 2001 and approved during the 119th Congress of the IOC. The first Summer Youth Games will be in Singapore in 2010, while the inaugural Winter Games will be hosted in Innsbruck, Austria, two years later. These Games will be shorter than the senior Games; the summer version will last twelve days, while the winter version will last nine days. The IOC will allow 3,500 athletes and 875 officials to participate at the Summer Youth Games, and 970 athletes and 580 officials at the Winter Youth Games. The sports to be contested will coincide with those scheduled for the traditional senior Games, however there will be a reduced number of disciplines and events.

Recent Games

From 241 participants representing 14 nations in 1896, the Games have grown to 10,500 competitors from 204 countries at the 2008

Summer Olympics. The scope and scale of the Winter Olympics is smaller. For example, Turin hosted 2,508 athletes from 80 countries competing in 84 events, during the 2006 Winter Olympics. During the Games most athletes and officials are housed in the Olympic village. This village is intended to be a self-contained home for all the Olympic participants. It is furnished with cafeterias, health clinics, and locations for religious expression.

The number of participating countries is higher than the 193 that are current members of the United Nations. The IOC allows nations to compete that do not meet the strict requirements for political sovereignty that other international organizations demand. As a result, colonies and dependencies are permitted to set up their own National Olympic Committees. Examples of this include territories such as Puerto Rico, Bermuda, and Hong Kong, all of which compete as separate nations despite being legally a part of another country.

International Olympic Committee

The Olympic Movement encompasses a large number of national and international sporting organizations and federations, recognized media partners, as well as athletes, officials, judges, and every other person and institution that agrees to abide by the rules of the Olympic Charter. As the umbrella organization of the Olympic Movement, the International Olympic Committee (IOC) is responsible for selecting the host city, overseeing the planning of the Olympic Games, updating and approving the sports program, and negotiating sponsorship and broadcasting rights. The Olympic Movement is made of three major elements:

- International Federations (IFs) are the governing bodies that supervise a sport at an international level. For example, the International Federation of Association Football (FIFA) is the IF for football (soccer), and the Federation International de Volleyball (FIVB) is the international governing body for volleyball. There are currently 35 IFs in the Olympic Movement, representing each of the Olympic sports.
- National Olympic Committees (NOCs) represent and regulate the Olympic Movement within each country. For example, the United States Olympic Committee (USOC) is the NOC of the

United States. There are currently 205 NOCs recognized by the IOC.

- Organizing Committees for the Olympic Games (OCOGs) constitute the temporary committees responsible for the organization of a specific celebration of the Olympics. OCOGs are dissolved after each Games, once the final report is delivered to the IOC.

French and English are the official languages of the Olympic Movement. The other language used at each Olympic Games is the language of the host country. Every proclamation (such as the announcement of each country during the parade of nations in the opening ceremony) is spoken in these three languages, or the main two depending on whether the host country is an English or French speaking country.

Criticism

The IOC has often been criticized for being an intractable organization, with several members on the committee for life. The leadership of IOC presidents Avery Brundage and Juan Antonio Samaranch was especially controversial. Brundage was president for over 20 years, and during his tenure he protected the Olympics from untoward political involvement. He was accused of both racism, for his handling of the apartheid issue with the South African delegation, and anti-Semitism. Under the Samaranch presidency, the office was accused of both nepotism and corruption. Samaranch's ties with the Franco regime in Spain was also a source of criticism.

In 1998, it was uncovered that several IOC members had taken bribes from members of the Salt Lake City bid committee for the hosting of the 2002 Winter Olympics, to ensure their votes were cast in favour of the American bid. The IOC pursued an investigation which led to the resignation of four members and expulsion of six others. The scandal set off further reforms that would change the way host cities are selected, to avoid similar cases in the future.

A BBC documentary entitled *Panorama: Buying the Games*, aired in August 2004, investigated the taking of bribes in the bidding process for the 2012 Summer Olympics. The documentary claimed it was possible to bribe IOC members into voting for a particular candidate city. After being narrowly defeated in their bid for the 2012 Summer Games, Parisian Mayor Bertrand Delanoë specifically accused the British Prime Minister Tony Blair and the London Bid Committee (headed by former Olympic champion Sebastian Coe) of breaking the bid rules. He cited French President Jacques Chirac as a witness; Chirac gave guarded interviews regarding his involvement. The allegation was never fully explored. The Turin bid for the 2006 Winter Olympics was also shrouded in controversy. A prominent IOC member, Marc Hodler, strongly connected with the rival bid of Sion, Switzerland, alleged bribery of IOC officials by members of the Turin Organizing Committee. These accusations led to a wide-ranging investigation. The allegations also served to sour many IOC members against Sion's bid and potentially helped Turin to capture the host city nomination.

Commercialization

The IOC originally resisted funding by corporate sponsors. It was not until the retirement of IOC president Avery Brundage, in 1972, that the IOC began to explore the potential of the television medium and the lucrative advertising markets available to them. Under the leadership of Juan Antonio Samaranch the Games began to shift toward international sponsors who sought to link their products to the Olympic brand.

Budget

During the first half of the 20th century the IOC was run on a small budget. As president of the IOC from 1952 to 1972, Avery Brundage rejected all attempts to link the Olympics with commercial interest. Brundage believed the lobby of corporate interests would unduly impact the IOC's decision-making. Brundage's resistance to this revenue stream meant the IOC left organizing committees to negotiate their own sponsorship contracts and use the Olympic symbols. When Brundage retired the IOC had US$2 million in assets; eight years later the IOC coffers had swelled to US$45 million. This was primarily due to a shift in ideology toward expansion of the Games through corporate sponsorship and the sale of television rights. When Juan Antonio Samaranch was elected IOC president in 1980 his desire was to make the IOC financially independent.

The 1984 Summer Olympics became a watershed moment in Olympic history. The Los Angeles-based organizing committee, led by Peter Ueberroth, was able to generate a surplus of US$225 million, which was an unprecedented amount at that time. The organizing committee had been able to create such a surplus in part by selling exclusive sponsorship rights to select companies. The IOC sought to gain control of these sponsorship rights. Samaranch helped to establish The Olympic Program (TOP) in 1985, in order to create an Olympic brand. Membership in TOP was, and is, very exclusive and expensive. Fees cost US$50 million for a four year membership. Members of TOP received exclusive global advertising rights for their product category, and use of the Olympic symbol, the interlocking rings, in their publications and advertisements.

Impact of Television

The 1936 Summer Olympics in Berlin were the first Games to be broadcast on television, though only to local audiences. The 1956 Winter Olympics were the first internationally televised Olympic Games, and the following Winter Games had their broadcasting rights sold for the first time to specialized television broadcasting networks—CBS paid US$394,000 for the American rights, and the European Broadcasting Union (EBU) allocated US$660,000. In the following decades the Olympics became one of the ideological fronts of the Cold War. Superpowers jockeyed for political supremacy, and the IOC wanted to take advantage of this heightened interest via the broadcast medium. The sale of broadcast rights enabled the IOC to increase the exposure of the Olympic Games, thereby generating more interest, which in turn created more appeal to advertisers who purchased advertising time on television. This cycle allowed the IOC to charge ever-increasing fees for those rights. For example, CBS paid US$375 million for the rights of the 1998 Nagano Games, while NBC spent US$3.5 billion for the broadcast rights of all the Olympic Games from 2000 to 2008.

Viewership increased exponentially from the 1960s until the end of the century. Worldwide audience estimates for the 1968 Mexico City Games was 600 million, whereas at the Los Angeles Games of 1984, the audience numbers had increased to 900 million; that number swelled to 3.5 billion by the 1992 Summer Olympics in Barcelona. However, at the 2000 Summer Games in Sydney, NBC drew the lowest ratings for any Summer or Winter Olympics since 1968. This was attributed to two factors: one was the increased competition from cable channels, the second was the internet, which was able to display results and video in real time. Television companies were still relying on tape-delayed content, which was becoming outdated in the information era. A drop in ratings meant that television studios had to give away free advertising time. With such high costs charged to broadcast the Games, the added pressure of the internet, and increased competition from cable, the television lobby demanded concessions from the IOC to boost ratings. The IOC responded by making a number of changes to the Olympic program. At the Summer Games, the gymnastics competition was expanded from seven to nine nights, and a Champions Gala was added to draw greater interest. The IOC also expanded the swimming and diving programs, both popular sports with a broad base of television viewers. Finally, the American television lobby was able to dictate when certain events were held so that they could be broadcast live during prime time in the United States. The result of these efforts was mixed: the ratings for the 2006 Winter Games, held in Europe, were significantly lower than those for the 2002 Games, while there was a sharp increase in viewership for the 2008 Summer Olympics, staged in Beijing.

Controversy

The sale of the Olympic brand has been controversial. The argument is that the Games have become indistinguishable from any other commercialized sporting spectacle. Specific criticism was levelled at the IOC for market saturation during the 1996 Atlanta and 2000 Sydney Games. The cities were awash in corporations and merchants attempting to sell Olympic-related wares.

The IOC responded by indicating they would address this to prevent further spectacles of over-marketing at future Games. Another criticism is that the Games are funded by host cities and national governments; the IOC incurs none of this cost, yet controls all the rights and profits from the Olympic symbols. The IOC also takes a percentage of all sponsorship and broadcast income. Host cities continue to compete ardently for the right to host the Games, even though there is no certainty that they will earn back their investments.

Symbols and Ceremonies

Symbols

The Olympic Movement uses symbols to represent the ideals embodied in the Olympic Charter. The Olympic symbol, better known as the Olympic rings, consists of five intertwined rings and represents the unity of the five inhabited continents (considering North and South America as a single continent). The coloured version of the rings—blue, yellow, black, green, and red—over a white field forms the Olympic flag. These colours were chosen because every nation had at least one of them on its national flag. The flag was adopted in 1914 but flown for the first time only at the 1920 Summer Olympics in Antwerp, Belgium. It has since been hoisted during each celebration of the Games.

The Olympic motto is *Citius, Altius, Fortius*, a Latin expression meaning "Faster, Higher, Stronger". Coubertin's ideals are further expressed in the Olympic creed:

> *The most important thing in the Olympic Games is not to win but to take part, just as the most important thing in life is not the triumph but the struggle. The essential thing is not to have conquered but to have fought well.*

Months before each Games, the Olympic flame is lit in Olympia in a ceremony that reflects ancient Greek rituals. A female performer, acting as a priestess, ignites a torch by placing it inside a parabolic mirror which focuses the sun's rays; she then lights the torch of the first relay bearer, thus initiating the Olympic torch relay that will carry the flame to the host city's Olympic stadium, where it plays an important role in the opening ceremony. Though the flame has been an Olympic symbol since 1928, the torch relay was introduced at the 1936 Summer Games, as part of the German government's attempt to promote its National Socialist ideology.

The Olympic mascot, an animal or human figure representing the cultural heritage of the host country, was introduced in 1968. It has played an important part on the Games identity promotion since the 1980 Summer Olympics, when the Russian bear cub Misha reached international stardom. The mascots of the most recent Summer

Olympics, in Beijing, were the Fuwa, five creatures that represent the five fengshui elements important in Chinese culture.

Ceremonies

As mandated by the Olympic Charter, various elements frame the opening ceremony of the Olympic Games. Most of these rituals were established at the 1920 Summer Olympics in Antwerp. The ceremony typically starts with the hoisting of the host country's flag and a performance of its national anthem. The host nation then presents artistic displays of music, singing, dance, and theatre representative of its culture. The artistic presentations have grown in scale and complexity as successive hosts attempt to provide a ceremony that outlasts its predecessor's in terms of memorability. The opening ceremony of the Beijing Games reportedly cost $100 million, with much of the cost incurred in the artistic segment.

After the artistic portion of the ceremony, the athletes parade into the stadium grouped by nation. Greece is traditionally the first nation to enter in order to honour the origins of the Olympics. Speeches are given, formally opening the Games. Finally, the Olympic torch is brought into the stadium and passed on until it reaches the final torch carrier—often a well-known and successful Olympic athlete from the host nation—who lights the Olympic flame in the stadium's cauldron.

Closing

The closing ceremony of the Olympic Games takes place after all sporting events have concluded. Flag-bearers from each participating country enter the stadium, followed by the athletes who enter together, without any national distinction. Three national flags are hoisted while the corresponding national anthems are played: the flag of Greece, to honour the birthplace of the Olympic Games; the flag of the current host country, and the flag of the country hosting the next Summer or Winter Olympic Games. The president of the organizing committee and the IOC president make their closing speeches, the Games are officially closed, and the Olympic flame is extinguished. In what is known as the Antwerp Ceremony, the mayor of the city that organized the Games transfers a special Olympic flag to the president of the IOC, who then passes it on to the mayor of the city hosting the next Olympic

Games. After these compulsory elements, the next host nation briefly introduces itself with artistic displays of dance and theatre representative of its culture.

Medal Presentation

A medal ceremony is held after each Olympic event is concluded. The winner, second and third-place competitors or teams stand on top of a three-tiered rostrum to be awarded their respective medals. After the medals are given out by an IOC member, the national flags of the three medalists are raised while the national anthem of the gold medalist's country plays. Volunteering citizens of the host country also act as hosts during the medal ceremonies, as they aid the officials who present the medals and act as flag-bearers. For every Olympic event, the respective medal ceremony is held, at most, one day after the event's final. For the men's marathon, the competition is usually held early in the morning on the last day of Olympic competition and its medal ceremony is then held in the evening during the closing ceremony.

Sports

The Olympic Games program consists of 33 sports, 52 disciplines and nearly 400 events. For example, wrestling is a Summer Olympic sport, comprising two disciplines: Greco-Roman and Freestyle. It is further broken down into fourteen events for men and four events for women, each representing a different weight class. The Summer Olympics program includes 26 sports, while the Winter Olympics program features 7 sports. Athletics, swimming, fencing, and artistic gymnastics are the only summer sports that have never been absent from the Olympic program. Cross-country skiing, figure skating, ice hockey, Nordic combined, ski jumping, and speed skating have been featured at every Winter Olympics program since its inception in 1924. Current Olympic sports, like badminton, basketball, and volleyball, first appeared on the program as demonstration sports, and were later promoted to full Olympic sports. Some sports that were featured in earlier Games were later dropped from the program.

Olympic sports are governed by international sports federations (IFs) recognized by the IOC as the global supervisors of those sports. There are 35 federations represented at the IOC. There are sports recognized by the IOC that are not included on the Olympic program. These sports are not considered Olympic sports, but they can be promoted to this status during a program revision that occurs in the first IOC session following a celebration of the Olympic Games. During such revisions, sports can be excluded or included in the program based on a two-thirds majority vote of the members of the IOC. There are recognized sports that have never been on an Olympic program in any capacity, including chess and surfing.

In October and November 2004, the IOC established an Olympic Programme Commission, which was tasked with reviewing the sports on the Olympic program and all non-Olympic recognized sports. The goal was to apply a systematic approach to establishing the Olympic program for each celebration of the Games. The commission formulated seven criteria to judge whether a sport should be included on the Olympic program. These criteria are history and tradition of the sport, universality, popularity of the sport, image, athletes' health, development of the International Federation that governs the sport, and costs of holding the sport. From this study five recognized sports emerged as candidates for inclusion at the 2012 Summer Olympics: golf, karate, rugby, roller sports and squash. These sports were reviewed by the IOC Executive Board and then referred to the General Session in Singapore in July 2005. Of the five sports recommended for inclusion only two were selected as finalists: karate and squash. Neither sport attained the required two-thirds vote and consequently they were not promoted to the Olympic program. In October 2009 the IOC voted to in state golf and rugby as Olympic sports for the 2016 and 2020 Summer Olympic Games.

The 114th IOC Session, in 2002, limited the Summer Games program to a maximum of 28 sports, 301 events, and 10,500 athletes. Three years later, at the 117th IOC Session, the first major program revision was performed, which resulted in the exclusion of baseball and softball from the official program of the 2012 London Games. Since there was no agreement in the promotion of two other sports, the 2012 program will feature just 26 sports. The 2016 and 2020 Games will return to the maximum of 28 sports given the addition of rugby and golf.

Amateurism and Professionalism

The ethos of the aristocracy as exemplified in the English public schools greatly influenced Pierre de Coubertin. The public schools subscribed to the belief that sport formed an important part of education, an attitude summed up in the saying *mens sana in corpore sano*, a sound mind in a sound body. In this ethos, a gentleman was one who became an all-rounder, not the best at one specific thing.

There was also a prevailing concept of fairness, in which practising or training was considered tantamount to cheating. Those who practiced a sport professionally were considered to have an unfair advantage over those who practiced it merely as a hobby.

The exclusion of professionals caused several controversies throughout the history of the modern Olympics. The 1912 Olympic pentathlon and decathlon champion Jim Thorpe was stripped of his medals when it was discovered that he had played semi-professional baseball before the Olympics. His medals were restored by the IOC in 1983 on compassionate grounds. Swiss and Austrian skiers boycotted the 1936 Winter Olympics in support of their skiing teachers, who were not allowed to compete because they earned money with their sport and were thus considered professionals.

As class structure evolved through the 20th century, the definition of the amateur athlete as an aristocratic gentleman became outdated. The advent of the state-sponsored "full-time amateur athlete" of the Eastern Bloc countries further eroded the ideology of the pure amateur, as it put the self-financed amateurs of the Western countries at a disadvantage. Nevertheless, the IOC held to the traditional rules regarding amateurism.

Beginning in the 1970s, amateurism requirements were gradually phased out of the Olympic Charter. Eventually the decisions on professional participation were left to the IFs. As of 2004, the only sport in which no professionals compete is boxing, although even this requires a definition of amateurism based on fight rules rather than on payment, as some boxers receive cash prizes from their National Olympic Committees. In men's football (soccer), only three players over the age of 23 are eligible to participate per team in the Olympic tournament. This is done in order to maintain a level of amateurism.

Controversies

Boycotts

The 1956 Melbourne Olympics were the first Olympics to be boycotted. The Netherlands, Spain, and Switzerland refused to attend because of the repression of the Hungarian uprising by the Soviet Union.

Cambodia, Egypt, Iraq and Lebanon boycotted the Games due to the Suez Crisis.

In 1972 and 1976 a large number of African countries threatened the IOC with a boycott to force them to ban South Africa and Rhodesia, because of their segregationist regimes. New Zealand was also one of the African boycott targets, due to the "All Blacks" (national rugby team) having toured apartheid-ruled South Africa.

The IOC conceded in the first two cases, but refused to ban New Zealand on the grounds that rugby was not an Olympic sport. Fulfilling their threat, twenty African countries were joined by Guyana and Iraq in a Tanzania-led withdrawal from the Montreal Games, after a few of their athletes had already competed.

Taiwan also decided to boycott these Games because the People's Republic of China (PRC) exerted pressure on the Montreal organizing committee to keep the delegation from the Republic of China (ROC) from competing under that name.

The ROC refused a proposed compromise that would have still allowed them to use the ROC flag and anthem as long as the name was changed. Taiwan did not participate again until 1984, when it returned under the name of Chinese Taipei and with a special flag and anthem.

In 1980 and 1984, the Cold War opponents boycotted each other's Games. Sixty-five nations refused to compete at the Moscow Olympics in 1980 because of the Soviet invasion of Afghanistan. This boycott reduced the number of nations participating to 81, the lowest number since 1956.

The Soviet Union and 14 of its Eastern Bloc partners (except Romania) countered by boycotting the Los Angeles Olympics of 1984, contending that they could not guarantee the safety of their athletes. Soviet officials defended their decision to withdraw from the Games by saying that "chauvinistic sentiments and an anti-Soviet hysteria are being whipped up in the United States".

The boycotting nations of the Eastern Bloc staged their own alternate event, the Friendship Games, in July and August.

There had been growing calls for boycotts of Chinese goods and the 2008 Olympics in Beijing in protest of China's human rights record, and in response to the disturbances in Tibet and ongoing conflict in Darfur. Ultimately, no nation supported a boycott.

In August 2008, the government of Georgia called for a boycott of the 2014 Winter Olympics, set to be held in Sochi, Russia, in response to Russia's participation in the 2008 South Ossetia war. The International Olympic Committee responded to concerns about the status of the 2014 games by stating that it is "premature to make judgments about how events happening today might sit with an event taking place six years from now".

Politics

Contrary to the founding principles, the Olympic Games have been used as a platform to promote political ideologies. Nazi Germany wished to demonstrate the Nationalist Socialist Party's benevolence and desire for peace when they hosted the 1936 Games.

The Games were also intended to show the superiority of the Aryan race; a goal that was not met due in part to the achievements of athletes such as Jesse Owens, who won four gold medals at this Olympics. The Soviet Union did not participate until the 1952 Summer Olympics in Helsinki.

Instead, starting in 1928, the Soviets organized an international sports event called Spartakiads. Other communist countries organized Workers Olympics during the interwar period of the 1920s and 1930s. These events were held as an alternative to the Olympics, which were perceived as a capitalist and aristocratic event. It was not until the 1956 Summer Games that the Soviets emerged as a sporting superpower and, in doing so, took full advantage of the publicity that came with winning at the Olympics.

Individual athletes have also used the Olympic stage to promote their own political agenda. At the 1968 Summer Olympics, in Mexico City, two American track and field athletes, Tommie Smith and John Carlos, who finished first and third in the 200 meter sprint race, performed the Black Power salute on the victory stand.

The second place finisher Peter Norman wore an Olympic Project for Human Rights badge in support of Smith and Carlos. In response to the protest, IOC President Avery Brundage told the United States Olympic Committee (USOC) to either send the two athletes home or withdraw the track and field team. The USOC opted for the former.

Currently, the government of Iran has taken steps to avoid any competition between its athletes and those from Israel. An Iranian judoka did not compete in a match against an Israeli during the 2004 Summer Olympics. Although he was officially disqualified for excessive weight, Arash Miresmaeli was awarded US$125,000 in prize money by the Iranian government, an amount paid to all Iranian gold medal winners. He was officially cleared of intentionally avoiding the bout, but his receipt of the prize money raised suspicion.

Use of Performance Enhancing Drugs

In the early 20th century, many Olympic athletes began using drugs to improve their athletic abilities. For example, the winner of the marathon at the 1904 Games, Thomas J. Hicks, was given strychnine and brandy by his coach. The only Olympic death linked to doping occurred at the Rome Games of 1960. During the cycling road race, Danish cyclist Knud Enemark Jensen fell from his bicycle and later died. A coroner's inquiry found that he was under the influence of amphetamines. By the mid-1960s, sports federations were starting to ban the use of performance enhancing drugs; in 1967 the IOC followed suit.

The first Olympic athlete to test positive for the use of performance enhancing drugs was Hans-Gunnar Liljenwall, a Swedish pentathlete at the 1968 Summer Olympics, who lost his bronze medal for alcohol use. The most publicized doping-related disqualification was that of Canadian sprinter Ben Johnson, who won the 100 meter dash at the 1988 Seoul

Olympics but tested positive for stanozolol. His gold medal was subsequently stripped and awarded to runner-up Carl Lewis, who himself had tested positive for banned substances prior to the Olympics.

In the late 1990s, the IOC took the initiative in a more organized battle against doping, by forming the World Anti-Doping Agency (WADA) in 1999. There was a sharp increase in positive drug tests at the 2000 Summer Olympics and 2002 Winter Olympics. Several medalists in weightlifting and cross-country skiing were disqualified due to doping offenses.

During the 2006 Winter Olympics, only one athlete failed a drug test and had a medal revoked. The IOC-established drug testing regimen (now known as the Olympic Standard) has set the worldwide benchmark that other sporting federations around the world attempt to emulate. During the Beijing games, 3,667 athletes were tested by the IOC under the auspices of the World Anti-Doping Agency. Both urine and blood tests were used to detect banned substances. Several athletes were barred from competition by their National Olympic Committees prior to the Games; only three athletes failed drug tests while in competition in Beijing.

Violence

Despite what Coubertin had hoped for, the Olympics did not bring total peace to the world. In fact, three Olympiads had to pass without a celebration of the Games because of war: the 1916 Games were cancelled due to World War I, and the summer and winter games of 1940 and 1944 were cancelled because of World War II.

The South Ossetia War between Georgia and Russia erupted on the opening day of the 2008 Summer Olympics in Beijing. Both President Bush and Prime Minister Putin were attending the Olympics at that time and spoke together about the conflict at a luncheon hosted by Chinese President Hu Jintao. When Nino Salukvadze of Georgia won the bronze medal in the 10 meter air pistol competition, she stood on the medal podium with Natalia Paderina, a Russian shooter who had won the silver. In what became a much-publicized event from the Beijing Games, Salukvadze and Paderina embraced on the podium after the ceremony had ended.

Terrorism has also threatened the Olympic Games. In 1972, when the Summer Games were held in Munich, Bavaria, Germany, eleven members of the Israeli Olympic team were taken hostage by the terrorist group Black September in what is now known as the Munich massacre. A bungled liberation attempt led to the deaths of the nine abducted athletes who had not been killed prior to the rescue. Also killed were five of the terrorists and a German policeman. During the Summer Olympics in 1996 in Atlanta, a bomb was detonated at the Centennial Olympic Park, which killed 2 and injured 111 others. The bomb was set by Eric Robert Rudolph, an American domestic terrorist, who is currently serving a life sentence for the bombing.

Champions and Medalists

The athletes or teams who place first, second, or third in each event receive medals. The winners receive gold medals, which were solid gold until 1912, then made of gilded silver and now gold plated silver. Every gold medal must contain at least six grams of pure gold.

The runners-up receive silver medals and the third-place athletes are awarded bronze medals. In events contested by a single-elimination tournament (most notably boxing), third place might not be determined and both semifinal losers receive bronze medals. At the 1896 Olympics only the first two received a medal; silver for first and bronze for second. The current three medal format was introduced at the 1904 Olympics From 1948 onward athletes placing fourth, fifth, and sixth have received certificates, which became officially known as victory diplomas; in 1984 victory diplomas for seventh and eighth-place finishers were added. At the 2004 Summer Olympics in Athens, the gold, silver, and bronze medal winners were also given olive wreaths. National Olympic Committees and the media record medal statistics as a measure of success.

All-time Individual Medal Count

The IOC does not keep an official record of individual medal counts, though unofficial medal tallies abound. These provide one method of determining the most successful Olympic athletes of the modern era. Below are the top ten individual medal winners of the modern Olympics (the gender of the athlete is denoted in the "Sport" column):

Athlete	*Nation*	*Sport*	*Olympics*	*Gold*	*Silver*	*Bronze*	*Total*
Michael	United	Swimming	2000-2008	14	0	2	16
Phelps,	States	(m)	1956-1964	9	5	4	18
Larissa	Soviet	Gymnastics	1920-1928	9	3	0	12
Latynina	Union	(f)					
Paavo	Finland	Athletics					
Nurmi		(m)					
Mark	United	Swimming					
Spitz		(m)					
Carl	United	Athletics	1984-1996	9	1	0	10
Lewis	States	(m)					
Bjørn	Norway	Crosss	1992-1998	8	4	0	12
Dæhlie		-country					
		kiing (m)					
Birgit	East	Canoeing	1980-2004	8	4	0	12
Fischer	Germany	(flatwater)					
	Germany	(f)					
Sawao	Japan	Gymnastics	1968-1972	9	1	1	11
Kato		(m)					
Jenny	United	Swimming	1992-2004	8	3	1	12
Thompson	States	(f)					
Matt	United	Swimming	1984-1992	8	2	1	11
Biondi	States	(m)					

Host Nations and Cities

The host city for an Olympic Games is usually chosen seven years ahead of their celebration. The process of selection is currently carried out in two phases that span over a two-year period. The prospective host city first applies to its country's Olympic Committee; if more than one city from the same country submits a proposal to its NOC, the national committee typically holds an internal selection, since only one city per NOC can be presented to the International Olympic Committee for consideration. Once the deadline for submission of proposals by the NOCs is reached, the first phase (Application) begins with the applicant cities asked to complete a questionnaire regarding several key criteria related to the organization of the Olympic Games. In this form, the applicants must give assurances that they will comply with the Olympic Charter and with any other regulations established by the IOC Executive Committee. The evaluation of the filled questionnaires by a specialized group provides the IOC with an overview of each applicant's project and their potential to host the Games. Based on this technical evaluation, the IOC Excutive Board selects the applicants that will proceed to the candidature stage.

Once the candidate cities are selected, they must submit to the IOC a bigger and more detailed presentation of their project as part of a candidature file. Each city is thoroughly analysed by an evaluation commission. This commission will also visit the candidate cities, interviewing local officials and inspecting prospective venue sites, and submits a report on its findings one month prior to the IOC final decision. During the interview process the candidate city must also guarantee that it will be able to fund the Games. After the work of the evaluation commission, a list of candidates is presented to the General Session of the IOC, which is assembled in a country that must not have a candidate city in the running. The IOC members gathered in the Session have the final vote on the host city. Once elected, the host city bid committee (together with the NOC of the respective country) signs a Host City Contract with the IOC, officially becoming an Olympic host nation and host city.

By 2016, the Olympic Games will have been hosted by 44 cities in 23 countries, but by cities outside Europe and North America on only eight occasions. Since the 1988 Summer Olympics in Seoul, South Korea, the Olympics have been held in Asia or Oceania four times, a sharp increase compared to the previous 92 years of modern Olympic history. The 2016 Games in Rio de Janeiro will be the first for a South American country. No bids from countries in Africa have ever succeeded. The countries that sent the most athletes to the 2008 Summer Olympics are China with 639, the United States with 596, and Russia who brought 455 athletes.

The United States has hosted four Summer and four Winter Olympics, more than any other nation. Among Summer Olympics host nations, the United Kingdom has been the host of two Games, and will host its third Olympics in 2012. Germany, Australia, France, and Greece are the other nations to have hosted the Summer Olympics twice. Concerning the Winter Olympics, France took the hosting job for three times, while Switzerland, Austria, Norway, Japan, and Italy have done it twice. The next Games, to be held in Vancouver, will be Canada's second Winter Olympics and third overall.

Summer Olympic Games

The Summer Olympic Games or the Games of the Olympiad are an international multisport event, occurring every four years, organized by the International Olympic Committee. Medals are awarded in each event, with gold medals for first place, silver for second and bronze for third, a tradition that started in 1904. The Winter Olympics were also created due to the success of the summer Olympics.

The games have expanded from a 42-event competition with fewer than 250 male athletes to a 300-event sporting tradition with over 10,000 competitors of both sexes from 205 nations. Organizers for the 2008 Summer Olympics in Beijing expected approximately 10,500 athletes to take part in the 302 events on the program for the games.

The United States has hosted four Summer Olympics Games, more than any other nation. The United Kingdom will have hosted three Summer Olympics Games when they return to the British capital in 2012, all of them have been (and will be in) London, making it the first city to hold the Summer Olympic Games three times. Australia, France, Germany and Greece have all hosted the Summer Olympic Games twice.

Other countries that have hosted the summer Olympics are Belgium, Canada, Finland, Italy, Japan, Mexico, Netherlands, South Korea, Spain, the Soviet Union and Sweden. The People's Republic of China hosted the Summer Olympics for the first time in Beijing in 2008. In the 2016 Summer Olympics, Rio de Janeiro will host the first Summer Games in South America. Four cities have hosted two Summer Olympic Games: Los Angeles, London, Paris and Athens. Stockholm, Sweden, has hosted events at two Summer Olympic Games, having hosted the games in 1912 and the equestrian events at the 1956 Summer Olympics—which they are usually listed as jointly hosting. Events at the summer Olympics have also been held in Hong Kong and The Netherlands (both represented by their own NOCs), with the equestrian events at the 2008 Summer Olympics being held in Hong Kong and two sailing races at the 1920 Summer Olympics being held in The Netherlands.

Five countries—France, Australia, Great Britain, Greece, and Switzerland—have been represented at all Summer Olympic Games. The only country to have won at least one gold medal at every Summer Olympic Games is Great Britain, ranging from one gold in 1904, 1952 and 1996 to fifty-six golds in 1908.

Qualification

Qualification rules for each of the Olympic sports are set by the International Federation (IF) that governs that sport's international competition.

For individual sports, competitors typically qualify through attaining a certain place in a major international event or on the IF's ranking list. National Olympic committees may enter a limited number of qualified competitors in each event, and the NOC decides which qualified competitors to select as representatives in each event if more have attained the benchmark than can be entered. Many events provide for a certain number of wild card entries, given to athletes from developing nations.

Nations qualify teams for team sports through continental qualifying tournaments, in which each continental association is given a certain number of spots in the Olympic tournament. The host nation is generally given an automatic qualification.

The modern Olympic Games were founded in 1894 when Pierre Fredi, Baron de Coubertin sought to promote international understanding through sporting competition. He based his Olympics on the Wenlock Olympian Society Annual Games, which had been contested in Much Wenlock since 1850.

The first edition of de Coubertin's games, held in Athens in 1896, attracted just 245 competitors, of whom more than 200 were Greek, and only 14 countries were represented. Nevertheless, no international events of this magnitude had been organized before. Female athletes were not allowed to compete, though one woman, Stamata Revithi, ran the marathon course on her own, saying "if the committee doesn't let me compete I will go after them regardless".

The 1896 Summer Olympics, officially known as the Games of the I Olympiad, was an international multisport event which was celebrated in Athens, Greece, from April 6 to April 15, 1896. It was the first Olympic Games held in the Modern era. Ancient Greece was the birthplace of the Olympic Games, consequently Athens was perceived to be an appropriate choice to stage the inaugural modern Games. It was unanimously chosen as the host city during a congress organized by Pierre de Coubertin, a French pedagogue and historian, in Paris, on June 23, 1894. The International Olympic Committee (IOC) was also established during this congress.

Despite many obstacles and setbacks, the 1896 Olympics were regarded as a great success. The Games had the largest international participation of any sporting event to that date. Panathinaiko Stadium, the first big stadium in the modern world, overflowed with the largest crowd ever to watch a sporting event. The highlight for the Greeks was the marathon victory by their compatriot Spiridon Louis. The most successful competitor was German wrestler and gymnast Carl Schuhmann, who won four gold medals.

After the Games, Coubertin and the IOC were petitioned by several prominent figures including Greece's King George and some of the American competitors in Athens, to hold all the following Games in Athens. However, the 1900 Summer Olympics were already planned for Paris and, except for the 1906 Intercalated Games, the Olympics did not return to Greece until the 2004 Summer Olympics.

Four years later the 1900 Summer Olympics in Paris attracted more than four times as many athletes, including 11 women, who were allowed to officially compete for the first time, in croquet, golf, sailing, and tennis. The Games were integrated with the Paris World's Fair and lasted over 5 months. It is still disputed which events exactly were *Olympic*, since few or maybe even none of the events were advertised as such at the time.

Numbers declined for the 1904 Games in St. Louis, Missouri, United States, due in part to the lengthy transatlantic boat trip required of the European competitors, and the integration with the Louisiana Purchase Exposition World's Fair, which again spread the event out over an extended period. In contrast with Paris 1900, the word *Olympic* was used for practically every contest, including those exclusively for school boys or for Irish-Americans.

A series of smaller games were held in Athens in 1906. These were to be the first of an in 1906 to celebrate the "tenth birthday" of the games. The IOC does not currently recognize these games as being official Olympic Games, although many historians do. The 1906 Athens alternating series of games to be held in Athens, but the series failed to materialize. The games were more successful than the 1900 and 1904 games, with over 900 athletes competing, and contributed positively to the success of future games. The 1908 London Games saw numbers rise again, as well as the first running of the marathon over its now-standard distance of 42.195 km (26 miles 385 yards). The winner of the first Olympic Marathon in 1896 (a male-only race) was Spiridon "Spiros" Louis, a Greek water-carrier. He won at the Olympics in 2 hours 58 minutes and 50 seconds at a distance of 40 km (24 miles 85 yards). The new marathon distance of 42.195 km (26 miles 385 yards) was chosen to ensure that the race finished in front of the box occupied by the British royal family. Thus the marathon had been 40 km for the first games in 1896, but was subsequently varied by up to 2 km due to local conditions such as street and stadium layout. At the six Olympic games between 1900 and 1920, the marathon was raced over six different distances.

At the end of the 1908 marathon the Italian runner Dorando Pietri was first to enter the stadium, but he was clearly in distress, and collapsed of exhaustion before he could complete the event. He was helped over the finish line by concerned race officials, but later he was disqualified and the gold medal was awarded to John Hayes, who had trailed him by around 30 seconds.

The Games continued to grow, attracting 2,504 competitors, to Stockholm in 1912, including the great all-rounder Jim Thorpe, who won both the decathlon and pentathlon. Thorpe had previously played a few games of baseball for a fee, and saw his medals stripped for this breach of amateurism after complaints from Avery Brundage. They were reinstated in 1983, 30 years after his death. The Games at Stockholm were the first to fulfil Pierre de Coubertin's original idea. For the first time since the Games started in 1896 were all continents represented with athletes competing in the same stadium. The scheduled Berlin Games of 1916 were cancelled following the onset of World War I.

The Interwar Era

The 1920 Antwerp games in war-ravaged Belgium were a subdued affair, but again drew a record number of competitors. This record only stood until 1924, when the Paris Games would involve 3,000 competitors, the greatest of whom was Finnish runner Paavo Nurmi. "The Flying Finn", won three team gold medals and the individual 1,500 and 5,000 meter runs, the latter two on the same day.

The 1928 Amsterdam games were notable for being the first games which allowed females to compete at track & field athletics, and benefited greatly from the general prosperity of the times alongside the first appearance of sponsorship of the games, from Coca-Cola. This was in stark contrast to 1932 when the Los Angeles games were affected by the Great Depression, which contributed to the fewest competitors since the St. Louis games.

The 1936 Berlin Games were seen by the German government as a golden opportunity to promote their ideology. The ruling Nazi Party commissioned filmmaker Leni Riefenstahl to film the games. The result, *Olympia*, was a masterpiece, despite Hitler's theories of Aryan racial superiority being repeatedly shown up by "non-Aryan" athletes. In particular, African-American sprinter and long jumper Jesse Owens won 4 gold medals. The tale of Hitler snubbing Owens at the ensuing medal ceremony is a fabrication. The 1936 Berlin Games also saw the reintroduction of the Torch Relay.

Due to World War II, the Games of 1940 (due to be held in Tokyo and temporarily relocated to Helsinki upon the outbreak of war) were cancelled. The Games of 1944 were due to be held in London but were also cancelled; instead, London hosted the first games after the end of the war, in 1948.

After World War II

The first postwar Games were held in 1948 in London, with both

Germany and Japan excluded. Dutch sprinter Fanny Blankers-Koen won four gold medals on the track, emulating Owens' achievement in Berlin.

At the 1952 Games in Helsinki the USSR team competed for the first time and immediately became one of the dominant teams. Finland made a legend of an amiable Czech army lieutenant named Emil Zátopek, who was intent on improving on his single gold and silver medals from 1948. Having first won both the 10,000 and 5,000 meter races, he also entered the marathon, despite having never previously raced at that distance. Pacing himself by chatting with the other leaders, Zatopek led from about half way, slowly dropping the remaining contenders to win by two and a half minutes, and completed a trio of wins.

The 1956 Melbourne Games were largely successful, barring a water polo match between Hungary and the Soviet Union, which political tensions caused to end as a pitched battle between the teams. Due to a foot-and-mouth disease outbreak in Britain at the time and the strict quarantine laws of Australia, the equestrian events were held in Stockholm.

The 1960 Rome Games saw the arrival on the world scene of a young light-heavyweight boxer named Cassius Clay, later known as Muhammad Ali, who would later throw his gold medal away in disgust after being refused service in a whites-only restaurant in his home town, Louisville, Kentucky. Soviet women's artistic gymnastics team members won 15 of 16 possible medals. Other performers of note in 1960 included Wilma Rudolph, a gold medalist in the 100 meters, 200 meters and 4x100 meters relay events.

The 1964 Games held in Tokyo are notable for heralding the modern age of telecommunications. These games were the first to be broadcast worldwide on television, enabled by the recent advent of communication satellites. The 1964 Games were thus a turning point in the global visibility and popularity of the Olympics.

Performances at the 1968 Mexico City games were affected by the altitude of the host city. No event was affected more than the long jump. American athlete Bob Beamon jumped 8.90 meters, setting a new world record and, in the words of fellow competitor and then-reigning champion Lynn Davies, "making the rest of us look silly." Beamon's world record would stand for 23 years. The 1968 Games also saw the introduction of the now-universal Fosbury flop, a technique which won American high jumper Dick Fosbury the gold medal. Politics took centre stage in the medal ceremony for the men's 200 meter dash, where Tommie Smith and John Carlos made a protest gesture on the podium against the segregation in the United States; their political act was condemned within the Olympic Movement, but was praised in the American Civil Rights Movement.

Politics again intervened at Munich in 1972, with lethal consequences. A Palestinian terrorist group named Black September invaded the Olympic village and broke into the apartment of the Israeli delegation. They killed two Israelis and held 9 others as hostages. The terrorists demanded that Israel release numerous prisoners. When the Israeli government refused their demand, a tense stand-off ensued while negotiations continued. Eventually the captors, still holding their hostages, were offered safe passage and taken to an airport, where they were ambushed by German security forces. In the firefight that followed, 15 people, including the nine Israeli athletes and five of the terrorists, were killed. After much debate, it was decided that the Games would continue, but proceedings were obviously dominated by these events. Some memorable athletic achievements did occur during these Games, notably the winning of a then record seven gold medals by United States swimmer Mark Spitz, Lasse Viren's, of Finland, back to back gold in the 5,000 meters and 10,000 meters, defeating American distance great Steve Prefontaine in the former, and the winning of three gold medals by 16-year-old Soviet gymnast Olga Korbut, who, however failed to win the all-around to her teammate Ludmilla Tourischeva.

There was no such tragedy in Montreal in 1976, but bad planning and fraud led to the Games' cost far exceeding the budget. The Montreal Games were the most expensive in Olympic history, until the 2008 Summer Olympics, costing over $5 billion (equivalent to $20 billion in 2006). For a time, it seemed that the Olympics might no longer be a viable financial proposition. In retrospect, the belief that contractors (suspected of being members of the Montreal Mafia) skimmed large sums of money from all levels of contracts while also profiting from the substitution of cheaper building materials of lesser quality, may have contributed to the delays, poor construction and excessive costs. In 1988, one such contractor, Giuseppe Zappia "was cleared of fraud charges that resulted from his work on Olympic facilities after two key witnesses died before testifying at his trial."

There was also a boycott by African nations to protest against a recent tour of apartheid-run South Africa by a New Zealand rugby side. The Romanian gymnast Nadia Comãneci won the women's individual all around gold medal with two of four possible perfect scores, thus giving birth to a gymnastics dynasty in Romania. Another female gymnast to earn the perfect score and three gold medals there was Nellie Kim of the USSR. Lasse Viren repeated his double gold in the 5,000 meters and 10,000 meters, making him the only athlete to ever win the distance double twice.

End of the 20th Century

Closing Ceremony of the 1980 Summer Olympics, in Moscow, Soviet Union, with bear cub Misha, the mascot of that year's games, flying into the sky.

Following the Soviet Union's participation in the Afghan Civil War, 66 nations, including the United States, Canada, West Germany and Japan, boycotted the 1980 games held in Moscow. The boycott contributed to the 1980 Games being a less publicised and less competitive affair, which was dominated by the host country.

In 1984 the Soviet Union, and 13 Soviet Allies, reciprocated by boycotting the 1984 Summer Olympics in Los Angeles. These games were perhaps the first games of a new era to make a profit. The games were again viable, but had become more commercial. Again, without the participation of the Eastern European countries, the 1984 Games were dominated by their host country. The game was also the first time Mainland China (People's Republic) participated.

The 1988 Seoul games were very well planned but the games were tainted when many of the athletes, most notably men's 100 metres winner Ben Johnson, failed mandatory drug tests. Despite splendid drug-free performances by many individuals, the number of people who failed screenings for performance-enhancing chemicals overshadowed the games.

On the bright side, drug testing and regulation authorities were catching up with the cheating that had been endemic in athletics for some years. The 1992 Barcelona Games were cleaner, although not without incident. In evidence there was increased professionalism amongst Olympic athletes, exemplified by US basketball's "Dream Team". 1992 also saw the reintroduction to the Games of several smaller European states which had been incorporated into the Soviet Union since World War II. These games also saw gymnast Vitaly Scherbo equal the record for most individual gold medals at a single Games set by Eric Heiden in the 1980 Winter Games, with five.

By then the process of choosing a location for the Games had itself become a commercial concern; allegations of corruption rocked the International Olympic Committee, in particular with reference to Salt Lake City's bid to host the 2002 Winter Olympics. It was also widely rumored that The Coca-Cola Company, a key IOC sponsor, was highly influential in the 1996 Summer Olympics being hosted by its home city of Atlanta. In the stadium in 1996, the highlight was 200 meters runner Michael Johnson annihilating the world record in front of a home crowd. Canadians savored Donovan Bailey's record-breaking gold medal run in the 100-meter dash. This was popularly felt to be an appropriate recompense for the previous national disgrace involving Ben Johnson. There were also emotional scenes, such as when Muhammad Ali, clearly affected by Parkinson's disease, lit the Olympic torch and received a replacement medal for the one he had discarded in 1960. The latter event took place not at the boxing ring but in the basketball arena, at the demand of US television. The atmosphere at the Games was marred however when a bomb exploded during the celebration in Centennial Olympic Park. In June 2003, the principal suspect in this bombing, Eric Robert Rudolph, was captured.

A New Millennium

The 2000 Games were held in Sydney, Australia, and showcased individual performances by local favourite Ian Thorpe in the pool, Briton Steve Redgrave who won a rowing gold medal in an unprecedented fifth consecutive Olympics, and Cathy Freeman, an Indigenous Australian whose triumph in the 400 meters united a packed stadium. Eric "the Eel" Moussambani, a swimmer from Equatorial Guinea, had a memorably slow 100 meter freestyle swim that showed that, even in the commercial world of the twentieth century, some of de Coubertin's original vision still remained. The Sydney Games were also memorable for the first appearance of a joint North and South Korean contingent (to a standing ovation) at the opening ceremonies, even if they competed as different countries. Controversy did not escape the 2000 Games in Women's Artistic Gymnastics, in which the vaulting horse was set to the wrong height during the All Around Competition. Several athletes faltered, including Russian Svetlana Khorkina, who had been favoured to win gold after qualifying for the competition in first place.

2004 saw the Games return to their birthplace in Athens, Greece. Greece spent at least $7.2 billion on the Games, including $1.5 billion on security alone. The games were praised and appreciated for their excellent quality in terms of organization, hospitality, symbolism, the level of the competition and athleticism, and the overall image transmitted worldwide. Nonetheless, the Men's Gymnastics events were mired in controversy when it was discovered that Korean gymnast Yang Tae Young had been incorrectly credited with a lower start value, which placed him third behind American Paul Hamm, who won the competition. Later in the event finals, fans halted the Men's High Bar competition with chants of disapproval following the release of the score for Russian Alexei Nemov. Allegations of corrupt judging also mired the Event Finals in Men's Still Rings. Although unfounded and wildly sensationalized reports of potential terrorism drove crowds away from the preliminary competitions of first weekend of the games (August 14-15), attendance picked up as the games progressed. Still, a third of the tickets failed to sell. The Athens Games witnessed all 202 NOCs participate with over 11,000 participants.

The 2008 Summer Olympics were held in Beijing, People's Republic of China. Several new events, including the new discipline of BMX for both men and women, were held. For the first time, women competed in the steeplechase. The fencing program was expanded to include all six events for both men and women. Women had not previously been able to compete in team foil or saber events (although women's team epee and men's team foil were dropped for these Games). Marathon swimming events, over the distance of 10 kilometres, were added. In addition, the doubles events in table tennis were replaced by team events.

List of Olympic Sports

Sport	*Years*	*Sport*	*Years*
Archery	1900–1912, 1920, since 1972	Modern pentathlon	since 1912
		Polo	1900, 1908, 1920, 1924, 1936
Athletics	all	Rackets	1908
Badminton	since 1992	Roque	1904
Baseball	1992–2008	Rowing	since 1900
Basketball	since 1936	Rugby union	1900, 1908, 1920, 1924
Basque pelota	1900	Rugby sevens	2016
Boxing	1904, 1908, since 1920	Sailing	1900, since 1908
Canoeing	since 1936	Shooting	1896, 1900, 1908–1924, since 1932
Cricket	1900	Softball	1996–2008
Croquet	1900	Swimming	all
Cycling	all	Synchronized swimming	since 1984
Diving	since 1904		
Equestrian	1900, since 1912	Table tennis	since 1988
Fencing	all	Taekwondo	since 2000
Football	1900–1928, since 1936	Tennis	1896–1924, since 1988
Golf	1900, 1904, 2016	Triathlon	since 2000
Gymnastics	all	Tug of war	1900–1920
Handball	1936, since 1972	Volleyball	since 1964
Hockey (field)	1908, 1920, since 1928	Water motorsports	1908
Jeu de paume	1908	Water polo	1900, since 1908
Judo	1964, since 1972	Weightlifting	1896, 1904, since 1920
Lacrosse	1904, 1908	Wrestling	1896, since 1904

American swimmer Michael Phelps set a record for gold medals at a single Games, with eight, and tied the record of Heiden and Scherbo for most individual golds at a single Games. Another major star of the Games was Jamaican sprinter Usain Bolt, who became the first male athlete ever to set world records in the finals of both the 100 and 200 metres in the same Games.

London, United Kingdom will hold the 2012 Summer Olympics, making London the first city to host the Games three times. The International Olympic Committee has removed baseball and softball from the 2012 program. However, it may be re-added in programs in later years. The International Olympic Committee has announced that the 2016 Summer Olympics are going to be held in Rio de Janeiro, Brazil. Of historic importance, Brazil is the first South American country to host the Summer Olympic Games.

43 different sports, spanning 56 different disciplines, have been part of the Olympic program at one point or another. 28 sports have comprised the schedule for the 2000, 2004, and 2008 Summer Olympics, though baseball and softball have been removed to give a list of 26 for the 2012 Games.

The Summer Olympic Sports or Federations are regrouped under a common umbrella association, called the Association of Summer Olympic International Federations (ASOIF).

List of Modern Summer Olympic Games

Note: *Although the Games of 1916, 1940, and 1944 had been cancelled, the Roman numerals for those Games were still used because the Summer Games' official titles count Olympiads, not the Games themselves; those Olympiads occurred anyway per the Olympic Charter. This is in contrast to the Roman numerals in the official titles of the Winter Olympic Games, which ignore the cancelled Winter Games of 1940 & 1944; those titles count Games instead of Olympiads.*

Games	Year	Host	Dates	Nations	Competitors			Sports	Events
					Total	Men	Women		
I	1896	Athens, Greece	6–15 April	14	241	241	0	9	43
II	1900	Paris, France	14 May–28 Oct.	24	997	975	22	18	95

Games	Year	Host	Dates	Nations	Competitors			Sports	Events
					Total	Men	Women		
III	1904	St.Louis, US	1 July- 23 Nov.	12	651	645	6	17	91
Int'd [A]	*1906*	*Athens, Greece*	*22 April- 2May*	*20*	*903*	*883*	*20*	*13*	*78*
IV	1908	London, UK	27 April- 31 Oct.	22	2008	1971	37	22	110
V	1912	Stockholm, Sweden	12 May- 27 July	28	2407	2359	48	14	102
VI	*1916*	*Originally awarded to Berlin, cancelled because of World War I*							
VII	1920	Antwerp, Belgium	20 April- 12 Sep.	29	2626	2561	65	22	154
VIII	1924	Paris, France	4 May- 27 July	44	3089	2954	135	17	126
IX	1928	Amsterdam, Netherlands	17 May- 12 Aug.	46	2883	2606	277	14	109
X	1932	Los Angeles, US	30 July- 14 Aug.	37	1332	1206	126	14	117
XI	1936	Berlin, Germany	1-16 Aug	49	3963	3632	331	19	129
XII	*1940*	*Originally awarded to Tokyo, then awarded to Helsinki, cancelled because of World War II*							
XIII	*1944*	*Originally awarded to London, cancelled because of World War II*							
XIV	1948	London, UK	29 July- 14 Aug	59	4104	3714	390	17	136
XV	1952	Helsinki, Finland	19 July- 3 Aug.	69	4955	4436	519	17	149
XVI	1956	Melbourne, Australia	22 Nov. 9 Dec.	72	3314	2938	376	17	145
		Stockholm, Sweden[B]	10-17 June						
XVII	1960	Rome, Italy	25 Aug. 11 Sept.	83	5338	4727	611	17	150
XVIII	1964	Tokyo, Japan	10-24 Oct.	93	5151	4473	678	19	163

Games	Year	Host	Dates	Nations	Competitors Total	Men	Women	Sports	Events
XIX	1968	Mexico City, Mexico	12-27 Oct.	112	5516	4735	781	18	172
XX	1972	Munich, West Germany	26 Aug. 11 Sept.r	121	7134	6075	1059	21	195
XXI	1976	Montreal, Canada	17 July- 1 Aug.	92	6084	4824	1260	21	198
XXII	1980	Moscow, Soviet Union	19 July- 3 Aug.	80	5179	4064	1115	21	203
XXIII	1984	Los Angeles, US	28 July- 12 Aug.	140	6829	5263	1566	21	221
XXIV	1988	Seoul, South Korea	17 Sept. 2 Oct.	160	8391	6197	2194	23	237
XXV	1992	Barcelona, Spain	25 July 9 Aug.	169	9356	6652	2704	25	257
XXVI	1996	Atlanta, US	19 July 4 Aug.	197	10318	6806	3512	26	271
XXVII	2000	Sydney, Australia	15 Sept. 1 Oct.	199	10651	6582	4069	28	300
XXVIII	2004	Athens, Greece	13–29 Aug.	201	10625	6296	4329	28	301
XXIX	2008	Beijing, China	8-24 Aug.	204	11028			28	302
XXX	2012	London, UK	27 July 12 Aug.					*future event*	
XXXI	2016	Rio de Janeiro, Brazil	5-21 Aug.					*future event*	

A: The 1906 Intercalated Games are no longer considered official Games by the IOC.

B: Due to Australian quarantine laws, the equestrian events were held in Stockholm several months before the rest of the 1956 Games in Melbourne.

Winter Olympic Games

The Winter Olympic Games is a winter multisport event held every four years. They feature winter sports held on snow or ice, such as Alpine skiing, cross-country skiing, figure skating, bobsledding and ice hockey. Cross-country skiing, figure skating, ice hockey, Nordic combined, ski jumping, and speed skating have been competed at every Winter Olympics since 1924. Other athletic events have been added as the Games have progressed. Some of these events, such as luge, short track speed skating, and freestyle skiing have earned a permanent spot on the Olympic programme. Others, like speed skiing, bandy, and skijoring have been demonstration sports but never incorporated officially as an Olympic sport.

Fewer countries participate in the Winter Olympics than the Summer Olympics. The first Winter Olympics were held in Chamonix, France. Figure skating and ice hockey had been events at the Summer Olympics prior to 1924. The Games were held every four years from 1924 until 1940 when they were interrupted by World War II. The Winter and Summer Games resumed in 1948 and were celebrated on the same year until 1992. At that time the Winter Games split from the Summer Games. The Summer and Winter Olympics are currently celebrated on alternating even years. The first Winter Olympic Games to be held on this new schedule was in 1994 in Lillehammer, Norway.

The Winter Games have undergone significant changes since their inception. The rise of television as a global medium for communication has greatly enhanced the profile of the Games. It has also created an income stream, in the form of the sale of broadcast rights, and advertising, which has become very lucrative. This has also allowed outside interests, such as television companies and corporate sponsors, to influence the various aspects of the Games. The International Olympic Committee (IOC) has had to address several internal scandals, and the use of performance enhancing drugs by Winter Olympic athletes. The Winter Games have also been used by countries to demonstrate the superiority of their political systems.

Many countries have played home to the Winter Olympics. France has been host to the Games three times. The United States has hosted the Games four times, more than any other country. Several countries including Italy, Japan, Austria and Norway have hosted the Games twice. The next host city will be Vancouver, Canada in 2010. This will be the second time the Games will be held in Canada. The Games will then be hosted by Sochi, Russia in 2014. This will be the first time that Russia has hosted a Winter Olympic Games.

Early Years

The first international multisport event specifically for winter sports were the Nordic Games, held in 1901 in Sweden. The Nordic Games were organized by General Viktor Gustaf Balck. They were held again in 1903, again in 1905, and then every four years there after until 1926. Balck was a charter member of the International Olympic Committee (IOC) and a close personal friend of Olympic Games founder Pierre de Coubertin. He attempted to have winter sports, specifically figure skating, added to the Olympic programme. Balck was unsuccessful until the 1908 Summer Olympics in London, which featured four figure skating events. Ulrich Salchow (10 time World champion) and Madge Syers won the individual titles.

Three years later, Italian count Eugenio Brunetta d'Usseaux proposed that the IOC stage a week with winter sports as part of the 1912 Summer Olympics in Stockholm. The organizers opposed this idea, their reasoning was twofold: they desired to protect the integrity of the Nordic Games; and they were concerned about a lack of facilities that could accommodate winter sports. The idea was resurrected for the 1916 Games, which were to be held in Berlin. A winter sports week with speed skating, figure skating, ice hockey and Nordic skiing was planned, but the 1916 Olympics were cancelled after the outbreak of World War I.

The first Olympics after the war, the 1920 Games in Antwerp featured figure skating with the addition of ice hockey. At the IOC Congress held the following year, it was decided that the organizers of the 1924 Summer Olympics, France, would also host a separate "International Winter Sports Week", under the patronage of the IOC. This "week" (it actually lasted 11 days) of events in Chamonix proved to be a great success. More than 200 athletes from 16 nations, competed in 16 events. Less than 15 of the athletes were women and they were only allowed to compete in figure skating events. Finnish and Norwegian athletes dominated the events. In 1925 the IOC decided to create a separate Olympic Winter Games, and the 1924 Games in Chamonix were retroactively designated as the first Winter Olympics.

St. Moritz was appointed by the IOC to host the second Olympic Winter Games in 1928. Fluctuating weather conditions made these Olympics memorable. The opening ceremonies were held in a blizzard. In contrast, warm weather conditions plagued the Olympics for the remainder of the Games. Due to the weather the 10,000 metre (6.2 miles) speed skating event had to be abandoned and officially cancelled with no winner.

The 50 km (31 miles) cross-country event was officially contested but ended with a temperature of 25 °C (77 °F), which caused significant problems with snow and waxing conditions. The weather was not the only note-worthy aspect of the 1928 Games; Sonja Henie of Norway created a sensation when she won the figure skating competition at the age of 15. She became the youngest Olympic champion in history, a distinction she would hold for 74 years.

The next Winter Olympics was the first to be hosted outside of Europe. Fewer athletes participated than in 1928, as the journey to Lake Placid, United Sates, was a long and expensive one for most competitors, and there was little money for sports in the midst of the Great Depression. These Games were also marred by warm weather. Virtually no snow fell for two months preceding the Games.

It was not until mid-January that there was enough snow to hold all the events. Sonja Henie defended her Olympic title. Eddie Eagan, who had been an Olympic champion in boxing in 1920, won the gold in the men's bobsled event to become the first, and so far only, Olympian to have won gold medals in both the Summer and Winter Olympics. The Bavarian towns of Garmisch and Partenkirchen joined to organize the 1936 edition of the Winter Games, held from February 6–16. 1936 marked the last year that the Summer and Winter Olympics were held in the same country.

Alpine skiing made its Olympic debut in Germany, but skiing teachers were barred from entering because they were considered to be professionals. This decision caused the Swiss and Austrian skiers to refuse to compete in the Olympics.

World War II

The Second World War interrupted the celebration of the Winter Olympics. The 1940 Winter Olympics had originally been awarded to Sapporo, Japan, but was rescinded in 1938, because of the Japanese invasion of China in the Sino-Japanese War. Subsequently, St. Moritz, Switzerland, was chosen by the IOC to host the Games, but three months later the IOC withdrew St. Moritz from the Games, because of quarrels with the Swiss organizing team.

Garmisch-Partenkirchen, the hosts of the previous Olympics, stepped in to host the Winter Games again, but both Summer and Winter Olympics were cancelled in their entirety in November 1939 following Germany's invasion of Poland. The 1944 Winter Olympics, scheduled to take place in Cortina d'Ampezzo, Italy, were cancelled in the Summer of 1941, due to the continuing World War.

1948 to 1960

The IOC selected the Swiss town of St. Moritz to host the first postwar Games in 1948. St. Moritz was untouched by World War II because of Switzerland's neutrality. Since most of the venues were already constructed for the 1928 Games it was a logical choice to become the first city to host a Winter Olympics twice. Twenty-eight countries competed in Switzerland. Athletes from Germany and Japan were not invited. The Games were marred by controversy, and theft. Two hockey teams from the United States arrived. Both teams claimed to be the legitimate U.S. Olympic hockey representative. The Olympic flag presented at the 1920 Summer Olympics in Antwerp, was stolen. Its replacement was also stolen. The Games were declared a success, due mainly to the fact that they were the most competitive in history. Ten countries won gold medals at these Games, more than any Games to that point.

The city of Oslo, Norway, was selected to host the 1952 Winter Olympics. The Olympic Flame was lit in the fireplace of the home of skiing pioneer Sondre Nordheim. The torch relay was conducted by 94 participants and held entirely on skis. Bandy, a popular sport in the Nordic countries, was held as a demonstration sport though only Norway, Sweden, and Finland fielded teams.

After not being able to host the Games in 1944 due to the War, Cortina d'Ampezzo, Italy, was selected to organize the 1956 Winter Olympics. At the opening ceremonies the final torch bearer, Guido Caroli, entered the Olympic Stadium on ice skates. As he skated around the stadium rink his skate caught on a cable and he fell, nearly extinguishing the flame. He was able to recover and lit the cauldron. These were the first Winter Games to be televised, though no television rights would be sold until the 1960 Summer Olympics in Rome. The Cortina Games were used as an experiment on the feasibility of televising sporting events on such a large scale. These Games marked the debut of the Soviet Union at the Winter Olympics. The Soviet team won more medals than any other nation. The IOC awarded the 1960 Olympics to Squaw Valley, United States. Since the village was underdeveloped, there was a rush to construct roads, hotels, restaurants, and bridges, as well as the ice arena, the speed skating track, ski lifts, and the ski jump hill. The opening and closing ceremonies were produced by Walt Disney. These Games were the first to have a dedicated athlete's village, and the first to use a computer (courtesy of IBM) to tabulate results. The bobsled events were absent for the first and only time because the organizing committee found it too expensive. Women first took part in speed skating at these Games.

1964 to 1980

The Tyrolean city of Innsbruck was the host in 1964. Despite being a traditional winter sports resort, warm weather caused a lack of snow during the Games and the Austrian army was called in to bring snow and ice to the sport venues. Soviet speed skating star Lidia Skoblikova made history by sweeping all four speed skating events. Her career total of six gold medals set a record for the most medals by a Winter Olympics athlete. Luge was first contested in these Olympics, although the sport received bad publicity when a competitor was killed in a pre-Olympic training run.

Held in the French town of Grenoble, the 1968 Winter Olympics was the first Olympic Games to be broadcast in colour. Frenchman Jean-Claude Killy became only the second person to sweep all the men's alpine skiing events. The effects of television began to show at the Grenoble Games. The organizing committee sold the television rights for $2 million, a significant increase over the price of the broadcast rights for the Innsbruck Games, which totalled $936,667. Venues were spread over long distances requiring three athletes' villages at these Games. The organizers claimed this was required to accommodate technological advances. Critics disputed this, alleging the layout was necessary to provide the best possible venues for television broadcasts at the expense of the athletes.

The 1972 Winter Games, held in Sapporo, Japan, were the first to be hosted outside North America or Europe. The issue of professionalism became very contentious during these Games. Three days before the Olympics, IOC president Avery Brundage threatened to bar a large number of alpine skiers from competing because they participated in a ski camp at Mammoth Mountain in the United States. Brundage reasoned that the skiers had financially benefited from their status as athletes and were therefore no longer amateurs. Eventually, only Austrian Karl Schranz, who earned more than all the other skiers, was not allowed to compete. Canada did not send teams to the 1972 or 1976 ice hockey tournaments in protest of their inability to use players from professional leagues. Francisco Ochoa became the only Spaniard to ever win a Winter Olympic gold medal, when he triumphed in the slalom.

Originally, the 1976 Winter Games had been awarded to Denver, United States, but in 1972 the voters of Colorado expressed unwillingness to host the Games through a state referendum. Innsbruck, which still had maintained the infrastructure from the 1964 Games, was chosen in 1973 to replace Denver. Two Olympic flames were lit because it was the second time the Austrian town had hosted the Games. The 1976 Games also featured the first combination bobsled and luge track in neighbouring Igls. The Soviet Union won its fourth straight ice hockey gold medal at these Games.

The Olympic Winter Games returned to Lake Placid, which had hosted the 1932 Games. The threat of a boycott of the 1980 Summer Olympics clouded these Olympics, due to the fact that much of the debate regarding this eventuality took place during the Winter Games. American Speed skater Eric Heiden set either an Olympic or world record winning each of the five events he competed in. Hanni Wenzel won both the Slalom and Giant Slalom. Her country, Liechtenstein, became the smallest nation to produce an Olympic gold medallist. In the "Miracle on Ice", the American hockey team beat the favoured Soviets and went on to win the gold medal.

1984 to 1998

The cities of Sapporo, Japan, and Gotheburg, Sweden, were front-runners to host the 1984 Winter Olympics. It was therefore a surprise when Sarajevo, Yugoslavia was chosen to host the Games. The Games were well-organized and displayed no indication of the war that would soon engulf the country.

Yugoslavia also won its first Olympic medal when alpine skier Jure Franko won a silver medal in the giant slalom. Another sporting highlight was the free dance performance of British ice dancers Jayne Torvill and Christopher Dean. Their performance to Ravel's Bolero earned the pair unanimous perfect scores in artistic impression, and the gold medal. The Republic of China boycotted the 1980 Olympics due to a conflict with China over the use of the name "Republic of China". They returned to the 1984 Games after an agreement was reached that the athletes would compete under the new name "Chinese Taipei", and use a special flag and national anthem. In 1988 the Canadian city of Calgary, hosted the first Winter Olympics to span 16 days. New events were added in ski jumping and speed skating, while future Olympic sports curling, short track speed skating and freestyle skiing made their appearance as demonstration sports. For the first time, the speed skating events were held indoors, on the Olympic Oval.

Dutch skater Yvonne van Gennip won three gold medals, and set two work records, in speed skating, beating the skaters from the favoured East German team in every race. Her total was equalled by Finnish ski jumper Matti Nykänen, who won all the events in his sport.

Alberto Tomba, an Italian skier made his Olympic debut at these Games winning both the Giant Slalom and Slalom. East German Christa Rothenburger won the women's 1000 metre speed skating event. Seven months later, she would earn a silver in track cycling at the Summer Games in Seoul. She became the first and only athlete to win medals in both a Summer and Winter Olympics in the same year.

The 1992 Games were the last to be held in the same year as the Summer Games. They were hosted in the French Savoie region. The town of Albertville was the host city though only 18 events were competed in the city. The rest of the events were spread out over the Savoie. Political changes of the time were reflected in the Olympic teams appearing in France. This was the first Games to be held after the fall of Communism and the dismantling of the Berlin Wall. Germany competed as a single nation for the first time since the 1964 Games, and former Yugoslavian republics Croatia and Slovenia made their debut. Most of former Soviet republics still competed as a single team known as the Unified Team, but the Baltic States made independent appearances for the first time since before World War II. At 16 years old, Finnish ski jumper Toni Nieminen made history by becoming the youngest male/Winter Olympic champion. New Zealand skier Annelise Coberger became the first Winter Olympic medallist from the southern hemisphere when she won a silver medal in the women's slalom. In 1986, the IOC voted to separate the Summer and Winter Games and place them in alternating even-numbered years starting in 1994.

The Lillehammer Games were the first Winter Olympics to be held without the Summer Games in the same year. After the division of Czechoslovakia in 1993, the Czech Republic and Slovakia made their Olympic debut in Lillehammer, Norway. The women's figure skating competition garnered significant media attention. American skater Nancy Kerrigan had been injured on January 6 in an assault planned by the ex-husband of opponent Tonya Harding. Both skaters competed in the Games, but neither of them won the gold medal, which went to Oksana Baiul, who won Ukraine's first Olympic title.

The 1998 Winter Olympics was the first Games to host more than 2,000 athletes. The Games were held in the Japanese city of Nagano. The men's ice hockey tournament was open to all professionals for the first time. Canada and the United States, with their many NHL players, were favoured for the gold. However, neither nation won any medals, as the Czech Republic prevailed. Women's ice hockey made its debut at these Games, with the United States winning the gold medal. Bjørn Dæhlie of Norway won three gold medals in Nordic skiing. He became the most decorated Winter Olympic athlete with eight gold medals and twelve medals overall. Austrian Hermann Maier survived a crash during the downhill competition and returned to win gold in the Super-G and the Giant Slalom A wave of new world records were set in speed skating due to the use of the clap skate.

2002 to Present

The 19th Olympic Winter Games were held in Salt Lake City, United States. German Georg Hackl won a silver in the singles luge, becoming the first athlete in Olympic history to medal in the same individual event in five consecutive Olympics. Canada achieved an unprecedented double by winning both the men's and women's Ice Hockey gold medals. Canada became embroiled with Russia in a controversy that involved the judging of the pairs figure skating competition. The Russian pair of Yelena Berezhnaya and Anton Sikharulidze competed against the Canadian pair of Jamie Sale and David Pelletier for the gold medal.

The Canadians appeared to have skated well enough to win the competition, yet the Russians were awarded the gold. The judging broke along Cold War lines with the exception of the French judge, Marie-Reine Le Gougne, who awarded the gold to the Russians. An investigation revealed that she had been pressured to give the gold to the Russian pair regardless of how they skated; in return the Russian judge would look favourably on the French entrants in the ice dancing competition. The IOC decided to award both pairs the gold medal in a second medal ceremony held later in the Games. Australian Steven Bradbury became the first gold medallist from the Southern Hemisphere when he won the 1,000 metre short-track speed skating event.

The Italian city of Turin hosted the 2006 Winter Olympics. It was the second time that Italy held the Winter Olympic Games. South Korean athletes dominated the short-track speed skating events at these Games. Sun-Yu Jin won three gold medals while her teammate Hyun-Soo Ahn won three gold medals and a bronze. In the women's Cross-Country team pursuit Canadian Sara Renner broke one of her poles.

When he saw her dilemma, Norwegian coach Bjørnar Håkensmoen decided to lend her a pole. In so doing she was able to help her team win a silver medal in the event. Norway finished fourth. Duff Gibson of Canada became the oldest athlete to win a Winter Olympic gold medal in an individual event. He won the skeleton event at 39 years of age.

Future

In 2003 the IOC awarded the 2010 Winter Olympics to Vancouver, thus allowing Canada to host its second Winter Olympics. With a population of more than 2.5 million people, Vancouver will be the largest metropolitan area to ever host a Winter Olympic Games. Vancouver is a low-altitude, seaport city with a relatively mild oceanic climate. Most of the venues will be located in the Vancouver metropolitan area, with the exception of the alpine, nordic, and sliding events, which will be held in Whistler.

The decision for the location of the 2014 Winter Olympics was made on 4 July 2007. Sochi, Russia, was elected as the host city over the other two finalists: Salzburg, Austria, and Pyeongchang, South Korea. Sochi will be the first city with a subtropical climate to host the Winter Games. The Olympic Village and Olympic Stadium will be located on the Black Sea coast. All of the mountain venues will be 50 kilometres (30 mi) away in the alpine region known as Krasnaya Polyana.

Commercialization

As president of the IOC from 1952 to 1972, Avery Brundage rejected all attempts to link the Olympics with commercial interests. He felt that the Olympic movement should be completely separate from financial influence. The 1960 Winter Olympics marked the beginning of corporate sponsorship of the Games. Brundage saw this as an unwelcome development. He resisted any efforts to commercialize the Games, but as the decade of the 1960s continued the revenue generated by corporate sponsorship swelled.

By the Grenoble Games, Brundage had become so concerned about the direction of the Winter Olympic Games towards commercialization that if they could not be corrected, then he felt the Winter Olympics should be abolished. Brundage's resistance to this revenue stream meant the IOC was slow to seek a share of the financial windfall that was coming to host cities, and also slow to control how sponsorship deals would be structured. When Brundage retired, the IOC had $2 million in assets, eight years later the IOC coffers had swelled to $45 million.

This was primarily due to a shift in ideology among IOC members toward expansion of the Games through corporate sponsorship and the sale of television rights. Brundage's concerns did prove to be prophetic to a degree. The power and influence of the television lobby has expanded as the cost of the broadcast rights for each successive Games has increased. At the 1998 Nagano Games, CBS paid $375 million, whereas the 2006 Turin Games cost NBC $613 million to broadcast. The more television companies have paid the greater their persuasive power with the IOC has been. For example, the television lobby has influenced the Olympic programme by dictating when event finals were held so that they would appear in prime time for television audiences.

In 1986, the IOC decided to stagger the Summer and Winter Games on separate years. Instead of holding both Games in the same calendar year, it was decided to alternate them every two years. Both Games would still be held on four-year cycles. The rationale given by the IOC for this change was in order to give more prominence to the Winter Olympic Games. It was decided that 1992 would be the last year to have both a Winter and Summer Olympic Games.

There were two groups pushing for this change. One was the television lobby, who had applied pressure to reschedule the Games due to the difficulty in raising advertising revenue for two Games in the same year. Television studios would now be able to emphasize story-lines and generate interest for each separate Games, thereby maximizing viewership and consequently profit. The second was the IOC's desire to gain more control over the revenue generated by the Games. The financial success of the 1984 Summer Olympics, which created a surplus of $227 million, exposed the importance of maximizing television rights and corporate sponsorships.

The IOC also realized that under the current structure they had little access to the corporate sponsorship funds raised by individual host cities. They determined that by staggering the Games, corporations would be more likely to sponsor individual Olympic Games thereby maximizing revenue potential. The IOC also sought to directly organize sponsorship contracts so that they had more control over the Olympic "brand". The first Winter Olympics to be hosted in this new format was the 1994 Games in Lillehammer.

Controversy

The Winter Olympics have not been immune to improprieties. Two of the more recent controversies occurred around the 2002 Winter Olympics. The first happened prior to the Games. After Salt Lake City had been awarded the right to host the 2002 Games it was discovered that the organizers had engaged in an elaborate scheme to bribe IOC officials in order to win favour and ultimately the bid to host the Games. Gifts and other financial considerations were given to IOC officials.

These gifts included medical treatment for relatives, a college scholarship for one member's son, and a land deal in Utah. Even IOC president Juan Antonio Samaranch received two rifles valued at $2,000. Samaranch defended the gift as inconsequential since as president he was a non-voting member. He also indicated that the rifles would go on display at the Olympic museum. The subsequent investigation resulted in the expulsion of ten members of the IOC and the sanctioning of another ten.

It also uncovered improprieties in the bids for every Games (both summer and winter) since 1988. It was discovered, for example, that the gifts received by IOC members from the Japanese Organizing Committee in exchange for their support of the bid for the 1998 Winter Olympics were described as "astronomical". Although nothing strictly illegal had been done, the fear was that corporate sponsors would lose faith in the integrity of the IOC, and that the Olympic brand would be tarnished to such an extent that advertisers would begin to pull their support. Stricter rules were adopted for future bids and ceilings were put into place as to how much IOC members could accept from bid cities. Additionally new term and age limits were established for IOC membership, and fifteen former Olympic athletes were added to the committee.

Steroids

In 1967 the IOC began enacting drug testing protocols. They started randomly testing athletes at the 1968 Winter Olympics. The first Winter Games athlete to test positive for a banned substance was Alois Schloder, a West German hockey player who had ephedrine in his system. He was disqualified from the rest of the tournament but his team was still allowed to compete. During the 1970s, testing out of competition was escalated and found to be a useful deterrent to athletes. The problem with testing during this time was a lack of standardization of test procedures, which undermined the credibility of the test process.

It was not until the late 1980s that international sporting federations, of which the IOC was a member, began to coordinate efforts to standardize the drug testing protocols. The IOC decided to take a leadership role in the fight against steroids when they established an independent World Anti-Doping Agency (WADA) in November 1999. The 2006 Winter Olympics in Turin, became notable for a scandal involving the emerging trend of blood doping, which is the use of blood transfusions or synthetic hormones like Erythropoietin (EPO), to improve oxygen flow in order to reduce fatigue.

The Italian police conducted a raid during the Games on the Austrian cross-country ski team's residence. They seized blood doping specimens and equipment. This event followed the pre-Olympics suspension of 12 cross-country skiers who tested positive for unusually high levels of hemoglobin, which is evidence of blood doping. This particular method of cheating has been used by cross-country athletes before. At the 2002 Games three skiers were stripped of their medals after they tested positive for blood doping.

Politics

Cold War

The Winter Olympics have been an ideological front in the Cold War since the Soviet Union first participated at the 1956 Winter Games. It did not take long for the Cold War combatants to discover what a powerful propaganda tool the Olympic Games could be. Soviet and American politicians used the Olympics, and other international sporting events, as an opportunity to prove the advantages of their respective political systems. The successful Soviet athlete was feted and honoured. Irina Rodnina, three-time Olympic gold medallist in figure skating, was awarded the Order of Lenin after her victory at the 1976 Winter Olympics in Innsbruck. With the award would come monetary compensation anywhere from $4,000–$8,000 depending on the prestige of the sport. A world record was worth $1,500. The United States responded to the propaganda pressure of the Soviet Union. In 1978, the U.S. Congress passed legislation completely reorganizing the United States Olympic Committee (USOC). This sort of political intrusion in a sports federation was unheard of in a democratic country. It was a direct response to the increasing international profile that television gave to the Olympic Games. The USOC also pays its athletes for Olympic medals won: $25,000 for gold, $15,000 for silver and $10,000 for bronze. Multiple medals garner multiple amounts of money.

The Cold War also created tensions among countries allied to the two super powers. A particularly thorny issue for the IOC to navigate was the question of how to recognize both East and West Germany. Germany was not allowed to compete at the 1948 Winter Olympics. In 1950, the IOC recognized the West German Olympic Committee. It was a West German team who represented Germany at the 1952 Winter Olympics in Oslo.

The East Germans were invited to cooperate as a unified team in 1952 but they declined this offer. In 1955 the Soviet Union recognized East Germany as a sovereign state, thereby giving more credibility to East Germany's campaign to become an independent participant at the Olympics. The IOC agreed to provisionally accept the East German National Olympic Committee with the condition that they compete as a unified team with the West Germans. This was done because the West Germans had adopted the Hallstein Doctrine, which forbade West Germany from entering into diplomatic relations with any country that recognized East Germany. The situation became tenuous when the Berlin Wall was constructed in 1962. Many western countries, including France and the United States, refused visas to East German athletes competing in world championships in their countries. The uneasy compromise of a unified team held until the Grenoble Games of 1968 when the IOC officially split both teams and threatened to reject the host city bids of any country that refused entry visas to East German athletes.

Boycott

While their Summer counterpart has experienced several boycotts, the Winter Games have had only one national team boycott. Taiwan decided to boycott the 1980 Winter Olympics held in Lake Placid. The reason for the boycott was due to the fact that the IOC had agreed to allow China to compete in the Olympics for the first time since 1952. They were allowed to compete as the People's Republic of China and to use the Chinese flag and anthem. Until 1980, the island of Taiwan had been competing under the name Republic of China and had been using the Chinese flag and anthem. As part of their decision, the IOC demanded that Taiwan cease to call itself the "Republic of China". Instead the IOC renamed it Chinese Taipei and forced it to adopt a different flag and national anthem. The IOC initially attempted to have the countries compete together, but this proved to be unacceptable. Taiwan would not concede to the IOC's demand that it be renamed and use different national symbols. Despite numerous appeals and court hearings the IOC's decision stood. When the Taiwanese athletes arrived at the Olympic village with their Republic of China identification cards they were not admitted. They subsequently left the Olympics in protest just before the opening ceremonies.

Sports

Chapter 1, article 6 of the 2007 edition of the Olympic Charter defines winter sports as "sports which are practised on snow or ice." Through the years, the number of sports and events conducted at the Winter Olympic Games has increased. There have also been Demonstration sports, which are contests held but for which no medals are awarded.

Discontinued Sports or Disciplines

- Military patrol, a precursor to the biathlon, was a medal sport in 1924. It was also demonstrated in 1928, 1936 and 1948, and in 1960 biathlon became an official sport.
- The special figures figure skating event was only contested at the 1908 Summer Olympics.

Demonstration Events

- Bandy, a sport described as ice hockey with a ball, very popular in the Nordic countries, was demonstrated at the Oslo Games.

- Ice stock sport, a German variant to curling, was demonstrated in 1936 in Germany and in 1964 in Austria.
- The ski ballet event, later known as ski-acro, was demonstrated in 1988 and 1992. The sport has significantly declined in popularity in recent years. The International Ski Federation ceased all formal competition of this sport after 2000.
- Skijöring, skiing behind dogs, was a demonstration sport in St. Moritz in 1928.

Current Sport Disciplines

Sport	*Years*	*# of events*	*Medal events scheduled for 2010*
Alpine skiing	Since 1936	10	Men's and women's downhill, super giant slalom, giant slalom, and Alpine combined.
Biathlon	Since 1960	10	The Sprint (men: 10 km; women: 7.5 km), the individual (men: 20 km; women: 15 km), the pursuit (men: 12.5 km; women: 10 km), the relay (men: 4x7.5 km; women: 4x6 km), and the mass start (men: 15 km; women: 12.5 km).
Bobsled	1924–1956		
	1964–present	3	Four-man race, two-man race and two-woman race. Cross-country skiing Since 1924 12 Men's sprint, team sprint, 30 km pursuit, 15 km, 50 km and 4x10 km relay; women's sprint, team sprint, 15 km pursuit, 10 km, 30 km (women) and 4x5 km relay.
Curling	1924		
	1998–present	2	Men's and women's tournaments.
Figure skating	Since 1924	4	Men's and women's singles; pairs; and ice dancing.
Freestyle skiing	Since 1992	6	Men's and women's moguls, aerials and skicross.

Sport	*Years*	*# of events*	*Medal events scheduled for 2010*
Ice hockey	Since 1924	2	Men's and women's tournaments.
Luge	Since 1964	3	Men's and women's singles, men's doubles.
Nordic combined	Since 1924	3	Men's 10 km individual normal hill, 10 km individual large hill and team.
Short track speed skating	Since 1992	8	Men's and women's 500 metres, 1000 metres, 1500 metres; women's 3000 metre relay; and men's 5000 metre relay.
Skeleton	1924; 1948 Since 2002	2	Men's and women's events.
Ski jumping	Since 1924	3	Men's individual large hill, individual small hill and team large hill.
Snowboarding	Since 1998	6	Men's and women's parallel giant slalom, half-pipe and snowboard cross.
Speed skating	Since 1924	12	Men's and women's 500 metres, 1000 metres, 1500 metres, 5000 metres and team pursuit; women's 3000 metres; men's 10000 metres.

Note 1. Figure skating events were also held at the 1908 and 1920 Summer Olympics.

Note 2. A men's ice hockey tournament was also held at the 1920 Summer Olympics.

- Sled-dog racing contests were displayed at Lake Placid in 1932.
- Speed skiing was demonstrated in Albertville at the 1992 Winter Olympics.
- Winter pentathlon, a variant to the modern pentathlon, was included as a demonstration event at the 1948 Games in Switzerland. It was composed of cross country skiing, shooting, downhill skiing, fencing, and horse riding.

List of Games

Note: Unlike the Summer Olympics, the cancelled 1940 Winter Olympics and 1944 Winter Olympics are *not* included in the official Roman numeral counts for the Winter Games. While the official titles of the Summer Games actually count Olympiads (which occur even if the Games do not), the official titles of the Winter Games only count the Games themselves.

Games	*Year*	*Host*	*Dates*	*Nations*	*Competitors*			*Sports*	*Events*
					Total	*Men*	*Women*		
I	1924	Chamonix, France	25 Jan. 5 Feb.	16	258	247	11	6	16
II	1928	St. Moritz, Switzerland	11-19 Feb.	25	464	438	26	4	14
III	1932	Lake Placid, US	4-15 Feb.	17	252	231	21	4	14
IV	1936	Garmisch Partenkirchen, Germany	6-16 Feb.	28	646	566	80	4	17
	1940	*Originally awarded to Sapporo, Japan, cancelled because of World War II.*							
	1944	*Originally awarded to Cortina d'Ampezzo, Italy, cancelled because of World War II.*							
V	1948	St. Moritz, Switzerland	30 Jan. 8 Feb.	28	669	592	77	4	22
VI	1952	Oslo, Norway	14-25 Feb.	30	694	585	109	4	22
VII	1956	Cortina d' Ampezzo, Italy	26 Jan. 5 Feb.	32	821	687	134	4	24
VIII	1960	Squaw Valley, US	18-28 Feb. 30	665	521	144	4	27	
IX	1964	Innsbruck, Austria	29 Jan. 9 Feb.	36	1091	892	199	6	34
X	1968	Grenoble, France	6-18 Feb.	37	1158	947	211	6	35
XI	1972	Sapporo, Japan	3-13 Feb.	35	1006	801	205	6	35

Games	*Year*	*Host*	*Dates*	*Nations*	*Competitors*			*Sports*	*Events*
					Total	*Men*	*Women*		
XII	1976	Innsbruck, Austria	4-15 Feb.	37	1123	892	231	6	37
XIII	1980	Lake Placid, US	13-24 Feb.	37	1072	840	232	6	38
XIV	1984	Sarajevo, Yugoslavia	8-19 Feb.	49	1272	998	274	6	39
XV	1988	Calgary, Canada	13-28 Feb.	57	1423	1122	301	6	46
XVI	1992	Albertville, France	8-23 Feb.	64	1801	1313	488	7	57
XVII	1994	Lillehammer Norway	12-27 Feb.	67	1737	1215	522	6	61
XVIII	1998	Nagano, Japan	7-22 Feb.	72	2176	1389	787	7	68
XIX	2002	Salt Lake City, US	8-24 Feb.	77	2399	1513	886	7	78
XX	2006	Turin, Italy	10-26 Feb.	80	2508	1548	960	7	84
XXI	*2010*	*Vancouver, Canada*	*12-28 Feb.*	*future event*					
XXII	*2014*	*Sochi, Russia*	*7-23 Feb.*	*future event*					
XXIII	*2018*	*TBD* (2011)	*TBD*	*future event*					
XXIV	*2022*	*TBD* (2015)	*TBD*	*future event*					

Youth Olympic Games

The Youth Olympic Games (YOG) are planned to be an international multisport event held every four years in staggered summer and winter events complementing the current Olympic Games, and will feature athletes between the ages of 14 and 18.

The idea for such an event was envisioned in 2001 by International Olympic Committee (IOC) president Jacques Rogge. On July 6, 2007,

IOC members at the 119th IOC session in Guatemala City approved the creation of a youth version of the Olympic Games. The summer version will last at most twelve days, with the first edition taking place in mid-summer of 2010; the winter version will last a maximum of nine days, with the first edition taking place in early 2012. The IOC will allow a maximum of 3,500 athletes and 875 officials to participate at the summer games, while 970 athletes and 580 officials are expected at the winter games.

Several other Olympic events for youth, like the European Youth Olympic Festival held every other year with summer and winter versions, and the Australian Youth Olympic Festival, have proven successful; the Youth Games would most likely be modelled after these. The YOG are a successor to the discontinued World Youth Games.

Requirements of Host Cities

It has been stressed that the host city should not have to build any major venues, with the exception of some temporary structures or possibly an Olympic village. Also, all competitions must be held in the host city, ruling out any joint bids. According to bid procedures, the track and field stadium for the opening and closing ceremonies must hold 10,000 people, and a city must have a 2,500-seat aquatics facility (for Summer editions).

Education and culture are also key components for this Youth edition. Not only does the education/culture aspect apply to athletes and participants, but also youth around the world and inhabitants of the host city and surrounding regions. Multi-lingual, multi-cultural, and multi-age requirements are the targets of the program which stress the themes of "Learning to know, learning to be, learning to do, and learning to live together."

Each participating country would send at least four athletes. 170 countries are expected to participate in the 2010 Youth Summer Olympics. (There are over 200 National Olympic Committees, most of which participate at the regular Games). Participants will be grouped by age, for example, 14–15 years, and 16–18 years. One source indicates athletes will be chosen at least 18 months in advance, which suggests that some could be chosen as young as age 12. Other reports indicates the qualifications (which guidelines are being set in autumn of 2008) will occur between December 2009 and May 2010. At least one IOC member criticized the plan, noting that smaller teams from all countries may fail to capture the interest of the media, nations, and the athletes themselves.

Financing

Estimated costs are currently $30 million for the summer and $15 million-$20 million for winter games, primarily on infrastructure and lodging. The IOC will pay travel costs to the host city and room and board for the athletes and judges, estimated costs at $11 million. The funding will come from IOC funds and not revenues. The budgets for the final two bids for the inaugural Summer Games came in at $75 million (Singapore) and $175 million (Moscow), much higher than the estimated costs. Bids with lower budgets were eliminated early in the process. Budgets for the inaugural Winter Games were more in line, with a range of $22 million for Innsbruck and $14 million for Kuopio. It has been stated the IOC will "foot the bill" for the Youth Games, but whether or not they will pay the first $15–30 million is as of yet unclear.

Differences from the Main Olympic Games

The sports contested at these games will be the same as those scheduled for the traditional Games, but with a limited number of disciplines and events. Of the 26 sports, the IOC plans, for example, not to include the water polo and synchronized swimming disciplines of aquatics, as well as the slalom discipline of canoeing on the schedule of events.

The basketball competition may be "streetball," in which games are held outside and sometimes with fewer players. The cycling disciplines are mountain bike and BMX, and road and track cycling were left off the schedule. Baseball and Softball were also not included on the list of sports. Other youth-driven sports may eventually be contested if backed by international sports federations. In November 2007, it was revealed that pentathlon will be included, as well as sailing, giving an edge to candidate cities near water. The Winter edition will contest seven sports. Luge and bobsled are possible casualties considering the small number of worldwide venues and restrictions in building new venues. In the bidding for the first edition, one bid city was nevertheless planning to construct a bobsled/sleigh run, while another was not offering bobsled as an event. Another difference is that no national flags or anthems will be utilized. During medal ceremonies, only the Olympic flag and the Olympic anthem will be seen and heard in order to deemphasize international competition.

List of Youth Olympic Games

In early November 2007, Athens, Bangkok, Singapore, Moscow, and Turin were selected by the IOC as the five candidate cities among which the host city will be elected for the Inaugural Games. In January 2008, the candidates were further pared down to just Moscow and Singapore. Finally, on 21 February 2008, Singapore was declared host of the inaugural Youth Olympic Games 2010 via live telecast from Lausanne, Switzerland, winning by a tally of 53 votes to 44 for Moscow. Singapore is contesting all 26 sports.

On 2 September 2008 IOC announced that the IOC executive board had shortlisted four cities among the candidates to host the first Winter Youth Olympic Games in 2012. The four candidate cities were Harbin in China, Innsbruck in Austria, Kuopio in Finland and Lillehammer in Norway. IOC president Jacques Rogge appointed Pernilla Wiberg to chair the commission which analysed the projects. As with the Summer Games, the list was then shortened to two finalists, Innsbruck and Kuopio, in November 2008. On December 12, 2008, it was announced that Innsbruck beat Kuopio to host the games.

List of Summer Youth Olympic Games

Year	*Olympiad*	*Games*	*Location*
2010	XXIX	1st Summer Youth Olympic Games	Singapore
2014	XXX	2nd Summer Youth Olympic Games	TBA
2018	XXXI	3rd Summer Youth Olympic Games	TBA

List of Winter Youth Olympic Games

Year	*Olympiad*	*Games*	*Location*
2012	XXIX	1st Winter Youth Olympic Games	Innsbruck
2016	XXX	2nd Winter Youth Olympic Games	TBA

Commonwealth Games

The Commonwealth Games is a multinational, multisport event. Held every four years, it involves the elite athletes of the Commonwealth of Nations. Attendance at the Commonwealth Games is typically around 5,000 athletes. The Commonwealth Games Federation (CGF) is the organisation that is responsible for the direction and control of the Commonwealth Games.

The first such event, then known as the British Empire Games, was held in 1930 in Hamilton, Ontario, Canada. The name changed to British Empire and Commonwealth Games in 1954, to British Commonwealth Games in 1970 and assumed the current name of the Commonwealth Games in 1978.

As well as many Olympic sports, the Games also include some sports that are played mainly in Commonwealth countries, such as lawn bowls, rugby sevens and netball.

There are currently 53 members of the Commonwealth of Nations, and 71 teams participate in the Games. The four constituent countries of the United Kingdom-England, Scotland, Wales and Northern Ireland-send separate teams to the Commonwealth Games (unlike at the Olympic Games, where the United Kingdom sends a single team), and individual teams are also sent from the British Crown dependencies-Guernsey, Jersey and the Isle of Man-and many of the British overseas territories. The Australian external territory of Norfolk Island also sends its own team, as do the Cook Islands and Niue, two states in free association with New Zealand. Only six teams have attended every Commonwealth Games: Australia, Canada, England, New Zealand, Scotland and Wales. Australia has been the highest scoring team for ten games, England for seven and Canada for one. At the 1930 games, women competed in the Swimming events only. From 1934, women also competed in some Athletics events.

The next edition will be held in 2010 in Delhi, India. The nineteenth edition of Commonwealth Games will be held from October 3-14, 2010. The opening and closing ceremony is scheduled to take place at the Jawaharlal Nehru Stadium. In 2014 the Games will be held in Glasgow, Scotland.

Origins

A sporting competition bringing together the members of the British Empire was first proposed by the Reverend Astley Cooper in 1891 when he wrote an article in *The Times* suggesting a "Pan-Britannic-Pan-Anglican Contest and Festival every four years as a means of increasing the goodwill and good understanding of the British Empire".

In 1911, the Festival of the Empire was held in London to celebrate the coronation of King George V. As part of the festival an Inter-Empire Championships was held in which teams from Australia, Canada, South Africa and the United Kingdom competed in events such as boxing, wrestling, swimming and athletics.

In 1928, Melville Marks Robinson of Canada was asked to organise the first ever British Empire Games. These were held in Hamilton, Ontario two years later.

Opening Ceremony Traditions

- From 1930 through 1950, the parade of nations was led by a single flagbearer carrying the Union Flag, symbolising Britain's leading role in the British Empire.
- Since 1958, there has been a relay of athletes carrying a baton from Buckingham Palace to the Opening Ceremony. This baton has within it the Queen's Message of Greeting to the athletes. The baton's final bearer is usually a famous sporting personage of the host nation.
- All other nations march in English alphabetical order, except that the first nation marching in the Parade of Athletes is the host nation of the previous games, and the host nation of the current games marches last. In 2006 countries marched in alphabetical order in geographical regions.
- Three national flags fly from the stadium on the poles that are used for medal ceremonies: Previous host nation, Current host nation, Next host nation.
- The military is more active in the Opening Ceremony than in the Olympic Games. This is to honour the British Military traditions of the Old Empire.

Boycotts

The Commonwealth Games, like the Olympic Games, has also suffered from political boycotts. Nigeria boycotted the 1978 Games in protest of New Zealand's sporting contacts with apartheid-era South Africa, and 32 of 59 nations from Africa, Asia, and the Caribbean boycotted the 1986 Commonwealth Games due to the Thatcher government's attitude towards South African sporting contacts. Boycotts were also threatened in 1974, 1982, and 1990 because of South Africa.

Editions

British Empire Games

- 1930 games-Hamilton, Ontario, Canada.
- 1934 games-London, England, United Kingdom.
- 1938 games-Sydney, New South Wales, Australia.
- 1950 games-Auckland, New Zealand.

British Empire and Commonwealth Games

- 1954 games-Vancouver, British Columbia, Canada.
- 1958 games-Cardiff, Wales, United Kingdom.
- 1962 games-Perth, Western Australia, Australia.
- 1966 games-Kingston, Jamaica.

British Commonwealth Games

- 1970 games-Edinburgh, Scotland, United Kingdom.
- 1974 games-Christchurch, New Zealand.

Commonwealth Games

- 1978 games-Edmonton, Alberta, Canada.
- 1982 games-Brisbane, Queensland, Australia.
- 1986 games-Edinburgh, Scotland, United Kingdom.
- 1990 games-Auckland, New Zealand.
- 1994 games-Victoria, British Columbia, Canada.
- 1998 games-Kuala Lumpur, Malaysia.
- 2002 games-Manchester, England, United Kingdom.
- 2006 games-Melbourne, Victoria, Australia.

- 2010 games-Delhi, India.
- 2014 games-Glasgow, Scotland, United Kingdom.
- 2018 games-To Be Determined by 2011.

Numbers of Athletes, Sports, and Nations

This list shows the total number of athletes, male and female, the number of sports they were selected to compete in, and the number of nations (including dependencies) competing.

This list is incomplete; you can help by expanding it.

Year	*Athletes*	*Male*	*Female*	*Sports*	*Events*	*Officials*	*Nations*
2006	4500			16[2]	247		71
2002	3863			17[3]			72
1998	3638			15			70
1994	2669			12			63
1990	2073			10	205		55
1986	1660			10	165		27
1982	1580			12	143		45
1978	1475			11	126		47
1974	1276	977	299	10	121	372	38
1970	1744[1]			10	121		42
1966	1316[1]			10	110		34
1962	863			9		178	35
1958	1122			9		228	35
1954	662			9		127	24
1950	590	495	95	9			12
1938	464			7		43	15
1934	500			6			17
1930	400			6			11

Total including athletes and officials. Includes 4 team sports. Includes 3 team sports.

Approved Sports

There are a total of 31 sports (with two multi-disciplinary sports) and a further 7 para-sports which are approved by the Commonwealth

Games Federation. They are categorised into three types. Core sports must be included on each programme.

A number of optional sports may be picked by the host nation, which may include some team sports such as basketball. Recognised sports are sports which have been approved by the CGF but which are deemed to need expansion; host nations may not pick these sports for their programme until the CGF's requirements are fulfilled.

Sport	*Type*	*Years*
Archery	Optional	1982, *2010*
Athletics	Core	1930–present
Badminton	Core	1966–present
Basketball	Optional	2006
Billiards	Recognised	Never
Boxing	Core	1930–present
Canoeing	Recognised	Never
Cycling	Optional	1934–present
Diving	Optional	1930–present
Fencing	Recognised	1950–1970
Golf	Recognised	Never
Gymnastics (Artistic and Rhythmic)	Optional	1978, 1990–present
Handball	Recognised	Never
Field Hockey	Core	1998–present
Judo	Optional	1990, 2002, *2014*
Lawn bowls	Core	1930–present (except 1966)
Life saving	Recognised	Never
Netball	Core	1998–present
Rowing	Recognised	1930, 1938–62, 1986
Rugby sevens	Core	1998–present
Sailing	Recognised	Never
Shooting	Optional	1966, 1974–present
Softball	Recognised	Never
Squash	Core	1998–present

Sport	*Type*	*Years*
Swimming	Core	1930–present
Synchronized swimming	Optional	1986, 2006
Table tennis	Optional	2002–present
Tennis	Optional	*2010*
Tenpin bowling	Recognised	1998
Triathlon	Optional	2002, 2006, *2014*
Volleyball	Recognised	Never
Water polo	Recognised	1950
Weightlifting	Core	1950–present
Wrestling	Optional	1930–present (Except 1990 and 1998)

List of Nations/Dependencies to Competed

Nations/Dependencies that have Competed

- Aden 1962,
- Anguilla 1982, 1998,
- Antigua and Barbuda 1966-1970, 1978, 1994,
- Australia 1930,
- Bahamas 1954-1970, 1978-1982, 1990,
- Bangladesh 1978, 1990,
- Barbados 1954-1966, 1970-1982, 1990,
- Belize 1978, 1994,
- Bermuda 1930-1938, 1954-1982, 1990,
- Botswana 1974, 1982,
- British Guiana 1930-1938, 1954-1962,
- British Honduras 1962-1966,
- British Virgin Islands 1990,
- Brunei Darussalam 1958, 1990,
- Cameroon 1998,
- Canada 1930,
- Cayman Islands 1978,

- Ceylon 1938-1950, 1958-1970,
- Cook Islands 1974-1978, 1986,
- Cyprus 1978-1982, 1990,
- Dominica 1958-1962, 1970, 1994,
- England 1930,
- Falkland Islands 1982,
- Fiji 1938, 1954-1986, 1998-2006,
- The Gambia 1970-1982, 1990,
- Ghana 1958-1982, 1990,
- Gibraltar 1958,
- Gold Coast 1954,
- Grenada 1970-1974, 1994,
- Guernsey 1970,
- Guyana 1966-1970, 1978-1982, 1990,
- Hong Kong 1934, 1954-1962, 1970-1994,
- India 1934-1938, 1954-1958, 1966-1982, 1990,
- Ireland 1930,
- Irish Free State 1934,
- Isle of Man 1958,
- Jamaica 1934, 1954-1982, 1990,
- Jersey 1958,
- Kenya 1954-1982, 1990,
- Kiribati 1998,
- Lesotho 1974,
- Malawi 1970,
- Malaya 1950, 1958-1962,
- Malaysia 1966-1982, 1990,
- Maldives 1986,
- Malta 1958-1962, 1970, 1982,
- Mauritius 1958, 1966-1982, 1990,

- Montserrat 1994,
- Mozambique 1998,
- Namibia 1994,
- Nauru 1990,
- Newfoundland 1930-1934,
- New Zealand 1930,
- Nigeria 1950-1958, 1966-1974, 1982, 1990-1994, 2002,
- Niue 2002,
- Norfolk Island 1986,
- North Borneo 1958-1962,
- Northern Ireland 1934-1938, 1954,
- Northern Rhodesia 1954,
- Pakistan 1954-1970, 1990,
- Papua New Guinea 1962-1982, 1990,
- Rhodesia 1934-1950,
- Rhodesia and Nyasaland 1958-1962,
- Saint Helena 1982, 1998,
- Saint Kitts and Nevis (Saint Christopher-Nevis-Anguilla 1978), 1990,
- Saint Lucia 1962, 1970, 1978, 1994,
- Saint Vincent and the Grenadines 1958, 1966-1978, 1994,
- Samoa *and Western Samoa* 1974,
- Scotland 1930,
- Seychelles 1990,
- Sierra Leone 1966-1970, 1978, 1990,
- Singapore 1958,
- Solomon Islands 1982, 1990,
- South Africa 1930-1958, 1994,
- South Arabia 1966,
- Southern Rhodesia 1954,
- Sri Lanka 1974-1982, 1990,

- Swaziland 1970,
- Tanganyika 1962,
- Tanzania 1966-1982, 1990,
- Tonga 1974, 1982, 1990,
- Trinidad and Tobago 1934-1982, 1990,
- Turks and Caicos Islands 1978, 1998,
- Tuvalu 1998,
- Uganda 1954-1982, 1990,
- Vanuatu 1982,
- Wales 1930,
- Zambia 1970-1982, 1990,
- Zimbabwe 1982, 1990-2002.

Commonwealth Winter Games

There has been some speculation about the possibility of there being a Commonwealth Winter Games in 2010 held in Kashmir. Apparently Gulmarg, where the Indian National Winter Games have been held in the past, would be the venue of the games.

Jammu and Kashmir Chief Minister Ghulam Nabi Azad is reported as saying "Kashmir would be developed as an industrial destination and paradise of tourism. In this direction, Kashmir has been selected as spot across for holding 2010 Commonwealth Winter Sports".

The other possible venue for the Commonwealth Winter Games being mooted is Himachal Pradesh.

2010 Commonwealth Games

The 2010 Commonwealth Games are the nineteenth edition of the Commonwealth Games, and the ninth to be held under that name. The Games are scheduled to be held in Delhi, India between 3 October and 14 October 2010. The games will be the largest multisport event conducted to date in Delhi and India generally, which has previously hosted the Asian Games in 1951 and 1982. The opening ceremony is scheduled to take place at the Jawaharlal Nehru Stadium, Delhi. It will also be the first time the Commonwealth Games will be held in India and the second time the event has been held in Asia. In addition to the Commonwealth Games, the city of Pune, India hosted the 3rd Commonwealth Youth Games between October 12 and 18, 2008. The Youth Games offered nine sports: athletics, badminton, boxing, shooting, swimming, table tennis, tennis, weightlifting and wrestling.

Games Preparation

In January 2005, the Commonwealth Games Federation vice-president Raja Randhir Singh expressed concern that Delhi was behind schedule in forming an organising committee. On 18 January 2008, however, the Commonwealth Games Federation expressed its approval of Delhi's progress.

On 15 October 2009, Jarnail Singh, a former Secretary of the Government of India was appointed as the Chief Executive Officer of the Organising Committee. India's Sports Minister will head the apex committee for conducting the games while the Indian Olympic Association president Suresh Kalmadi will head the organising committee. The Games will be held from the 3rd to 14 October 2010.

The total budget estimated for hosting the 19th Commonwealth is US$ 1.6 billion and this amount excludes non sports related infrastructure development in the city like airports, roads and other structures.

This makes the 2010 Commonwealth Games as the most expensive Commonwealth Games ever (compared to Manchester 2002-approx. US$420 million, and Melbourne 2006-approx. US$ 1.1 billion).

Infrastructure

Delhi already has many international features of a modern and well-planned city. However, to get ready for the huge influx of tourists visiting Delhi during the Games, the Government of India has taken many steps to improve the city. This includes city beautification, transportation development, upgrading of many old structures etc.

Transport

Delhi proposed a four-lane, 2.2 km underground stretch from Lodhi Road to trans-Yamuna, linking the Games Village to the Jawaharlal Nehru Stadium and reducing travelling time for athletes travelling between the Village and the Stadium by six minutes. In response to concerns over the large number of trains that pass by the Delhi metropolitan region daily, construction of road under-bridges and over-bridges along railway lines has been started.

To expand road infrastructure, flyovers, cloverleaf flyovers, and bridges have been planned to provide connectivity to the Games Village, to sports venues, to hospitals, and for intra-city connectivity.

Road-widening projects have been under process, with an emphasis being placed on expanding national highways. To improve traffic flow on existing road, plans are underway to make both the inner and outer Ring roads signal free.

To support its commitment to mass transport, nine corridors have been identified and are being constructed as High Capacity Bus Systems. Six of these corridors are expected to be operational in 2010. Additionally, the Delhi Metro will be expanded to accommodate more people and boost the use of public transport during the 2010 games.

By then it will have the second longest network in the world and later the longest, which will be more than 420 km. To achieve this exponential increase in the network's length, the Delhi Metro has deployed 14 tunnel boring machines (TBMs). The Delhi Metro reports that no country in Asia has ever put to work so many TBMs at the same time. To further support air travel, the Indira Gandhi International Airport is being modernized, expanded, and upgraded.

By the 2010 games, a new terminal will have been constructed at a cost of nearly US$ 1.94 billion, with the capability to cater to more than 37 million passengers a year by 2010 and the planned expansion program will increase its capacity to handle 100 million passengers by 2030. Terminal 3 will be a two tier building, with the bottom floor being the arrivals area, and the top being a departures area.

This terminal will have over 130 check in counters, 55 aerobridges, 30 parking bays, 72 immigration counters, 15 X-ray screening areas, duty free shops, and much more. The airport will also have a new runway to cater more than 75 plus flights an hour; the runway will be more than 4400 meters long and one of Asia's longest. The entire airport will be connected to the city via a 6 lane highway and the Delhi Metro.

Energy Consumption

To prepare for the energy-usage spike during the Games and to end chronic power cuts in Delhi, the government is undertaking a large power-production initiative to increase power production to 7,000 MW (from the current 4,500 MW). To achieve this goal, the government plans to streamline the power distribution process, direct additional energy to Delhi, and construct new power plants. In fact, the government has promised that by 2010, Delhi will have a surplus of power.

Security

In preparation for the Games and to promote security at major tourist destinations, Indian states will be deploying a force of "tourist police" far before the Games begin.

These tourism police are regular state police forces, but will be trained to handle tourist-related aspects. A number of states have already implemented this program; other states are expected to emulate this model within the end of the year.

Delays

In September 2009, Commonwealth Games federation chief Mike Fennell reported that the games were at risk of falling behind schedule and that it was "reasonable to conclude that the current situation poses a serious risk to the Commonwealth Games in 2010".

A report by the Indian Government released several months prior found that construction work on 13 out of the 19 sports venues was behind schedule. The Chief of the Indian Olympic Association Randhir Singh has also called expressed his concerns regarding the current state of affairs.

Singh has called for the revamp of the games' organizing committees commenting that India now has to "retrieve the games". Other Indian officials have also expressed dismay at the ongoing delays but they have stated that they are confident that India will successfully host the games and do so on time.

The Queen's Baton Relay

The Queen's Baton 2010 Delhi containing Her Majesty Queen Elizabeth II's 'message to the athletes' left The Buckingham Palace on

29 October 2009. The baton will arrive at the Opening Ceremony of the XIX Commonwealth Games 2010 Delhi some 11 months later on 3 October 2010, after visiting the other 70 nations of the Commonwealth and travelling throughout India The Queen's Baton Relay 2010 Delhi will take the baton to the home of one third of the world's population, enabling many millions of people across the globe to join in the celebrations for the Games.

The Queen's Baton 2010 Delhi is a fusion of handcrafted elements interplayed with a precision engineered body, and ornamented with an intricate hand layered soil pattern. The shape and design of the baton is created using a triangular section of aluminium which has been twisted in the form of a helix and then coated with a diverse range of coloured soils collected from all corners of India.

The interweaving of coloured soils, including white sands, deep reds, warm yellows, dark browns and an array of other hues creates a very distinctive design, form and texture never before seen in the styling of a Queen's Baton.

The very essence of India with its diversity and unrelenting endeavour towards a harmonious and progressive nation has shaped the inspiration of the baton.

Culminating at the pinnacle of the Queen's Baton 2010 Delhi is a precious jewellery box containing the Queen's 'message to the athletes'. The Queen's message has been symbolically engraved onto a miniature 18 carat gold leaf, representative of the ancient Indian 'patras'. Modern laser technology known as micro calligraphy has been used for the first time to reproduce the Queen's message in this method.

The Queen's Baton 2010 Delhi stands at 664 millimetres high is 34 millimetres wide at the base, and 86 millimetres wide at the top and weighs a mere 1,900 grams. The baton's ergonomic contours allow for convenient holding and good balance. The Queen's Baton has been created using processes and technologies existing in India by Foley Design in partnership with Titan Industries and a technology consortium led by Bharat Electronics Limited.

The technology features of The Queen's Baton for Delhi 2010 include:

- The ability to capture images and sound as it travels throughout all nations of the Commonwealth;
- The latest global positioning system (GPS) technology through which the exact location of the baton can be tracked on the XIX Commonwealth Games 2010 Delhi website;
- Embedded light emitting diodes (LEDs) which will change into the colours of a country's flag whilst in that country; and
- Text messaging capability so that anyone anywhere can send their messages of congratulations and encouragement to the Batonbearers throughout the Queen's Baton Relay 2010 Delhi.

Mascot-Shera

Shera, mascot of the XIX Commonwealth Games 2010 Delhi, is the most visible face of the XIX Commonwealth Games 2010 Delhi.

His name comes from the Hindi word Sher – meaning tiger. Shera truly represents the modern Indian. He is an achiever with a positive attitude, a global citizen but justifiably proud of his nation's ancient heritage, a fierce competitor but with integrity and honesty. Shera is also a 'large-hearted gentleman' who loves making friends and enthusing people to 'come out and play'.

In Indian mythology, the tiger is associated with Goddess Durga, the embodiment of Shakti (or female power) and the vanquisher of evil. She rides her powerful vehicle – the tiger – into combat, especially in her epic and victorious battle against Mahishasur, a dreaded demon.

Shera embodies values that the nation is proud of: majesty, power, charisma, intelligence and grace. His athletic prowess, courage and speed on the field are legendary. He is also a reminder of the fragile environment he lives in and our responsibility towards the protection of his ecosystem.

Other Preparation

In addition to physical preparation, India and Delhi will be offering a myriad of amenities to all athletes. These include traditional Commonwealth Games services, such as free accommodation for all athletes, a modern, comfortable Games Village, cutting-edge health facilities, security, a pollution-free environment, entertainment for non-competition times, transportation, and other, unique amenities as well. Delhi will also be offering all athletes a free trip to the famed Taj Mahal and will provide a reserved lane for participants on selected highways.

The Delhi High Court is also set to implement a series of "mobile courts" to be dispatched throughout Delhi to relocate migrant beggars from Delhi streets. The mobile courts would consider each beggar on a case-by-case basis to determine whether the beggar should be sent back to his/her state of residence, or be permitted to remain in government-shelters.

In preparation for a rush of English-speaking tourists for the Games, the Delhi government is implementing a program to teach English to low-income individuals who will have a high-frequency of contact with tourists. This subset includes city cab drivers, waiters, gatemen, and service staff. Over the past two years, the city has successfully taught 2,000 drivers English, and is continuing the program to reach as many as possible before the Games. The city plans to teach 1,000 people English per month, and hopes to reach everyone necessary by March 2009. In addition to Delhi, the Indian Government plans to expand the program to teach people in local tourist destinations, including Agra and Mathura in Uttar Pradesh, Bhopal and Gwalior in Madhya Pradesh, Gaya in Bihar and Puri in Orissa.

Participating Nations

There are currently 71 nations planning to field teams at the 2010 Commonwealth Games. In alphabetical order, these nations are:

- Anguilla,
- Antigua and Barbuda,
- Australia,
- Bahamas,
- Bangladesh,
- Barbados,
- Belize,
- Bermuda,
- Botswana,
- British Virgin Islands,

- Brunei,
- Cameroon,
- Canada,
- Cayman Islands,
- Cook Islands,
- Cyprus,
- Dominica,
- England,
- Falkland Islands,
- Gambia,
- Ghana,
- Gibraltar,
- Grenada,
- Guernsey,
- Guyana,
- India,
- Isle of Man,
- Jamaica,
- Jersey,
- Kenya,
- Kiribati,
- Lesotho,
- Malawi,
- Malaysia,
- Maldives,
- Malta,
- Mauritius,
- Montserrat,
- Mozambique,
- Namibia,

- Nauru,
- New Zealand,
- Nigeria,
- Niue,
- Norfolk Island,
- Northern Ireland,
- Pakistan,
- Papua New Guinea,
- Saint Helena,
- Saint Kitts and Nevis,
- Saint Lucia,
- Saint Vincent and the Grenadines,
- Samoa,
- Scotland,
- Seychelles,
- Sierra Leone,
- Singapore,
- Solomon Islands,
- South Africa,
- Sri Lanka,
- Swaziland,
- Tanzania,
- Tokelau,
- Tonga,
- Trinidad and Tobago,
- Turks and Caicos Islands,
- Tuvalu,
- Uganda,
- Vanuatu,
- Wales,
- Zambia.

Sports

There are 17 disciplines planned for the 2010 Commonwealth Games.

- Aquatics,
- Archery,
- Athletics (track and field),
- Badminton,
- Boxing,
- Cycling,
- Gymnastics,
- Hockey,
- Lawn Bowls,
- Netball,
- Rugby sevens,
- Shooting,
- Squash,
- Table Tennis,
- Tennis,
- Weightlifting,
- Wrestling.

Kabaddi will also be a demonstration sport at the 2010 Games.

The triathlon appears likely to be excluded from these games as there is no suitable location for the swimming stage. The organisers have also proposed removing basketball, but want to include archery, tennis, and billiards and snooker for men. Cricket, although in strong demand, may not make a come-back as the Board of Control for Cricket in India were not keen on a Twenty 20 tournament, but the organisers did not want a one day tournament.

Venues

Existing and new stadiam will be used to house the following sports: Archery, Aquatics, Athletics, Badminton, Boxing, Cycling, Elite Athletes with a Disability (EAD) Events, Gymnastics, Hockey, Lawn

Bowls, Netball, Rugby 7s, Shooting, Squash, Table Tennis, Tennis, Weightlifting and Wrestling. Specific venues for 2010 games in Delhi are following:

- Jawaharlal Nehru Stadium-Opening and Closing ceremonies, Athletics, Lawn bowls, Weightlifting.
- Dhyan Chand National Stadium-Hockey.
- Indira Gandhi Arena-Archery, Cycling, Gymnastics, Wrestling.
- Delhi University sports complex-Rugby 7s.
- Tyagaraj Sports Complex-Netball.
- Siri Fort Sports Complex-Badminton, Squash.
- Dr. Karni Singh Shooting Range-Shooting.
- Talkatora Stadium-Boxing.
- SPM Swimming Pool Complex-Aquatics.
- RK Khanna Tennis Complex-Tennis.
- Yamuna Sports Complex-Table tennis.

Jawaharlal Nehru Stadium

The opening and closing ceremonies, athletics, lawn bowls, and weightlifting will take place at the massive Jawaharlal Nehru Stadium, Delhi, which will have a capacity of 75,000 spectators for the Games. The stadium will be renovated and improved in time for the Games.

Indira Gandhi Arena

The events of archery, cycling, gymnastics, and wrestling will take place at the Indira Gandhi Arena, the largest indoor sports arena in India and the second-largest in Asia, which seats 25,000 people. Located at the Indraprastha Estate in the eastern region of New Delhi, the arena will be connected to other venues via dedicated bus lanes and mass transportation. The arena will be renovated for the Games.

8

Major Sports Events-II

FIFA World Cup

The FIFA World Cup, occasionally called the Football World Cup, but usually referred to simply as the World Cup, is an international football competition contested by the men's national teams of the members of *Fédération International de Football Association* (FIFA), the sport's global governing body. The championship has been awarded every four years since the first tournament in 1930, except in 1942 and 1946, because of World War II. The current format of the tournament involves 32 teams competing for the title at venues within the host nation(s) over a period of about a month – this phase is often called the *World Cup Finals*. A qualification phase, which currently takes place over the preceding three years, is used to determine which teams qualify for the tournament together with the host nation(s). The World Cup is the most widely-viewed sporting event in the world, with an estimated 715.1 million people watching the 2006 final.

Of the 18 tournaments held, seven nations have won the title. Brazil are the only team that have played in every tournament and have won the World Cup a record five times. Italy are the current champions and have won four titles, and Germany are next with three. The other former champions are Uruguay, winners of the inaugural tournament, and Argentina, with two titles each, and England and France, with one title each. The most recent World Cup was held in Germany in 2006. The next World Cup will be held in South Africa, between 11 June and 11 July 2010, and the 2014 World Cup will be held in Brazil.

History

Previous International Competitions

The world's first international football match was a challenge match played in Glasgow in 1872 between Scotland and England, with the first international tournament, the inaugural edition of the British Home Championship, taking place in 1884.

At this stage the sport was rarely played outside the United Kingdom. As football began to increase in popularity in other parts of the world at the turn of the century, it was held as a demonstration sport with no medals awarded at the 1900 and 1904 Summer Olympics (however, the IOC has retroactively upgraded their status to official events), and at the 1906 Intercalated Games.

After FIFA was founded in 1904, there was an attempt made by FIFA to arrange an international football tournament between nations outside of the Olympic framework in Switzerland in 1906. These were very early days for international football, and the official history of FIFA describes the competition as having been a failure.

At the 1908 Summer Olympics in London, football became an official competition. Planned by The Football Association (FA), England's football governing body, the event was for amateur players only and was regarded suspiciously as a show rather than a competition. Great Britain (represented by the England national amateur football team) won the gold medals. They repeated the feat in 1912 in Stockholm, where the tournament was organized by the Swedish Football Association.

With the Olympic event continuing to be contested only between amateur teams, Sir Thomas Lipton organized the Sir Thomas Lipton Trophy tournament in Turin in 1909. The Lipton tournament was a championship between individual clubs (not national teams) from different nations, each one of which represented an entire nation.

The competition is sometimes described as *The First World Cup*, and featured the most prestigious professional club sides from Italy, Germany and Switzerland, but the FA of England refused to be associated with the competition and declined the offer to send a professional team. Lipton invited West Auckland, an amateur side from County Durham, to represent England instead. West Auckland won the tournament and returned in 1911 to successfully defend their title, and were given the trophy to keep forever, as per the rules of the competition.

In 1914, FIFA agreed to recognise the Olympic tournament as a "world football championship for amateurs", and took responsibility for managing the event. This paved the way for the world's first intercontinental football competition, at the 1920 Summer Olympics, contested by Egypt and thirteen European teams, and won by Belgium. Uruguay won the next two Olympic football tournaments in 1924 and 1928.

First World Cup

Due to the success of the Olympic football tournaments, FIFA, with President Jules Rimet the driving force, again started looking at staging its own international tournament outside of the Olympics. On 28 May 1928, the FIFA Congress in Amsterdam decided to stage a world championship organised by FIFA. With Uruguay now two-time official football world champions (as 1924 was the start of FIFA's professional era) and to celebrate their centenary of independence in 1930, FIFA named Uruguay as the host country of the inaugural World Cup tournament.

The national associations of selected nations were invited to send a team, but the choice of Uruguay as a venue for the competition meant a long and costly trip across the Atlantic Ocean for European sides. Indeed, no European country pledged to send a team until two months before the start of the competition. Rimet eventually persuaded teams from Belgium, France, Romania, and Yugoslavia to make the trip. In total thirteen nations took part: seven from South America, four from Europe and two from North America.

The first two World Cup matches took place simultaneously on 18 July 1930, and were won by France and USA, who beat Mexico 4–1 and Belgium 3–0 respectively. The first goal in World Cup history was scored by Lucien Laurent of France. In the final, Uruguay defeated Argentina 4–2 in front of a crowd of 93,000 people in Montevideo, and in doing so became the first nation to win the World Cup.

Growth

After the creation of the World Cup, the 1932 Summer Olympics, held in Los Angeles, did not plan to include football as part of the schedule due to the low popularity of the sport in the United States, as American football had been growing in popularity. FIFA and the IOC also disagreed over the status of amateur players, and so football was dropped from the Games. Olympic football returned at the 1936 Summer Olympics, but was now overshadowed by the more prestigious World Cup.

The issues facing the early World Cup tournaments were the difficulties of intercontinental travel, and war. Few South American teams were willing to travel to Europe for the 1934 and 1938 tournaments, with Brazil the only South American team to compete in both. The 1942 and 1946 competitions were cancelled due to World War II and its aftermath.

The 1950 World Cup, held in Brazil, was the first to include British participants. British teams withdrew from FIFA in 1920, partly out of unwillingness to play against the countries they had been at war with, and partly as a protest against foreign influence on football, but rejoined in 1946 following FIFA's invitation.

The tournament also saw the return of 1930 champions Uruguay, who had boycotted the previous two World Cups. Uruguay won the tournament again by defeating the host nation Brazil in one of the most famous matches in World Cup history, which was later called the "Maracanazo" (Portuguese: *Maracanaço*).

In the tournaments between 1934 and 1978, 16 teams competed in each tournament, except in 1938, when Austria were absorbed into Germany after qualifying, leaving the tournament with 15 teams, and in 1950, when India, Scotland and Turkey withdrew, leaving the tournament with 13 teams. Most of the participating nations were from Europe and South America, with a small minority from North America, Africa, Asia and Oceania.

These teams were usually defeated easily by the European and South American teams. Until 1982, the only teams from outside Europe and South America to advance out of the first round were: USA, semi-finalists in 1930; Cuba, quarter-finalists in 1938; Korea DPR, quarter-finalists in 1966; and Mexico, quarter-finalists in 1970.

The tournament was expanded to 24 teams in 1982, and then to 32 in 1998, allowing more teams from Africa, Asia and North America to take part. The one exception is Oceania, who have never had a guaranteed spot in the tournament. In recent years, teams from these regions have enjoyed more success, and those who have reached the quarter-finals include: Mexico, quarter-finalists in 1986; Cameroon, quarter-finalists in 1990; Korea Republic, finishing in fourth place in 2002; and Senegal and USA, both quarter-finalists in 2002. However, European and South American teams have remained the stronger forces. For example, the quarter-finalists in 2006 were all from Europe or South America.

198 nations attempted to qualify for the 2006 FIFA World Cup, and a record 204 will attempt to qualify for the 2010 FIFA World Cup.

Other FIFA Tournaments

An equivalent tournament for women's football, the FIFA Women's World Cup, was first held in 1991 in the People's Republic of China. The women's tournament is smaller in scale and profile than the men's, but is growing; the number of entrants for the 2007 tournament was 120, more than double that of 1991.

Football has been included in every Summer Olympic Games except 1896 and 1932. Unlike many other sports, the men's football tournament at the Olympics is not a top-level tournament, and since 1992, an under-23 tournament with each team allowed three over-age players. Women's football made its Olympic debut in 1996, and is contested between full national sides with no age restrictions.

The FIFA Confederations Cup is a tournament held one year before the World Cup at the World Cup host nation(s) as a dress-rehearsal for the upcoming World Cup. It is contested by the winners of each of the six FIFA confederation championships, along with the FIFA World Cup champion and the host country.

FIFA also organizes international tournaments for youth football (FIFA U-20 World Cup, FIFA U-17 World Cup, FIFA U-20 Women's World Cup, FIFA U-17 Women's World Cup), club football (FIFA Club World Cup), and football variants such as futsal (FIFA Futsal World Cup) and beach soccer (FIFA Beach Soccer World Cup).

Trophy

From 1930 to 1970, the *Jules Rimet Trophy* was awarded to the World Cup winner. It was originally simply known as the *World Cup* or *Coupe du Monde*, but in 1946 it was renamed after the FIFA president Jules Rimet who set up the first tournament. In 1970, Brazil's third victory in the tournament entitled them to keep the trophy permanently. However, the trophy was stolen in 1983, and has never been recovered, apparently melted down by the thieves.

After 1970, a new trophy, known as the *FIFA World Cup Trophy*, was designed. The experts of FIFA, coming from seven different countries, evaluated the 53 presented models, finally opting for the work of the Italian designer Silvio Gazzaniga.

The new trophy is 36 cm (14.2 in) high, made of solid 18 carat (75%) gold and weighs 6.175 kg (13.6 lb). The base contains two layers of semi-precious malachite while the bottom side of the trophy bears the engraved year and name of each FIFA World Cup winner since 1974.

The description of the trophy by Gazzaniga was: "The lines spring out from the base, rising in spirals, stretching out to receive the world. From the remarkable dynamic tensions of the compact body of the sculpture rise the figures of two athletes at the stirring moment of victory."

This new trophy is not awarded to the winning nation permanently. World Cup winners retain the trophy until the next tournament and are awarded a gold-plated replica rather than the solid gold original.

Format

Qualification

Since the second World Cup in 1934, qualifying tournaments have been held to thin the field for the final tournament. They are held within the six FIFA continental zones (Africa, Asia, North and Central America and Caribbean, South America, Oceania, Europe), overseen by their respective confederations.

For each tournament, FIFA decides the number of places awarded to each of the continental zones beforehand, generally based on the relative strength of the confederations' teams, but also subject to lobbying from the confederations. The qualification process can start as early as almost three years before the final tournament and last over a two-year period. The formats of the qualification tournaments differ between confederations. Usually, one or two places are awarded to winners of intercontinental play-offs.

For example, the winner of the Oceanian zone and the fifth-placed team from the Asian zone will enter a play-off for a spot in the 2010 World Cup. From the 1938 World Cup onwards, host nations have received automatic qualification to the final tournament.

This right was also granted to the defending champions between 1938 and 2002, but was withdrawn from the 2006 FIFA World Cup onward, requiring the champions to qualify. Brazil, winners in 2002, thus became the first defending champions to play in a qualifying match.

Final Tournament

The current final tournament features 32 national teams competing over a month in the host nation(s). There are two stages: a *group stage* followed by a *knockout stage.*

In the group stage, teams compete within eight groups of four teams each. Eight teams are seeded (including the hosts, with the other teams selected using a formula based on both the FIFA World Rankings and performances in recent World Cups) and drawn to separate groups.

The other teams are assigned to different "pots", usually based on geographical criteria, and teams in each pot are drawn at random to the eight groups. Since 1998, constraints have been applied to the draw to ensure that no group contains more than two European teams or more than one team from any other confederation.

Each group plays a round-robin tournament, guaranteeing that every team will play at least three matches. The last round of matches of each group is scheduled at the same time to preserve fairness among all four teams. The top two teams from each group advance to the knockout stage. Points are used to rank the teams within a group. Since 1994, three points have been awarded for a win, one for a draw and none for a loss (prior to this, winners received two points rather than three). If two or more teams end up with the same number of points, tiebreakers are used: first is goal difference, then total goals scored, then head-to-head results, and finally drawing of lots (i.e. determining team positions at random).

The knockout stage is a single-elimination tournament in which teams play each other in one-off matches, with extra time and penalty shootouts used to decide the winner if necessary. It begins with the "round of 16" (or the second round) in which the winner of each group plays against the runner-up of another group. This is followed by the quarter-finals, the semi-finals, the third-place match (contested by the losing semi-finalists), and the final.

Selection of Hosts

Early World Cups were given to countries at meetings of FIFA's congress. The choice of location gave rise to controversies, a consequence of the three-week boat journey between South America and Europe, the two centres of strength in football. The decision to hold the first World Cup in Uruguay, for example, led to only four European nations competing. The next two World Cups were both held in Europe. The decision to hold the second of these, the 1938 FIFA World Cup, in France was controversial, as the American countries had been led to understand that the World Cup would rotate between the two continents. Both Argentina and Uruguay thus boycotted the tournament.

Since the 1958 FIFA World Cup, to avoid future boycotts or controversy, FIFA began a pattern of alternating the hosts between the Americas and Europe, which continued until the 1998 FIFA World Cup. The 2002 FIFA World Cup, hosted jointly by South Korea and Japan, was the first one held in Asia, and the only tournament with multiple hosts. In 2010, South Africa will become the first African nation to host the World Cup. The 2014 FIFA World Cup will be hosted by Brazil, the first held in South America since 1978, and will be the first occasion where consecutive World Cups are held outside Europe.

The host country is now chosen in a vote by FIFA's Executive Committee. This is done under a single transferable vote system. The national football association of a country desiring to host the event receives a "Hosting Agreement" from FIFA, which explains the steps and requirements that are expected from a strong bid. The bidding association also receives a form, the submission of which represents the official confirmation of the candidacy. After this, a FIFA designated group of inspectors visit the country to identify that the country meets the requirements needed to host the event and a report on the country is produced. The decision on who will host the World Cup is usually made six or seven years in advance of the tournament. However, there have been occasions where the hosts of multiple future tournaments were announced at the same time, as will be the case for the 2018 and 2022 World Cups.

For the 2010 and 2014 World Cups, the final tournament is rotated between confederations, allowing only countries from the chosen confederation (Africa in 2010, South America in 2014) to bid to host the tournament.

The rotation policy was introduced after the controversy surrounding Germany's victory over South Africa in the vote to host the 2006 tournament. However, the policy of continental rotation will not continue beyond 2014, so any country, except those belonging to confederations that hosted the two preceding tournaments, can apply as hosts for World Cups starting from 2018. This is partly to avoid a similar scenario to the bidding process for the 2014 tournament, where Brazil was the only official bidder.

Organization and Media Coverage

The World Cup was first televised in 1954 and is now the most widely-viewed and followed sporting event in the world, exceeding even the Olympic Games. The cumulative audience of all matches of the 2006 World Cup is estimated to be 26.29 billion. 715.1 million individuals watched the final match of this tournament (a ninth of the entire population of the planet). The 2006 World Cup draw, which decided the distribution of teams into groups, was watched by 300 million viewers.

Each FIFA World Cup since 1966 has its own mascot. *World Cup Willie*, the mascot for the 1966 competition, was the first World Cup mascot. Recent World Cups have also featured official match balls specially designed for each World Cup.

Summaries of previous tournaments

Year	Host Nation(s)	Winner	Final Score	Runner-up	Third Place match 3rd Place	Score	4th Place
1930 *Details*	Uruguay	Uruguay	4–2	Argentina	United States	[note 1]	Yugoslavia
1934 *Details*	Italy	Italy	2–1 (a.e.t.)	Czechoslovakia	Germany	3–2	Austria
1938 *Details*	France	Italy	4–2	Hungary	Brazil	4–2	Sweden
1950 *Details*	Brazil	Uruguay	[note 2]	Brazil	Sweden	[note 2]	Spain
1954 *Details*	Switzerland	West Germany	3–2	Hungary	Austria	3–1	Uruguay
1958 *Details*	Sweden	Brazil	5–2	Sweden	France	6–3	West Germany
1962 *Details*	Chile	Brazil	3–1	Czechoslovakia	Chile	1–0	Yugoslavia
1966 *Details*	England	England	4–2 (a.e.t.)	West Germany	Portugal	2–1	USSR
1970 *Details*	Mexico	Brazil	4–1	Italy	West Germany	1–0	Uruguay
1974 *Details*	West Germany	West Germany	2–1	Netherlands	Poland	1–0	Brazil
1978 *Details*	Argentina	Argentina	3–1 (a.e.t.)	Netherlands	Brazil	2–1	Italy
1982 *Details*	Spain	Italy	3–1	West Germany	Poland	3–2	France
1986 *Details*	Mexico	Argentina	3–2	West Germany	France	4–2 (a.e.t.)	Belgium
1990 *Details*	Italy	West Germany	1–0	Argentina	Italy	2–1	England
1994 *Details*	United States	Brazil	0–0 (a.e.t.) (3–2 pens.)	Italy	Sweden	4–0	Bulgaria
1998 *Details*	France	France	3–0	Brazil	Croatia	2–1	Netherlands
2002 *Details*	S. Korea & Japan	Brazil	2–0	Germany	Turkey	3–2	Korea Republic
2006 *Details*	Germany	Italy	1–1 (a.e.t.) (5–3 pens.)	France	Germany	3–1	Portugal

Notes

- * There was no official World Cup Third Place match in 1930; The United States and Yugoslavia lost in the semi-finals. FIFA now recognizes the United States as the third-placed team and Yugoslavia as the fourth-placed team, using the overall records of the teams in the tournament.
- * There was no official World Cup final match in 1950. The tournament winner was decided by a final round-robin group contested by four teams (Uruguay, Brazil, Sweden, and Spain). However, Uruguay's 2–1 victory over Brazil was the decisive match (and also coincidentally one of the last two matches of the tournament) which put them ahead on points and ensured that they finished top of the group as world champions. Therefore, this match is often considered the "final" of the 1950 World Cup. Likewise, Sweden's 3–1 victory over Spain (played at the same time as Uruguay vs Brazil) ensured that they finished third.

Winners and Finalists

In all, 75 nations have played in at least one World Cup. Of these, 11 have made it to the final match, and seven of them have won. The seven national teams that have won the World Cup have added stars to their crests, with each star representing a World Cup victory. (However, Uruguay are an exception to this unwritten rule; They choose to display four stars on their crest, representing their two gold medals at the 1924 and 1928 Summer Olympics and their two World Cup titles in 1930 and 1950). With five titles, Brazil are the most successful World Cup team and also the only nation to have played in every World Cup to date. Italy (1934 and 1938) and Brazil (1958 and 1962) are the only nations to have won consecutive titles. Below is a list of the 11 teams that have played in a World Cup final.

Team	*Titles*	*Runners-up*
Brazil	5 (1958, 1962, 1970, 1994, 2002)	2 (1950*, 1998)
Italy	4 (1934*, 1938, 1982, 2006)	2 (1970, 1994)
Germany^	3 (1954, 1974*, 1990)	4 (1966, 1982, 1986, 2002)
Argentina	2 (1978*, 1986)	2 (1930, 1990)
Uruguay	2 (1930*, 1950)	–
France	1 (1998*)	1 (2006)
England	1 (1966*)	–
Netherlands	–	2 (1974, 1978)
Czechoslovakia#	–	2 (1934, 1962)
Hungary	–	2 (1938, 1954)
Sweden	–	1 (1958*)

** = hosts; ^ = includes results representing West Germany between 1954 and 1990;*
 # = states that have since split into two or more independent nations

Performances by Host Nations

Six of the seven champions have won one of their titles while playing in their own homeland, the exception being Brazil, who finished as runners-up after losing the deciding match on home soil in 1950.

England (1966) and France (1998) won their only titles while playing as host nations.

Uruguay (1930), Italy (1934) and Argentina (1978) won their first titles as host nations but have gone on to win again, while Germany (1974) won their second title on home soil.

Other nations have also been successful when hosting the tournament. Sweden (runners-up in 1958), Chile (third place in 1962), Korea Republic (fourth place in 2002), Mexico (quarter-finals in 1970 and 1986), and Japan (second round in 2002) all have their best results when serving as hosts. So far, all host nations have progressed beyond the first round.

Best Performances by Continental Zones

To date, the final of the World Cup has only been contested by European and South American teams.

The two continents have won nine titles apiece. Only two teams from outside these two continents have ever reached the semi-finals of the competition: USA (North, Central America and Caribbean) in 1930 and Korea Republic (Asia) in 2002.

The best result of an African team is reaching the quarter-finals: Cameroon in 1990 and Senegal in 2002. Oceania has only been represented in the World Cup three times, and an Oceanian qualifier has reached the second round once, as Australia qualified as an Oceanian nation in 2005, although they moved to the Asian Football Confederation before the beginning of the tournament.

All World Cups won by European teams have taken place in Europe and the only teams to have won outside Europe come from South America. The only non-European team to win a tournament in Europe is Brazil in 1958. Only twice have consecutive World Cups been won by teams from the same continent – when Italy and Brazil successfully defended their titles in 1938 and 1962 respectively.

Awards

At the end of each World Cup, awards are presented to the players and teams for accomplishments other than their final team positions in the tournament. There are currently six awards:

- The *Golden Ball* for the best player, determined by a vote of media members (first awarded in 1982); the *Silver Ball* and the *Bronze Ball* are awarded to the players finishing second and third in the voting respectively;
- The *Golden Shoe* (sometimes called the *Golden Boot*) for the top goalscorer (first awarded in 1982, but retrospectively applied to all tournaments from 1930); most recently, the *Silver Shoe* and the *Bronze Shoe* have been awarded to the second and third top goalscorers respectively;
- The *Yashin Award* for the best goalkeeper, decided by the FIFA Technical Study Group (first awarded in 1994);
- The *Best Young Player Award* for the best player aged 21 or younger at the start of the calendar year, decided by the FIFA Technical Study Group (first awarded in 2006).
- The *FIFA Fair Play Trophy* for the team with the best record of fair play, according to the points system and criteria established by the FIFA Fair Play Committee (first awarded in 1978);
- The *Most Entertaining Team* for the team that has entertained the public the most during the World Cup, determined by a poll of the general public (first awarded in 1994);

An *All-Star Team* consisting of the best players of the tournament is also announced for each tournament since 1998.

Records and Statistics

Two players share the record for playing in the most World Cups; Mexico's Antonio Carbajal and Germany's Lothar Matthaus both played in five tournaments. Matthäus has played the most World Cup matches overall, with 25 appearances. Brazil's Pele is the only player to have won three World Cup winners' medals, with 20 other players who have won two World Cup medals.

The overall leading goalscorer in World Cups is Brazil's Ronaldo, scorer of 15 goals in three tournaments. West Germany's Gerd Müller is second, with 14 goals in two tournaments. The third placed goalscorer, France's Just Fontaine, holds the record for the most goals scored in a single World Cup.

All his 13 goals were scored in the 1958 tournament. Brazil are the leading scorers in the World Cup having scored 201 goals in 92 games, whilst Germany are the second highest with 190 goals in 93 games. Brazil's Mário Zagallo and West Germany's Franz Beckenbauer are the only people to date to win the World Cup as both player and head coach.

Zagallo won in 1958 and 1962 as a player and in 1970 as head coach. Beckenbauer won in 1974 as captain and in 1990 as head coach. Italy's Vittorio Pozzo is the only head coach to ever win two World Cups. All World Cup winning head coaches were natives of the country they coached to victory.

2010 FIFA World Cup

The 2010 FIFA World Cup will be the 19th FIFA World Cup, the premier international football tournament. It is scheduled to take place between 11 June and 11 July 2010 in South Africa. The 2010 FIFA World Cup will be the culmination of a qualification process that began in August 2007 and involved 204 of the 208 FIFA national teams. As such, it matches the 2008 Summer Olympics as the sports event with the most competing nations. This will be the first time that the tournament has been hosted by an African nation, after South Africa beat Morocco and Egypt in an all-African bidding process. Italy are the defending champions. The draw for the finals will take place on 4 December 2009 in Cape Town.

Host Selection

Africa was chosen as the host for the 2010 World Cup as part of a new policy to rotate the event between football confederations (which was later abandoned in October 2007). Five African nations placed bids to host the 2010 World Cup:

- Egypt,
- Libya/Tunisia (co-hosting),

- Morocco,
- South Africa.

Following the decision of the FIFA Executive Committee not to allow co-hosted tournaments, Tunisia withdrew from the bidding process. The committee also decided not to consider Libya's solo bid as it no longer met all the stipulations laid down in the official List of Requirements.

After one round of voting, the winning bid was announced by FIFA president Sepp Blatter at a media conference on 15 May 2004 in Zürich. South Africa was awarded the rights to host the tournament, defeating Morocco and Egypt.

Voting Results

Country	***Votes***
South Africa	14
Morocco	10
Egypt	0

- Tunisia *withdrew on 8 May 2004 after joint bidding was not allowed.*
- Libya *bid was rejected: bid did not meet the list of requirements and joint bidding was not allowed.*

Qualification

As the host nation, South Africa qualifies automatically for the tournament. However, South Africa did participate in World Cup qualifiers because the CAF qualifiers also serve as the qualifying tournament for the 2010 African Cup of Nations. They were the first host since 1934 to participate in preliminary qualifying. Like the previous tournament, the defending champions Italy do not qualify automatically.

The preliminary draw for the 2010 World Cup was held in Durban, South Africa, on 25 November 2007. The Final draw for the 2010 FIFA World Cup will be staged in Cape Town, South Africa, on 4 December 2009 at the Cape Town International Convention Centre.

List of Qualified Teams

The following 23 teams have qualified as of 14 October 2009.

Team	Qualified as	Qualification date	Appearance in finals	Consecutive Streak	Previous best performance	Current FIFA Ranking
South Africa	Host	15 May 2004	3rd	1 (first since 2002)	Group Stage (1998, 2002)	85
Japan	AFC Fourth Round Group A Runners-Up	6 June 2009	4th	4	Round of 16 (2002)	40
Australia	AFC Fourth Round Group A Winners	6 June 2009	3rd	2	Round of 16 (2006)	24
Korea Rep.	AFC Fourth Round Group B Winners	6 June 2009	8th	7	Fourth Place (2002)	48
Netherlands	UEFA Group 9 Winners	6 June 2009	9th	2	Runners-Up (1974, 1978)	3
Korea DPR	AFC Fourth Round Group B Runners-Up	17 June 2009	2nd	1 (first since 1966)	Quarter-finals (1966)	91
Brazil	CONMEBOL Winners	5 September 2009	19th	19	Winners (1958, 1962, 1970, 1994, 2002)	1
Ghana	CAF Third Round Group D Winners	6 September 2009	2nd	2	Round of 16 (2006)	38
England	UEFA Group 6 Winners	9 September 2009	13th	4	Winners (1966)	7
Spain	UEFA Group 5 Winners	9 September 2009	13th	9	Fourth Place (1950)	2
Paraguay	CONMEBOL Third Place	9 September 2009	8th	4	Round of 16 (1986, 1998, 2002)	21
Cote d'Ivoire	CAF Third Round Group E Winners	10 October 2009	2nd	2	Group Stage (2006)	19
Germany	UEFA Group 4 Winners	10 October 2009	17th2	15	Winners (1954, 1974, 1990)	5
Denmark	UEFA Group 1 Winners	10 October 2009	4th	1 (first since 2002)	Quarter-finals (1998)	27

Team	Qualified as	Qualification date	Appearance in finals	Consecutive Streak	Previous best performance	Current FIFA Ranking
Serbia	UEFA Group 7 Winners	10 October 2009	11th	2	Fourth Place (19305, 1962)	20
Italy	UEFA Group 8 Winners	10 October 2009	17th	13	Winners (1934, 1938, 1982, 2006)	4
Chile	CONMEBOL Runner-Up	10 October 2009	8th	1 (first since 98)	Third Place (1962)	17
Mexico	CONCACAF Fourth Round Runners-Up	10 October 2009	14th	5	Quarter-finals (1970, 1986)	18
US	CONCACAF Fourth Round Winners	10 October 2009	9th	6	Third Place (19305)	11
Switzerland	UEFA Group 2 Winners	14 October 2009	9th	2	Quarter-finals (1934, 1938, 1954)	13
Slovakia	UEFA Group 3 Winners	14 October 2009	9th	1 (first since 90)	Runners-Up (1934, 1962)	33
Argentina	CONMEBOL Fourth Place	14 October 2009	15th	10	Winners (1978, 1986)	6
Honduras	CONCACAF Fourth Round Third Place	14 October 2009	2nd	1 (first since 82)	Group Stage (1982)	35

Notes:

1. Standings are current as of 16 October 2009.
2. Competed as West Germany from 1954 to 1990; 6th appearance as Germany.
3. Competed as Yugoslavia from 1930 to 1998 and Serbia and Montenegro for 2006; 1st appearance as Serbia.
4. Competed as Czechoslovakia from 1934 to 1990; 1st appearance as Slovakia.
5. No official third place match took place in 1930 and no official third place was awarded at the time; both United States and Yugoslavia lost in the semi-finals. However, FIFA lists the teams as third and fourth respectively. 1930 FIFA World Cup Uruguay.

Mascot

The official mascot for the 2010 FIFA World Cup is Zakumi, a leopard with green hair. His name comes from "ZA", the international abbreviation for South Africa, and "kumi", a word that means "ten" in various African languages. The mascot's colours reflect those of the host nation's playing strip – yellow and green.

Venues

In 2005, the organisers released a provisional list of thirteen venues to be used for the World Cup: Mangaung/Bloemfontein, Cape Town, Durban, Johannesburg (two venues), Kimberley, Nelspruit, Orkney, Polokwane, Nelson Mandela Bay/Port Elizabeth, Tshwane/Pretoria (two venues), and Rustenburg. This was narrowed down to ten venues which were officially announced by FIFA on 17 March 2006:

Johannesburg	Durban	Cape Town	Johannesburg	Tshwane/Pretoria
Soccer City Capacity: 89,000	Moses Mabhida Stadium Capacity: 70,000	Cape Town Stadium Capacity: 69,070	Coca-Cola Park Capacity: 62,567	Loftus Versfeld Stadium Capacity: 51,760
Nelson Mandela Bay/ Port Elizabeth	Mangaung/ Bloemfontein	Polokwane	Nelspruit	Rustenburg
Nelson Mandela Bay Stadium	Free State Stadium	Peter Mokaba Stadium	Mbombela Stadium	Royal Bafokeng Stadium
Capacity: 48,000	Capacity: 48,070	Capacity: 46,000	Capacity: 44,000	Capacity: 42,000

Preparations

Five new stadiums are to be built for the tournament (three new match venues and two new practice grounds), and five of the existing venues are to be upgraded. Construction costs are expected to be R8.4bn.

In addition to the stadiums being built and upgraded, South Africa is also planning to improve its current public transport infrastructure within the various cities, with projects such as the Gautrain and the new Bus Rapid Transit system (BRT) titled Rea Vaya.

Danny Jordaan, the president of the 2010 World Cup organising committee has said that he expects all stadiums for the tournament to be completed by October 2009.

The country is also going to implement special measures to ensure the safety and security of local and international tourists attending the matches in accordance with standard FIFA requirements.

Construction Strike

70,000 construction workers who were supposed to be working on the new stadiums walked off their jobs on 8 July 2009. The majority of the workers receive R2500 per month (about £192, €224 or $313), but the unions allege that some workers are grossly underpaid – some receiving as little as R40 (£3.11) a week. A spokesperson for the National Union of Mineworkers said to the SABC that the "no work no pay" strike will go on until FIFA assesses penalties on the organisers. Other unions threatened to strike into 2011. The World Cup organising committee downplayed the strike and expressed confidence that the stadiums will be ready.

Relocation Rumours

During 2006 to 2007, rumours circulated in various news sources that the 2010 World Cup could be moved to another country. Some people, including Franz Beckenbauer, Horst R. Schmidt and, reportedly, some FIFA executives, expressed concern over the planning, organisation, and pace of South Africa's preparations. However, FIFA officials repeatedly expressed their confidence in South Africa as host, and stated that the event will not be moved, with FIFA president Sepp Blatter re-iterating that "Plan A... Plan B... Plan C is that the 2010 World Cup will be staged in South Africa". Blatter stated that there is a contingency plan to hold the World Cup elsewhere but only in the event of a natural catastrophe, and that the 2006 FIFA World Cup in Germany also had a similar contingency plan.

Despite reassurances by FIFA that the event would only be moved in the case of natural catastrophe, rumours continued to circulate about possible relocation of the event. These rumours were criticised by South Africa's Deputy Finance Minister Jabu Moleketi, saying that some have targeted the event to reflect their persistent negativity towards South Africa and Africa.

Controversies

As with many 'hallmark events' throughout the world, the 2010

FIFA World Cup has been connected to evictions in South Africa which many claim are meant to 'beautify the city', impress visiting tourists, and hide shackdwellers. On 14 May 2009, Durban-based shack-dwellers took the KwaZulu-Natal government to court over their controversial Elimination and Prevention of Re-Emergence of Slums Act, meant to eliminate slums in South Africa and put homeless shackdwellers in transit camps in time for the 2010 World Cup. They have gained a lot of publicity for their efforts even in the international media.

The most prominent controversy surrounding preparations for the World Cup is the N2 Gateway housing project in Cape Town, which plans to remove over 20,000 residents from Joe Slovo Informal Settlement along the busy N2 Freeway and build rental flats and bond houses in its place in time for the 2010 World Cup. The residents would be moved to the poverty stricken Delft township on the outskirts of the city and out of sight from the N2 Freeway.

In July 2009, South Africa was hit with rolling protests by poor communities who demanded access to basic services, jobs, adequate housing and the democratisation of service delivery. These protests have been linked to the World Cup as protesters complain that public funds are being diverted away from social issues to build stadiums and upgrade airports.

Matches

The Final draw for the 2010 FIFA World Cup will be staged in Cape Town, South Africa, on 4 December 2009 at the Cape Town International Convention Centre.

Group Stage

In the following tables:

- Pld = total games played,
- W = total games won,
- D = total games drawn (tied),
- L = total games lost,
- GF = total goals scored (goals for),
- GA = total goals conceded (goals against),

- GD = goal difference (GF"GA),
- Pts = total points accumulated.

The teams placed first and second (shaded in green) qualified to the round of 16.

Tie-breaking Criteria

In world football, there are various methods used to separate teams with equal points in a league. For the World Cup tournament, FIFA uses the following system.

The ranking in each group is determined as follows:

1. greatest number of points obtained in all group matches;
2. goal difference in all group matches;
3. greatest number of goals scored in all group matches.

If two or more teams are equal on the basis of the above three criteria, their rankings will be determined as follows:

4. greatest number of points obtained in the group matches between the teams concerned;
5. goal difference resulting from the group matches between the teams concerned;
6. greater number of goals scored in all group matches between the teams concerned;
7. drawing of lots by the FIFA Organising Committee or play-off depending on time schedule.

Cricket World Cup

The Cricket World Cup is the premier international championship of men's One Day International (ODI) cricket. The event is organised by the sport's governing body, the International Cricket Council (ICC), with preliminary qualification rounds leading up to a finals tournament which is held every four years. The tournament is the world's third largest and most viewed sporting event. According to the ICC, it is the most important tournament and the pinnacle of achievement in the sport. The first Cricket World Cup contest was organised in England in 1975. A separate Women's Cricket World Cup has been held every four years since 1973.The finals of the Cricket World Cup are contested by all ten Test-playing and ODI-playing nations, together with other nations that qualify through the World Cup Qualifier. Australia has been the most successful of the five teams to have won the tournament, taking four titles. The West Indies have won twice, while India, Pakistan, and Sri Lanka have each won once.

The 2007 Cricket World Cup matches were held between 13 March and 28 April 2007, in the West Indies. The 2007 tournament had sixteen teams competing in a pool stage (played in round-robin format), then a "super 8" stage, followed by semi-finals and a final. Australia defeated Sri Lanka in the final to retain the championship.

History

Before the first Cricket World Cup

The first ever international cricket match was played between Canada and the United States, on the 24th and 25th of September 1844. However, the first credited Test match was played in 1877 between Australia and England, and the two teams competed regularly for The Ashes in subsequent years. South Africa was admitted to Test status in 1889. Representative cricket teams were selected to tour each other, resulting in bilateral competition. Cricket was also included as an Olympic sport at the 1900 Paris Games, where Great Britain defeated France to win the gold medal. This was the only appearance of cricket at the Summer Olympics.

The first multilateral competition at international level was the 1912 Triangular Tournament, a Test cricket tournament played in England between all three Test-playing nations at the time: England, Australia and South Africa. The event was not a success: the summer was exceptionally wet, making play difficult on damp uncovered pitches, and attendances were poor, attributed to a "surfeit of cricket". In subsequent years, international Test cricket has been generally been organised as bilateral series: a multilateral Test tournament was not organised again until the quadrangular Asian Test Championship in 1999.

The number of nations playing Test cricket increased gradually over the years, with the addition of West Indies in 1928, New Zealand in 1930, India in 1932, and Pakistan in 1952, but international cricket continued to be played as bilateral Test matches over three, four or five days. In the early 1960s, English county cricket teams began playing a shortened version of cricket which only lasted for one day. Starting in 1962 with a four-team knockout competition known as the Midlands Knock-Out Cup, and continuing with the inaugural Gillette Cup in 1963, one-day cricket grew in popularity in England. A national Sunday League was formed in 1969. The first One-Day International event was played on the fifth day of a rain-aborted Test match between England and Australia at Melbourne in 1971, to fill the time available and as compensation for the frustrated crowd. It was a forty over match with eight balls per over.

The success and popularity of the domestic one-day competitions in England and other parts of the world, as well as the early One-Day Internationals, prompted the ICC to consider organising a Cricket World Cup.

Prudential World Cups

The inaugural Cricket World Cup was hosted in 1975 by England, the only nation able to put forward the resources to stage an event of such magnitude at that time. The first three events were held in England and officially known as the Prudential Cup after the sponsors Prudential plc. The matches consisted of 60 six-ball overs per team, played during the daytime in traditional form, with the players wearing cricket whites and using red cricket balls.

Eight teams participated in the first tournament: Australia, England, the West Indies, New Zealand, India, and Pakistan (the six Test nations at the time), together with Sri Lanka and a composite team from East Africa. One notable omission was South Africa, who were banned from international cricket due to apartheid. The tournament was won by the West Indies, who defeated Australia by 17 runs in the final at Lord's.

The 1979 World Cup saw the introduction of the ICC Trophy competition to select non-Test playing teams for the World Cup, with Sri Lanka and Canada qualifying. West Indies won a second consecutive World Cup tournament, defeating the hosts, England, by 92 runs in the final. At a meeting which followed the World Cup, the International Cricket Conference agreed to make the competition a quadrennial event.

The 1983 event was hosted by England for a third consecutive time. By this time, Sri Lanka had become a Test-playing nation, and Zimbabwe qualified through the ICC Trophy. A fielding circle was introduced, 30 yards (27 m) away from the stumps. Four fieldsmen needed to be inside it at all times. India, an outsider quoted at 66-1 to win by bookmakers before the competition began, were crowned champions after upsetting the West Indies by 43 runs in the final.

1987 – 1996

The 1987 tournament was held in India and Pakistan, the first time that the competition was held outside England. The games were reduced from 60 to 50 overs per innings, the current standard, because of the shorter daylight hours in the Indian subcontinent compared with England's summer. Australia won the championship by defeating England by 7 runs in the final, the closest margin in World Cup final history.

The 1992 World Cup, held in Australia and New Zealand, introduced many changes to the game, such as coloured clothing, white balls, day/night matches, and an alteration to the fielding restrictions. The South African cricket team participated in the event for the first time, following the fall of the apartheid regime and the end of the international sports boycott. Pakistan overcame a dismal start to emerge as winners, defeating England by 22 runs in the final.

The 1996 championship was held in the Indian subcontinent for a second time, with the inclusion of Sri Lanka as host for some of its group stage matches. In the semifinal, Sri Lanka, heading towards a crushing victory over India at Eden Gardens (Calcutta) after their hosts lost eight wickets while scoring 120 runs in pursuit of 254, were awarded victory by default after riots broke out in protest against the Indian performance. Sri Lanka went on to win their maiden championship by defeating Australia by seven wickets in the final, which was held in Lahore.

Australian treble

In 1999 the event was hosted by England, with some matches also being held in Scotland, Ireland, Wales and the Netherlands. Australia qualified for the semi-finals after reaching their target in their Super 6 match against South Africa off the final over of the match. They then proceeded to the final with a tied match in the semifinal (also against South Africa) where a mix-up between South African batsmen Lance Klusener and Allan Donald saw Donald drop his bat and stranded mid-pitch to be run out. In the final, Australia dismissed Pakistan for 132 and then reached the target in less than 20 overs, with eight wickets in hand.

A large crowd of over 10,000 fans welcome the Australian team on completing the first World Cup hat-trick-Martin Place, Sydney.

South Africa, Zimbabwe and Kenya hosted the 2003 World Cup. The number of teams participating in the event increased from twelve to fourteen. Kenya's victories over Sri Lanka and Zimbabwe, among others — and a forfeit by the New Zealand team, which refused to play in Kenya because of security concerns — enabled Kenya to reach the semi-finals, the best result by an associate. In the final, Australia made 359 runs for the loss of two wickets, the largest ever total in a final, defeating India by 125 runs.

In 2007 the tournament was hosted by the West Indies; the Cricket World Cup became the first such tournament to be hosted on all six populated continents. Bangladesh progressed to the second round for the first time, after defeating India, and they later went on to defeat South Africa in the second round.

Ireland making their World Cup debut tied with Zimbabwe and defeated Pakistan to progress to the second round, where they went on to defeating Bangladesh to get promoted to the main ODI table.

Following their defeat to Ireland, the Pakistani coach Bob Woolmer was found dead in his hotel room; it was later found out that he died of heart failure. Australia defeated Sri Lanka in the final by 53 runs (D/L), in farcical light conditions, extending their undefeated run in the World Cup to 29 matches and winning three straight World Cups.

Format

Qualification

The Test-playing nations and ODI-playing nations qualify automatically for the World Cup finals, while the other teams have to qualify through a series of preliminary qualifying tournaments.

Qualifying tournaments were introduced for the second World Cup, where two of the eight places in the finals were awarded to the leading teams in the ICC Trophy. The number of teams selected through the ICC Trophy has varied throughout the years; currently, six teams are selected for the Cricket World Cup. The World Cricket League (administered by the International Cricket Council) is the qualification system provided to allow the Associate and Affiliate members of the ICC more opportunities to qualify. In 2009, the name "ICC Trophy" will be changed to "ICC World Cup Qualifier".

Under the current qualifying process, the World Cricket League, all 91 Associate and Affiliate members of the ICC are able to qualify for the World Cup. Associate and Affiliate members must play between two and five stages in the ICC World Cricket League to qualify for the World Cup finals, depending on the Division in which they start the qualifying process.

Process summary in chronological order:

1. Regional tournaments: Top teams from each regional tournaments will be promoted to a division depending on the teams' rankings according to the ICC and each division's empty spots.
2. Division One: 6 Teams — All qualify for the World Cup Qualifier.
3. Division Three: 8 Teams — Top 2 promoted to Division Two.
4. Division Two: 6 Teams — Top 4 qualify for the World Cup Qualifier.
5. Division Five: 8 Teams — Top 2 promoted to Division Four.
6. Division Four: 5 Teams — Top 2 promoted to Division Three.
7. Division Three (second edition): 6 Teams — Top 2 qualify for the World Cup Qualifier.
8. World Cup Qualifier: 12 Teams — Top 6 are awarded ODI status and Top 4 qualify for the World Cup.

Tournament

The format of the Cricket World Cup has changed greatly over the course of its history. Each of the first four tournaments was played by eight teams, divided into two groups of four. There, competition comprised two stages, a group stage and a knock-out stage.

The four teams in each group played each other in the round-robin group stage, with the top two teams in each group progressing to the semi-finals.

The winners of the semi-finals played against each other in the final. With the return of South Africa in 1992 after the ending of the apartheid boycott, nine teams played each other once in the group phase, and the top four teams progressed to the semi-finals. The tournament was further expanded in 1996, with two groups of six teams. The top four teams from each group progressed to quarter-finals and semi-finals.

A new format was used for the 1999 and 2003 World Cups. The teams were split into two pools, with the top three teams in each pool advancing to the Super 6.

The "Super 6" teams played the three other teams that advanced from the other group. As they advanced, the teams carried their points forward from previous matches against other teams advancing alongside them, giving them an incentive to perform well in the group stages. The top four teams from the "Super 6" stage progressed to the semi-finals, with winners playing in the final.

The last format used in the 2007 World Cup, features 16 teams allocated into four groups of four. Within each group, the teams play each other in a round-robin format. Teams earn points for wins and half-points for ties. The top two teams from each group move forward to the Super 8 round.

The "Super 8" teams play the other six teams that progressed from the different groups.

Teams earned points in the same way as the group stage, but carrying their points forward from previous matches against the other teams who qualified from the same group to the "Super 8" stage. The top four teams from the "Super 8" round advance to the semi-finals, and the winners of the semi-finals play in the final.

The current format, approved by ICC to be used in 2011 World

Cup, features 14 teams allocated. Within each group, the teams will play in a round-robin format. The top four teams from each group will proceed to the knock out stage playing quarter-finals. Winners of the quarter-finals will play semi-finals and the winning semi-finalists will play in the final.

Trophy

The ICC Cricket World Cup Trophy is presented to the winners of the World Cup finals.

The current trophy was created for the 1999 championships, and was the first permanent prize in the tournament's history; prior to this, different trophies were made for each World Cup. The trophy was designed and produced in London by a team of craftsmen from Garrard & Co over a period of two months.

The current trophy is made from silver and gild, and features a golden globe held up by three silver columns. The columns, shaped as stumps and bails, represent the three fundamental aspects of cricket: batting, bowling and fielding, while the globe characterises a cricket ball. The trophy is designed with platonic dimensions, so that it can be easily recognised from any angle.

It stands 60 cm high and weighs approximately 11 kilograms. The names of the previous winners are engraved on the base of the trophy, with space for a total of twenty inscriptions.

The original trophy is kept by the ICC. A replica, which differs only in the inscriptions, is permanently awarded to the winning team.

Media Coverage

The tournament is the world's third largest and most viewed sporting events, being televised in over 200 countries to over 2.2 billion television viewers. Television rights, mainly for the 2011 and 2015 World Cup, were sold for over US$1.1 billion, and sponsorship rights were sold for a further US$500 million.

The 2003 Cricket World Cup matches were attended by 626,845 people, while the 2007 Cricket World Cup sold more than 672,000 tickets and recorded the highest ticketing revenue for a Cricket World Cup.

Statistical Summaries—Results

Year	Host Nation(s)	Final Venue	Final		
			Winner	Result	Runner-up
1975 *Details*	England	Lord's, London	West Indies 291 for 8 (60 overs)	WI won by 17 runs Scorecard	Australia 274 all out (58.4 overs)
1979 *Details*	England,	Lord's, London	West Indies 286 for 9 (60 overs)	WI won by 92 runs Scorecard	England 194 all out (51 overs)
1983 *Details*	England	Lord's, London	India 183 all out (54.4 overs)	Ind won by 43 runs Scorecard	West Indies 140 all out (52 overs)
1987 *Details*	India, Pakistan	Eden Gardens, Kolkata	Australia 253 for 5 (50 overs)	Aus won by 7 runs Scorecard	England 246 for 8 (50 overs)
1992 *Details*	Australia, New Zealand	MCG, Melbourne	Pakistan 249 for 6 (50 overs)	Pak won by 22 runs Scorecard	England 227 all out (49.2 overs)
1996 *Details*	Pakistan, India, Sri Lanka	Gaddafi Stadium, Lahore	Sri Lanka 245 for 3 (46.2 overs)	SL won by 7 wickets Scorecard	Australia 241 for 7 (50 overs)
1999 *Details*	England, Ireland, Netherlands, Scotland	Lord's, London	Australia 133 for 2 (20.1 overs)	Aus won by 8 wickets Scorecard	Pakistan 132 all out (39 overs)
2003 *Details*	Kenya, S. Africa, Zimbabwe	Wanderers, Johannesburg	Australia 359 for 2 (50 overs)	Aus won by 125 runs Scorecard	India 234 all out (39.2 overs)
2007 *Details*	West Indies	Kensington Oval, Bridgetown	Australia 281 for 4 (38 overs)	Aus won by 53 runs on D/L Method Scorecard	Sri Lanka 215 for 8 (36 overs)
2011 *Details*	India, Sri Lanka, Bangladesh	Wankhede Stadium, Mumbai	TBD	TBD	TBD
2015 *Details*	Australia, New Zealand	Not designated	TBD	TBD	TBD
2019 *Details*	England	Not designated	TBD	TBD	TBD

Successive World Cup tournaments have generated increasing media attention as One-Day International cricket has become more established. The 2003 World Cup in South Africa was the first to sport a mascot, *Dazzler* the zebra. An orange raccoon-like creature known as *Mello* was the mascot for the 2007 Cricket World Cup.

Selection of Hosts

The International Cricket Council's executive committee votes for the hosts of the tournament after examining the bids made by the nations keen to hold a Cricket World Cup.

England hosted the first three competitions. The ICC decided that England should host the first tournament because it was ready to devote the resources required to organising the inaugural event. India volunteered to host the third Cricket World Cup, but most ICC members believed England to be a more suitable venue because the longer period of daylight in England in June meant that a match could be completed in one day. The 1987 Cricket World Cup was the first hosted outside England, held in India and Pakistan.

Many of the tournaments have been jointly hosted by nations from the same geographical region, such as South Asia in 1987 and 1996, Australasia in 1992, Southern Africa in 2003 and West Indies in 2007. India, Sri Lanka, and Bangladesh are going to host the 2011 World Cup. Pakistan was the 4th country involved to host the 2011 World Cup; however, due to security reasons after the March 3, 2009 Lahore terror attacks on the Sri Lankan cricket team bus, the 14 scheduled matches in Pakistan (including one semifinal) have been reassigned to the remaining 3 countries by the ICC executive board. The final for the 2011 world cup will be in Mumbai. Every Test-playing nation now has hosted or co-hosted a Cricket World Cup at least once, except Bangladesh, the most recent country to achieve Test status.

Performance of Teams

Nineteen nations have qualified for the finals of the Cricket World Cup at least once (excluding qualification tournaments). Seven teams have competed in every finals tournament, five of which have won the title. The West Indies won the first two tournaments, and Australia has won four, while India, Pakistan and Sri Lanka have each won once.

Team	Appearances			Best result	Statistics				
	Total	First	Latest		Played	Won	Lost	Tie	NR
Australia	9	1975	2007	Champions (1987, 1999, 2003, 2007)	69	51	17	1	0
West Indies	9	1975	2007	Champions (1975, 1979)	57	35	21	0	1
India	9	1975	2007	Champions (1983)	58	32	25	0	1
Pakistan	9	1975	2007	Champions (1992)	56	30	24	0	2
Sri Lanka	9	1975	2007	Champions (1996)	57	25	30	1	1
England	9	1975	2007	Runners-up (1979, 1987, 1992)	59	36	22	0	1
New Zealand	9	1975	2007	Semifinals (1975, 1979, 1992, 1999, 2007)	62	35	26	0	1
Zimbabwe	7	1983	2007	Super Six (1999, 2003)	45	8	33	1	3
South Africa	5	1992	2007	Semifinals (1992, 1999, 2007)	40	26	12	2	0
Kenya	4	1996	2007	Semifinals (2003)	23	6	16	0	1
Bangladesh	3	1999	2007	Super 8 (2007)	20	5	14	0	1
Canada	3	1979	2007	Round 1	12	1	11	0	0
Netherlands	3	1996	2007	Round 1	14	2	12	0	0
Scotland	2	1999	2007	Round 1	8	0	8	0	0
Ireland	1	2007	2007	Super 8 (2007)	9	2	6	1	0
Bermuda	1	2007	2007	Round 1	3	0	3	0	0
Namibia	1	2003	2003	Round 1	6	0	6	0	0
United Arab Emirates	1	1996	1996	Round 1	5	1	4	0	0
East Africa	1	1975	1975	Round 1	3	0	3	0	0

The West Indies (1975 and 1979) and Australia (1999, 2003 and 2007) are the only nations to have won consecutive titles. Australia has played in 6 of the 9 final matches (1975, 1987, 1996, 1999, 2003, 2007) including the finals in the four most recent tournaments. England has yet to win the World Cup, but has been runners-up three times (1979, 1987, 1992). The best result by a non-Test playing nation is the semifinal appearance by Kenya in the 2003 tournament; while the best result by a non-Test playing team on their debut is the Super 8 (second round) by Ireland in 2007.

A Chart Showing each Country's Historical Performance in the Cricket World Cup

Sri Lanka, who co-hosted the 1996 Cricket World Cup, is the only host to win the tournament, though the final was held in Pakistan. England is the only other host to have made the final, in 1979. Other countries which have achieved or equalled their best World Cup results while co-hosting the tournament are New Zealand, semi-finalists in 1992; Zimbabwe, reaching the Super Six in 2003; and Kenya, semi-finalists in 2003. In 1987, co-hosts India and Pakistan both reached the semi-finals, but were eliminated by Australia and England respectively. The table below provides an overview of the performances of teams over past World Cups.

Individual awards

Since 1992, one player has been declared as "Man of the Tournament" at the end of the World Cup finals:

Year	*Player*	*Performance details*
1992	Martin Crowe	456 runs
1996	Sanath Jayasuriya	221 runs and 7 wickets
1999	Lance Klusener	281 runs and 17 wickets
2003	Sachin Tendulkar	673 runs and 2 wickets
2007	Glenn McGrath	26 wickets

Previously, there was no tournament award, although Man of the Match awards have always been given for individual matches. Winning the Man of the Match in the final is logically noteworthy, as this indicates the player deemed to have played the biggest part in the World

Cup final. To date the award has always gone to a member of the winning side. The Man of the Match award in the final of the competition has been awarded to:

Year	*Player*	*Performance details*
1975	Clive Lloyd	102 runs
1979	Viv Richards	138*
1983	Mohinder Amarnath	3/12 and 26
1987	David Boon	75 runs
1992	Wasim Akram	33 and 3/49
1996	Aravinda de Silva	107* and 3/42
1999	Shane Warne	4/33
2003	Ricky Ponting	140*
2007	Adam Gilchrist	149

Main Individual and Team Records

Sachin Tendulkar, the leading run-scorer in World Cup history.

World Cup Records

Batting

Most runs	Sachin Tendulkar	1796 (1992–2007)
Highest average (min. 20 inns.)	Viv Richards	63.31 (1975–1987)
Highest score	Gary Kirsten v UAE	188* (1996)
Highest partnership	Rahul Dravid & Sourav Ganguly (2nd wicket) v Sri Lanka	318 (1999)
Most runs in a tournament	Sachin Tendulkar	673 (2003)

Bowling

Most wickets	Glenn McGrath	71 (1996–2007)
Lowest average (min. 1000 balls bowled)	Glenn McGrath	19.21 (1996–2007)
Best bowling figures	Glenn McGrath v Namibia	7/15 (2003)
Most wickets in a tournament	Glenn McGrath	26 (2007)

Fielding

Most dismissals (wicketkeeper)	Adam Gilchrist	39 (1999–2007)
Most catches (fielder)	Ricky Ponting	24 (1996–2007)

Team

Highest score	India v Bermuda	413/5 (2007)
Lowest score	Canada v Sri Lanka	36 (2003)
Highest win %	Australia	75% (Played 69, Won 51)
Most consecutive wins	Australia	23 (1999–2007)
Most consecutive tournament wins	Australia	3 (1999–2007)

Glossary

ABTA: Association of British Travel Agents. Represents the interests of the larger UK tour operators and travel agents (with around 670 members as of 2000), and operates a bonding scheme whereby customers booking with ABTA members have their holidays protected should the operator/agent in question collapse.

Accommodation capacity: The measure of accommodation stock at a defined destination. May be given by various different measures: e.g. number of establishments; number of main units within an establishment (e.g. rooms, caravan stances); capacity in terms of residents.

Accounting period: Normally one year, the period for which accounts are drawn up.

AITO: Association of Independent Tour Operators. Performs a similar function to ABTA, although its membership (and therefore its agenda) differs in comprising some 160 of the smaller UK tour operators.

All-inclusive hotels: Resort facilities that offer all meals, activities and entertainments on site. All holiday expenses at these hotels are covered by one prepaid price. Caribbean destinations are noted for their high profile brands of all-inclusive hotels which offer unlimited alcoholic drinks, snacks between meals and motorised sports all included in one price.

All-inclusive: A form of package holiday where the majority of services offered at the destination are included in the price paid prior to departure (e.g. refreshments, excursions, amenities, gratuities, etc.).

Allocentric: Of a minority of tourists-adventurous, outgoing, self-confident, independent, needing little tourist infrastructure. Enjoys high contact with locals.

Alternative tourism: In essence, tourism activities or development that are viewed as non-traditional. It is often defined in opposition to large-scale mass tourism to represent small-scale sustainable tourism developments. AT is also presented as an 'ideal type', that is, an improved model of tourism development that redresses the ills of traditional, mass tourism.

Artefact: An object; an item of material culture.

Assets: Something of value that will provide future benefit or utility, can be used to generate revenue. Usually owned, so simply described as 'things we own'.

ATOL: Air Travel Organiser's License. A requirement of the Civil Aviation Authority for all UK tour operators wishing to sell air seats on chartered or scheduled services. Necessitates a financial 'health check' and the putting up of a bond to cover the expense of reimbursing/repatriating tourists in the event of operator failure.

Average Room Rate Achieved: The average of the room rates resulting in room sales which a hotel has experienced for a given time period.

Balance of payments: Record of one country's financial transactions with the rest of the world.

Benchmarking: Measuring your performance against that of best in class companies, determining how the best-in-class achieve those performance levels and using this information as a basis for your own company's targets, strategies and implementation.

Benchmarks: Points of reference or comparison, which may include standards, critical success factors, indicators, metrics.

Bureaucracy: An organisation typified by formal processes, standardisation, hierarchic procedures, and written communication.

Business travel: Travel for a purpose and to a destination determined by a business, and where all costs are met by that business.

Capacity management: A process that seeks to ensure that their organisations operate at optimum capacity whilst maintaining customer satisfaction levels.

Capital expenditure: The cost of long-term assets; such as computer equipment, vehicles and premises. Importantly these are bought to use over several years and not to resell.

Carrying-capacity analysis: Originally a term applied in ecology referring to the maximum number of animals of a given species that a particular habitat could support. In the context of tourism, it refers to the maximum number of tourists a destination can support.

Case: A case describes a dispute taken to court, and specific cases set legal precedents-a legal principle, created by a court decision, which provides an example or authority for judges deciding similar issues later.

Chain of distribution: The means by which products (package holidays in this instance) are distributed from producers (principals) to consumers (tourists), often via wholesalers and retailers (tour operators and travel agents).

Chaos theory: Views organisations/businesses as complex, dynamic, non-linear, co-creative and far-from-equilibrium systems the future performance of which cannot be decided alone by past and present events and actions. In a state of chaos, organisations behave in ways which are simultaneously both unpredictable (chaotic) and patterned (orderly).

Charter: A legal contract between an owner and an organisation for the hire of a means of transport for a particular purpose. An individual traveller will use an intermediary to arrange to be carried on the transport. Often applied to a flight which is the result of a charter.

Class action: A lawsuit filed by a number of people in a similar situation, e.g. participants in a particular package holiday might file a class action against the tour operator rather than take action individually.

Code of conduct: Guidelines advising a tourism stakeholder, including tourists, on how to behave in an environmentally responsible manner.

Collaboration: The process of working together in pursuit of common objectives.

Competitive strategies: Offensive or defensive strategies that aim at providing strategic competitive advantage and at increasing the competitiveness of an organisation.

Computer reservation systems (CRS): Computerised Reservation

Systems used for inventory management by airlines, hotels and other facilities. CRSs can allow direct access through terminals for intermediaries to check availability, make reservations and print tickets.

Conservation: Can be broadly interpreted as action taken to protect and preserve the natural world from harmful features of tourism, including pollution and overexploitation of resources.

Contract: A legal agreement entered into by two or more parties.

Control: Monitoring and if necessary adjusting the performance of the organisation and its members.

Cost-benefit analysis: Full analysis of public and private costs and benefits of project.

Cost-plus pricing: A method of pricing where an amount, to cover profit, is added to costs to establish the selling price, this is an internally orientated pricing method.

Critical incident point (CIP): A critical incident point or 'moment of truth' is any event which occurs when the customer has (or even perceives that he has) contact with a service organisation.

Culture: A set of shared norms and values which establish a sense of identity for those who share them. Typically applied at the level of nation and/or race.

Customer: "An organization or a person that receives a product".

Decision-making unit (DMU): The combination of inputs to a purchasing decision.

Delegation: The assignment to others of the authority for particular functions, tasks, and decisions.

Dependency theory: This theory maintains that developing countries are kept in a position of dependency and underdevelopment due to existing economic and institutional power structures sustained by leading Western nations. Dependency theorists argue that the policies and activities of multinational corporations, national bilateral and multinational aid agencies such as the World Bank and the International Monetary Fund (IMF) tend to widen the gap between rich and poor countries and perpetuate the dependency of developing nations.

Designation: The act of conferring a legal status on a building which requires compliance with specific legislation on conservation and preservation.

Discretionary income: Money received from employment or other sources which can be freely spent on leisure pursuits (such as travel and tourism) after general living costs, taxation etc. are taken into consideration.

Discrimination: Unequal treatment of persons on grounds which are not justifiable in law, e.g. in the UK, discrimination on the grounds of sex or race.

Disintermediation: A process by which the consumer 'bypasses' the services of an intermediary or intermediaries in the chain of distribution, in order to purchase products direct from those who supply them. In the travel industry, examples of disintermediation include airlines selling tickets direct to the public over the internet, thus cutting out the travel agent in the selling process.

Distribution: The process employed to provide customers access to the product. For travel products distribution focuses largely on the ways in which the customer can reserve or purchase the product.

Diversification: The process of developing new products for new markets, in order to achieve business growth.

Due diligence: Taking what is considered in law to be reasonable care.

E-Commerce: Internet facilitated commerce, using electronic means for promoting, selling, distributing, and servicing products.

Economic growth: An increase in real output per capita.

E-mediaries: Electronic booking systems (usually web-based) which combine commerce and the traditional intermediary role of travel agents. Products and services are usually sourced from a range of other product providers allowing customers to book a range of different tourism and travel services from one website, and may enable price/product comparisons between competing suppliers.

Employee Relations: Covers communications, employee participation in management decisions, conflict and grievance resolution, trade unions and collective bargaining.

Environmental auditing: Inspection of a tourism organisation to assess the environmental impact of its activities.

Environmental management systems: Systems established by tourism organisations with the aim of mitigating negative environmental impacts.

Environmental scanning: The process of collecting information to carry out a systematic analysis of the forces effecting the organisation and identifying potential threats and opportunities with view to generating future strategies.

Evolutionary theories: Theories of tourism which see destinations evolving, in the sense that the types of tourists change, or evolve, over time.

Exclusion clause: This is a term in a contract that tries to exclude or limit the liability of one of the parties if there is a breach. Such clauses often take the form of "small print" in the standard terms and conditions of the dominant partner in the contract e.g. tour operators.

Externalities: Those costs or benefits arising from production or consumption of goods and services which are not reflected in market prices.

Familiarisation trips: (Fam trips) Visits to tourism destinations made in order to experience and learn more about the destination. Such trips are usually organised either by tour operators or by destination managers to improve knowledge of the destination. When travel agents are taken on such trips it is expected that their increased knowledge will lead to greater level of sales of holidays to that destination.

Force majeure: This is an unforeseeable or uncontrollable situation or train of events that would excuse a breach of contract.

Global Distribution System (GDS): The reservation network which links bookers such as travel agencies to travel suppliers' booking systems.

Globalization: Generally defined as the network of connections of organisations and peoples are across national, geographic and cultural borders and boundaries. These global networks are creating a shrinking world where local differences and national boundaries are being subsumed into global identities. Within the field of tourism, globalization is also viewed in terms of the revolutions in

segmentation process also considers which of these segments to target.

Mass tourism: Traditional, large scale tourism commonly, but loosely used to refer to popular forms of leisure tourism pioneered in southern Europe, the Caribbean, and North America in the 1960s and 1970s.

Mature market: A market in which a wide range of substitutable products or services are available to consumers who exhibit a sophisticated approach to consumer decision making.

MAVERICS: Characterisation of tourists of the future as multi-holidaying, autonomous, variegated, energised, restless, irresponsible, constrained and segmented.

Mediation: An attempt to settle a dispute using a neutral third party.

Merit good: One with public as well as private benefits.

Midcentric: Of the majority of tourists-displaying a mix of allocentric and psychcentric characteristics. Prefers to be cushioned from contact with locals.

Mode of travel: The type of transport used to make a journey between an origin and a destination, and can include walking and cycling as well as all forms of mechanical transport.

Modernisation theory: The socioeconomic development and process that evolves from a traditional society to modern economies such as the United States and Western Europe. Harrison (1992) argues that modernisation is a process of westernisation where developing countries emulate Western development patterns.

Motivation: Internal and external forces and influences that drive an individual to achieving certain goals.

Mystery shoppers: These researchers investigate companies through using their services, whilst pretending to be customers (or potential customers). They usually monitor such areas as the level of customer service and product knowledge.

National income: A measure of the total level of economic activity which takes place in an economy over a year.

Negligence: Failing to exercise what is legally considered to be reasonable care.

Net worth / Total net assets: The net value of all operational assets and liabilities, shows the amount of money invested in operational capacity of the business. Calculated by deducting current and long-term liabilities from the value of Fixed assets and Current assets.

Niche tourism: Small specialised sector of tourism which appeals to a correspondingly tightly-defined market segment.

No-frills: A low-cost scheduled travel package based on minimising operator service and costs, which are passed to the consumer as a low price.

Non-profit: Non-profit organisations are those which are driven by non-financial organisational objectives, i.e. other than for profit or shareholder return.

Occupancy rate: The measure of capacity utilised within an accommodation unit for a given time period.

Online agency: Travel agencies who operate using the World Wide Web to provide information to potential customers as well as allowing the customer to book travel and related products without the necessity of speaking to a salesperson.

Operations management: "The ongoing activities of designing, reviewing and using the operating system, to achieve service outputs as determined by the organization for customers".

OPODO: A web based booking site linking the reservation systems of cooperating airlines, allowing bookers to compare times and prices for particular journeys.

Organisation: A deliberate arrangement of people to achieve a particular purpose.

Other recruitment difficulties: Includes poor recruitment/retention practices, poor image, low remuneration, poor employment conditions which arise despite sufficient skilled individuals.

Owners' equity: Combines the original investment and any retained profit to show the total value of the owners' interest in the business.

Package holiday: Also known as an inclusive tour. Defined in law as 'the prearranged combination of at least two of the following components when sold or offered for sale at an inclusive price and when the service covers a period of more than 24 hours or includes overnight accommodation: (a) transport; (b) accommodation; and (c) other tourist services not ancillary to transport or accommodation', as set out in Section 2 of the European Union's Package Travel Regulations, 1992.

Perishability: The characteristic of being perishable. In tourism the term is used to describe, for example, a particular hotel room on a specific night or a particular seat on a specific flight-they cannot be 'stored' and sold later, so they are perishable.

Personal disposable income: The amount an individual has left over for personal expenditure on goods and services, after payment of personal direct taxes, national insurance and pension contributions.

Personnel: Concerned with the practical management and administration of people at work.

PESTEL analysis: Examines the political, economic, sociocultural, technological, (physical) environmental and legal forces within which businesses operate and which act on them.

Physical evidence: The tangible evidence of a service, including everything which can be seen, touched, smelt and heard.

Politics: Politics has been defined in many ways. According to Heywood, politics is 'The activity through which people make, preserve and amend the general rules under which they live'. According to Davis et al., 'Politics is the process by which the structure, process and institutions are brought to a decision [including non-decisions] or outcome. It is an endless activity; while politics operates, all decisions [and non-decisions and actions] are provisional'. So politics means no decision or action is final. All decisions and actions of a government or institution of the state is open to question and is up for debate and argument and is, ultimately, subject to change.

Pollution: Harmful effects on the environment as a by-product of tourism activity. Types include: air; noise; water; and aesthetic.

Porter's forces: A model which suggests that the profit potential for companies is influenced by the interaction of five competitive forces: rivalry in the market place; the threat of substitutes; buyer power; supplier power; and barriers to entry into the market for new players.

Positioning: The process of ensuring potential customers have a desired perception of a product or service, relative to the competition.

Price elasticity of demand: A relationship between the changes in prices charged for a good or service (here taken as hotel rooms) and the change in the amount demanded.

Price elasticity of demand: A measure of the variability that can be expected in sales when prices are changed. Unity elasticity would see equal increase in sales to in reaction to a decrease in price. Inelastic demand would not change when prices went down or up.

Principal: A term that encompasses accommodation providers, carriers, ground handlers and any other provider of services to tourists, except for those whose primary function is to package and distribute tourism products.

Process control: A systematic use of tools to identify significant variations in operational performance and output quality, determine root causes, make corrections and verify results.

Process design: Involves specifying all practices needed, flowcharting, rationalisation and error prevention.

Process improvement: A pro-active task of management aimed at continual monitoring of a process and its outcome and developing ways to enhance its future performance.

Process management: Planning and administering the activities necessary to achieve a high level of performance in a process and identifying opportunities for improving quality, operational performance and ultimately customer satisfaction. It involves design, control and improvement of key business processes.

Process: "A set of interrelated or interacting activities which transforms inputs into outputs".

Product: "The result of a process" (i.e. output), which may be either a service, or a good (hardware or processed materials) or software (e.g. information) or their combination.

Profit: The excess of revenue over expenses, if expenses exceed revenues in a given period the organisation will make a loss.

Psychocentric: Of a minority of tourists-preferring 'away' to be like 'home'; requiring appropriate tourism infrastructure.

Public policy: Is whatever governments choose to do or not to do. Such a definition covers government action, inaction, decisions and non-decisions as it implies a very deliberate choice between alternatives.

Quality: The degree to which a set of inherent characteristics of a product fulfils customer requirements.

Regulation: Control through formalised processes.

Relationship marketing: Relationship marketing is a business philosophy which aims to develop strong relationships with a range of stakeholders, such as suppliers, media, intermediaries and public organisations, as well as with customers.

Requirements: Stated, generally implied (as a custom or common practice for the organisation, its customers and other interested parties) or obligatory needs.

Responsible tourism: Type of tourism which is practised by tourists who make responsible choices when choosing their holidays. These choices reflect responsible attitudes to the limiting of the extent of the sociological and environmental impacts their holiday may cause.

Retained profit: The profit left in the business at the end of the accounting period after all deductions and appropriations have been made.

Revenue expenditure: The cost of resources consumed or used up in the process of generating revenue, generally referred to as expenses.

Revenue management: Revenue management is a management approach to optimising revenue, often based on managing revenues around capacity and timing (yield management), for different market segments or from different sources of funding.

Sales: Revenue from ordinary activities-not necessarily cash.

Seasonality: A phenomenon created by either tourism supply or demand (or both) changing according to the time of the year.

Service encounter: The moments of interface between customer and supplier.

Service marketing mix: The addition of People, Physical Evidence and Process to the four areas of activity more usually associated with marketing products,-Price, Place, Promotion and Product.

Servicescape: The location in which the service encounter takes place.

Skills gaps: Employers perceive existing employees have lower skill levels than needed to achieve business objectives, or where new, apparently trained and qualified for specific occupations, entrants still lack requisite skills.

Skills shortages: Lack of adequately skilled individuals in the labour market due to low unemployment, sufficiently skilled people in the labour market but not easily geographically accessible or insufficient appropriately-skilled individuals.

Small business: A small business is one which has a small number of employees, profit and/or revenue. Often these are owner-managed, with few specialist managers. Some definitions of small businesses distinguish between businesses with under 10 employees, which are micro-businesses, and those with 10-49 employees, which are classified as small businesses.

Social: Relating to human society and interaction between its members.

Sports event tourism: Tourism where the prime purpose of the trip is to take part in sports events as either a participant or spectator.

Sports participation tourism: Active participation in sports that is the prime purpose of the tourism trip.

Sports tourism: A social, cultural and economic phenomenon arising from the unique interaction of activity, people and place.

Sports training tourism: Sports tourism trips where the prime purpose is sports instruction or training.

Sport-tourism link: Not just sports holidays, but all areas in which a link between sport and tourism might be of mutual benefit (e.g. joint facility development, marketing and information provision).

Stakeholder: Any person, group or organisation with an interest in, or who may be affected by, the activities of another organisation.

'The State': 'The state' is a set of officials with their own preferences and capacities to effect public policy, or in more structural terms a relatively permanent set of political institutions operating in relation to civil society'. The state includes elected politicians, interest or pressure groups, law enforcement agencies, the bureaucracy, and a plethora of rules, regulations, laws, conventions and policies.

Statute: The law as made by parliament, e.g. in the UK, the Disability Discrimination Act (1995). A statute is made up of many parts called 'sections' or 'provisions'.

Statutory instrument: The vast majority of delegated legislation in the UK is in the form of statutory instruments governed by the Statutory Instruments Act 1946.

Strategic information systems: Systems designed to support the strategic management decision processes and implementation.

Strategy pyramid: A visual way of representing the different levels of the strategy conceptualisation and implementation process. The most general assumptions are shown at the apex and the practical, implementation actions are at the base.

Suppliers: Individuals, companies or other organisations which provide goods or services to a recognisable customer or consumer.

Sustainable tourism: Tourism that is economically, socioculturally and environmentally sustainable. With sustainable tourism, sociocultural and environmental impacts are neither permanent nor irreversible.

SWOT analysis: Brings together the internal and external environmental scanning to identify the business's internal strengths and weaknesses and external opportunities and threats.

Tort: A civil wrong.

Tour operator: An individual or organisation in the business of (bulk) buying, and subsequently bundling, the various components that make up a package holiday, for sale via a travel agent or direct to the consumer.

Tourism flows: The major movements of tourists from specific home areas to destinations.

Tourism income multiplier (TIM): Exaggerated effect of a change in tourism expenditure on an area's income.

Tourism satellite account: System of accounting at national or regional level which reveals the total direct impact of tourism on the economy.

Tourism System: A framework that identifies tourism as being made up of a number of components, often taken to include the tourist, the tourist generating region, the transit route region, the tourist destination and the tourism industry.

Tourism with sports content: Tourism products that include participation in sport that is not the prime purpose of the trip.

Tourist attractions: Tourist attractions are defined as being destinations for visitors' excursions which are routinely accessible to visitors during opening hours. Visitors can include local residents, day-trippers or people who are travelling for business or leisure purposes. Formal definitions exclude shops, sports stadia, theatres and cinemas, as these meet a wider purpose, although in practice tourists may consider the excluded categories to be tourist attractions.

TOWS matrix: Uses a SWOT analysis to develop strategies by matching strengths with opportunities, using opportunities to reduce weaknesses, using strengths to overcome threats, and reducing weaknesses and avoiding threats.

Travel agent: The retailer of travel and related products. Whilst this refers to the sales person employed to sell travel products, the term is often applied in reference to the business that is established to sell travel products.

Variability: Because the production and the consumption of a tourism experience are inseparable and because differing circumstances and people will affect each experience, those experiences are prone to variance and create a challenge for tourism managers to achieve consistency of standards.

Virtual organisation: Organisation in which major processes are outsourced to partners.

Working Capital: Operational assets and liabilities needed for everyday operation, e.g. cash or bank overdraft, stock and trade creditors, known as net current assets/liabilities.

Yield Management: "A revenue maximization technique which aims to increase net yield through the predicted allocation of available ... capacity to predetermined market segments at optimal price".

Zoning: Different ecosystems may be zoned in terms of their robustness to pressures from tourism in an attempt to mitigate environmental damage.

Bibliography

Andrew, N; Flanagan, S & Ruddy, J: *Tourism Destination Planning*, Dublin, Dublin Institute of Technology, 2002.

Apostolopous, Y and Leivadi, S: *Sociology of Tourism, The: Theoretical And Empirical Investigations*, London, Retailed, 1996.

Ashworth, G J and Dietvorst, A G J: *Tourism and Spatial Transformations: Implications For Policy and Plan*, Wallingford, CAB International, 1995.

Ashworth, Greg and Larkham, P J: *Building a New Heritage: Tourism, Culture & Identity in the New Europe*, London, Routledge,1994.

Baum, Tom: *We're all Going on a Summer Holiday: Images of Tourism Past and Person*, Buckingham, University of Buckingham, 1995.

Beeho, A & Prentice, R: *Conceptualising The Experiences of Heritage Tourists*, 1997.

Beeton, Sue:: *Film-Induced Tourism*, Clevedon, Channel View, 2005.

Belie et al.: *Tourism and the Inner City: An Evaluation of / Impact of Grant Assist*, London, HMSO, 1990.

Benefice, Brian G, and Cooper, Chris: *Geography of Travel and Tourism*, The, London, Heinemann, 1987.

Bolshevism, Germy: *Coping with Tourists: European Reactions to Mass Tourism*, Oxford, Berghahn Books, 1995.

Boniface, Priscilla and Fowler, Peter: *Heritage and Tourism: In the Global Village*, London, Retailed, 1993.

Bosselman, Fred P: *In The Wake of the Tourist: Managing Special Places in Eight Countries*, Washington, DC, Conservation Foundation, The, 1978.

Briguglio, L and Vella, Leslie: *Competitiveness of the Maltese Islands in Mediterranean in Tourism*, Chichester, John Wiley, 1995.

Brown, Dona: *Inventing New England: Regional Tourism in the Nineteenth Century*, Washington DC, Smithsonian Institution, 1995.

Brunt, Paul: *Market Research in Travel and Tourism*, Oxford, Butterworth Heinemann, 1997.

Burkart, A and Medlik, S: *Management of Tourism*, The, London, Heinemann, 1975.

Chambers, Erve: *Native Tours: The Anthropology of Travel and Tourism*, Prospect Heights, Waveland Press, 2000.

Chandler, Harry and Carter, John: *Chandler's Travels: A Tour of the Life of Harry Chandler*, London, Quiller Press, 1985.

Clark, Colin: *Tourist Services and Guidance: Heritage and Information*, Strasbourg, Council of Europe Press, 1989.

Coccosis, Harry and Nijkamp, Peter: *Sustainable Tourism Development*, Aldershot, Avebury, 1995.

Cohen, Erik: *Towards a Sociology of International Tourism*, 1972.

Dann, Graham M S: *Language of Tourism*, The, Wallingford, CAB International, 1996.

Davidson, R and Maitland, R: *Tourism Destinations, London*, Hodder and Stoughton, 1997.

Davidson, Rob: *Travel and Tourism in Europe*, Harlow, Addison Wesley Longman, 1998.

Ecotec: *Calderdale: Tourism Impact Study*, Calderdale, ECOTEC/Calderdale Council, 1990.

Edensor, Tim: *Tourists at the Taj*, London, Retailed, 1998.

Edgell, David L: *International Tourism Policy, New York*, Van Nostrand and Reinhold, 1990.

Elliott, James: *Tourism: Politics and Public Sector Management*, London, Retailed, 1997.

Fairgrieve, James: *Geography in School*, London, University of London Press, 1926.

Foster, Douglas: *Travel and Tourism Management*, London, Macmillan Educational, 1985.

Frechtling, Douglas C: *Practical Tourism Forecasting*, Oxford, Butterworth Heinemann, 1996.

Gamble, P. R: *The Educational challenge for Hospitality and Tourism Studies*, Tourism Management, 13, 1992.

Ghimire, Krishna: *The Native Tourist*: Mass Tourism within Developing Regions, London, Earthscan, 2001.

Goeldner, C. R: *The Evaluation of Tourism as an Industry and a Discipline, Paper Presented to*, International Conference for Tourism Educators, Guildford, University of Surrey, 1988.

Gunn, Clare and Var, Turgut: *Tourism Planning*, London, Retailed, 2002.

Hall, C Michael *Tourism Planning: Policies, Processes and relationships*, Harlow, Prentice Hall, 2000.

Hall, Colin and Jenkins, John: *Tourism and Public Policy*, London, Retailed, 1995.

Hall, Colin Michael: *Tourism and Politics*: Policy, Power, & Place, Chichester, Wiley, 1994.

Harrison, Lyndon: *Tourism Means Jobs*, Chester, Lyndon Harrison, 1996.

Harron, S and Weiler, B: *Ethnic Tourism*, Belhaven/Wiley, 1992.

Inkpen, G: *Information Technology for Travel and Tourism*, Harlow, Addison Wesley Longman, 1998.

Inskeep, Edward *National and Regal Tourism Planing*: Methodologies & Case Studies, London, Routledge/WTO, 1994.

Irwin, William *The New Niagara: Tourism, Technology, And the Landscape of Niagara Fal*, University Park, PA, University of Pennsylvania, 1996.

Jack, G and Phipps, A: *Tourism and Intercultural Exchange: Why Tourism Matters*, Clevedon, Channel View, 2005.

Jakle, John: *Tourist, The: Travel in Twentieth Century North America*, University of North Nebraska, 1985.

Jennings, Gayle: *Tourism Research*, Chichester, Wiley, 2001.

Judd, D R: *Promoting Tourism* in US Cities, 1995.

Karski, A: *Urban Tourism* - A Key to Urban Regeneration?, 1990.

Kotler, Philip et al: *Marketing Places: Attracting Investment, Industry & Tourism etc*, New York, free press, 1993.

Labarge, Margaret Wade: *Medieval Travellers: The Rich and Restless*, London, Hamish Hamilton, 1982.

Laws, Eric: *Tourist Destination Management: Issues, Analysis & Policies*, London, Routledge, 1995.

Leed, Eric J: *Mind of the Traveller, The: From Gilgamesh to Global Tourism*, New York, 1991.

MacCannell, Dean: *Tourist, The: A New Theory of the Leisure Class*, London, Macmillan, 1976.

Machin, Alan: *Retracing the Steps: Tourism as Education, Janus*, Fin, ATLAS / FUNTS, 2001.

Opperman, Martin and Chon, Kye-Sung: *Tourism in Developing Countries, London*, International Thomson Business Press, 1997.

Patullo, Polly: *Last Resorts: The Cost of Tourism in the Caribbean*, London, Cassell, 1996.

Pearce, Douglas: *Tourism Today: A Geographical Analysis*, Harlow, Longman, 1995.

Pearce, P L: *Social Psychology Of Tourist Behaviour*, The, Oxford, Pergamon, 1982.

Peters, M: *International Tourism*, London, Hutchinson, 1969.

Ringer, Greg: *Destinations: Cultural Landscapes of Tourism*, London, Routledge, 1998.

Ritchie, Brent: *Managing Educational Tourism*, Clevedon, Channel View, 2003.

Robinson, H: *Geography of Tourism*, A, London, Macdonald and Evans, 1976.

Robinson, M, Evans, E & Chalazion, P: *Tourism and Cultural Change, Sunderland*, Business Education Publishers Ltd, 1996.

Rogers, H Anthea and Slinn, Judy A: *Tourism: Management of Facilities*, London, Pitman: M & E, 1993.

Schwaninger, M: *Trends in Leisure and Tourism for 2000 - 2010*, Prentice Hall, 1989.

Scottish Tourist Board: *Visitor Attractions: A Development Guide*, Edinburgh, Scottish Tourist Board, 1991.

Seaton, A V et al: *Tourism: The state of the Art*, Chichester, John Wiley, 1994.

Shaw, G and Williams, A: *Tourism and Tourism Spaces*, London, Sage, 2004.

Stevens, Terry: *Island Tourism*: Malta, , WTO, 1993.

Trench, R: *Travellers in Britain*, London, Aurum, 1990.

Tribe, John *Corporate Strategy for Tourism, London*, International Thomson Business Press, 1997.

Urry, John: *Tourist Gaze*, The, London, Sage, 1990.

Van den Berg et al: *Urban Tourism: Performance and Strategies in Eight European Cities*, Aldershot, Avebury, 1995.

Van Harssel, Jan: *Tourism: An Exploration*, New York, Prentice Hall, 1994.

Veal, A: *Leisure and Tourism*: Policy and Planning, Wallingford, CABI, 2001.

Wahab, S A: *Tourism Management*, Tourism International Press, 1975.

Walle, Alfred H: *Cultural Tourism*: A Strategic Focus, Boulder, Co, Westview Press, 1998.

Wilkinson, Paul: *Tourism Policy and Planning: As Studies from the Caribbean*, Elmsford New York, Cognizant Communications Corporation, 1997.

Yale, Pat: *From Tourist Attractions to Heritage Tourism*, Huntingdon, Elm, 1991.

Zarkia, Cornelia: *Philoxenia: Receiving Tourists*-but *not Guests-on a Greek Island*, Oxford, Berghahn Books, 1996.

Index

O

P

R

S

T

V

W

Y

□□□